Drawing Projects for Children

Paula Briggs

black dog
publishing
london uk

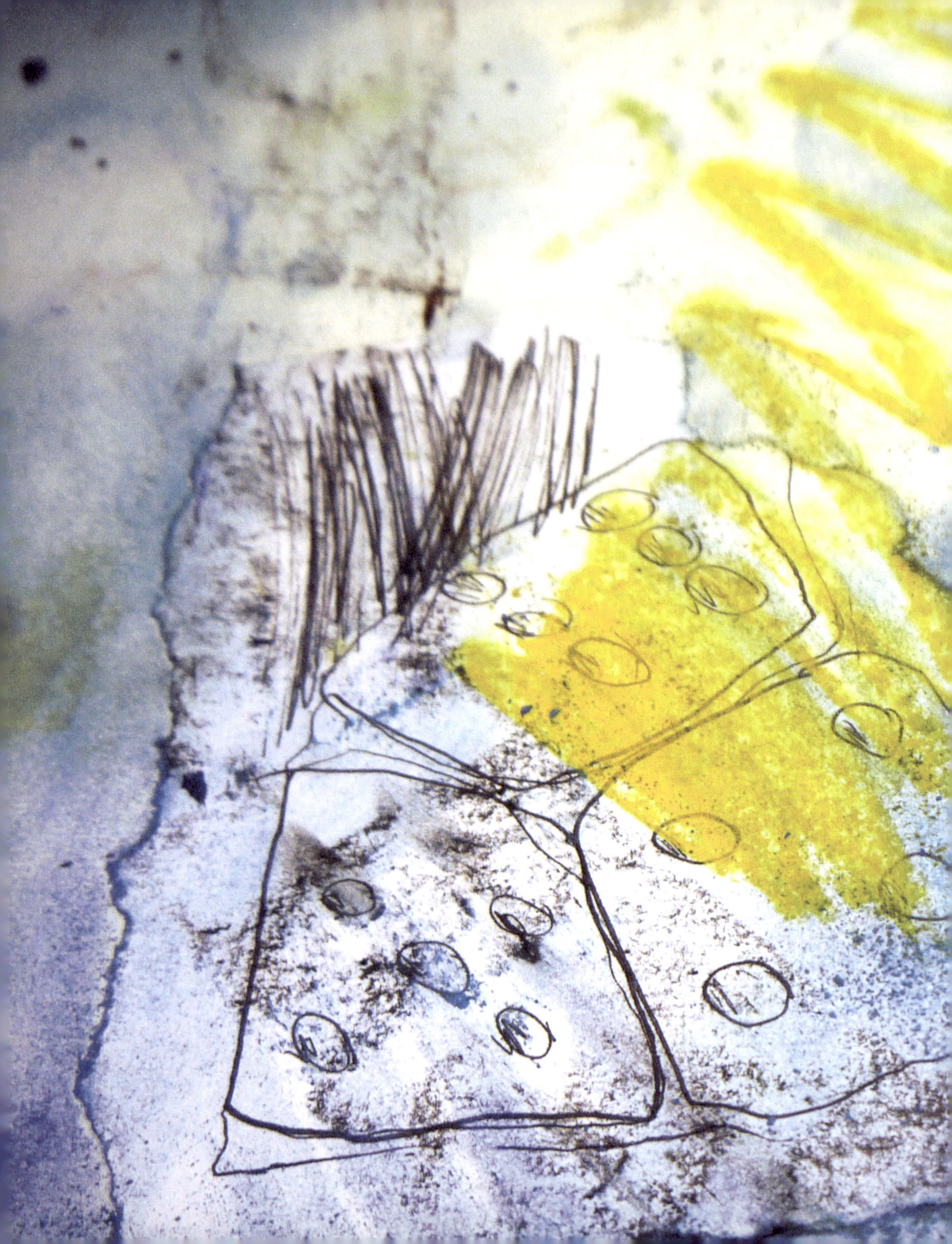

Drawing Projects for Children

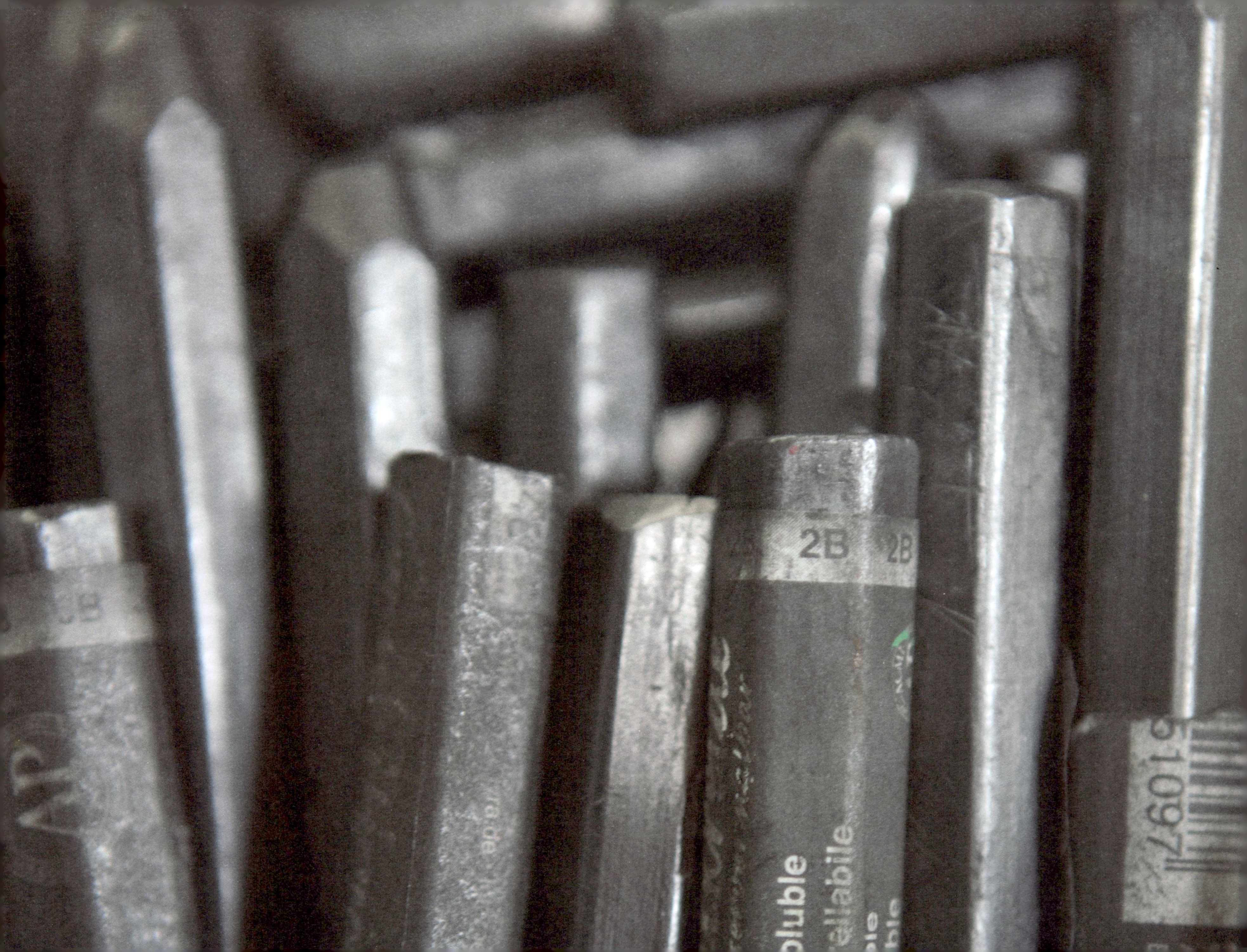
2B
2B 2B
AP
oluble
ellabile
ole
ble
51097

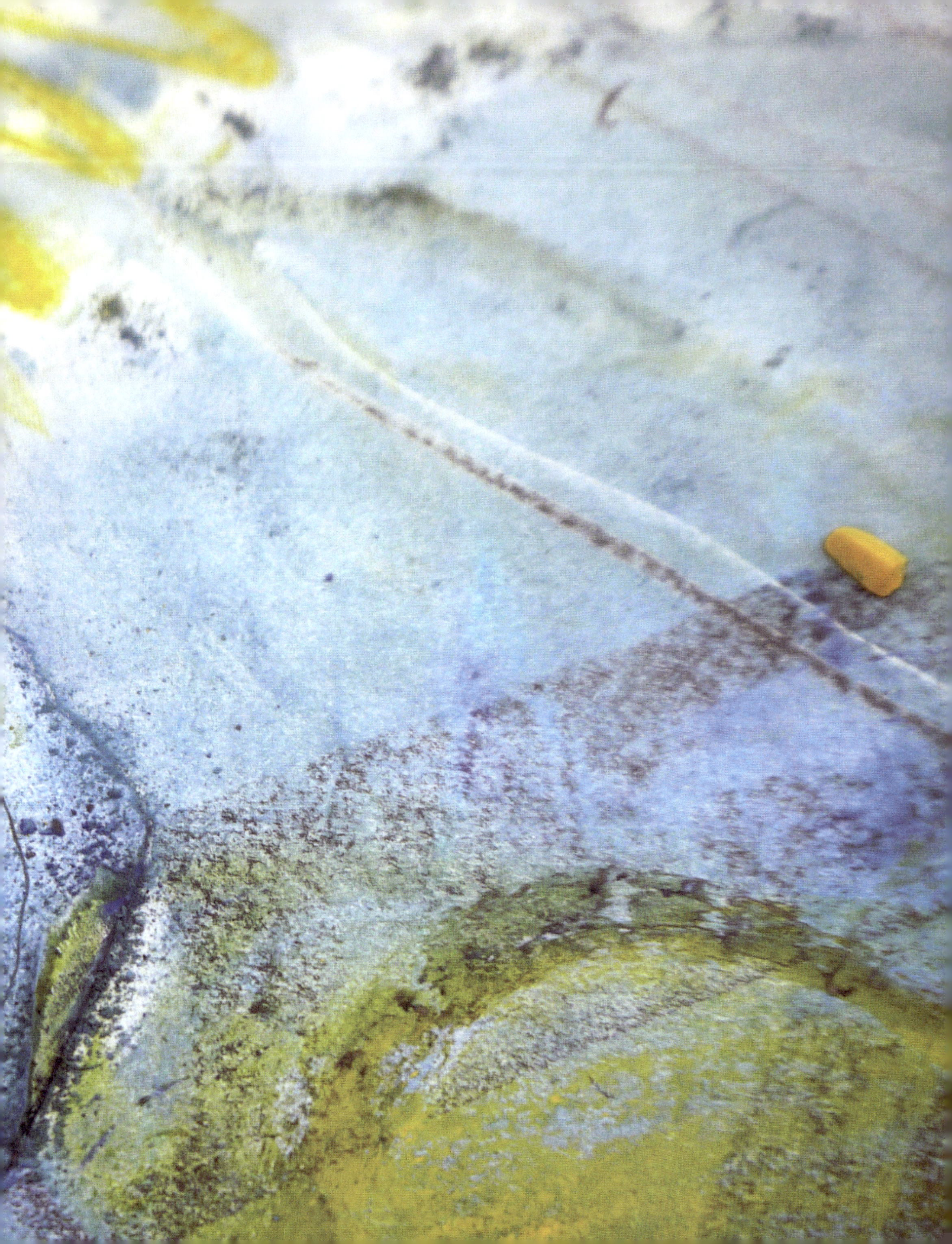

CONTENTS

WARM UPS

PROJECTS

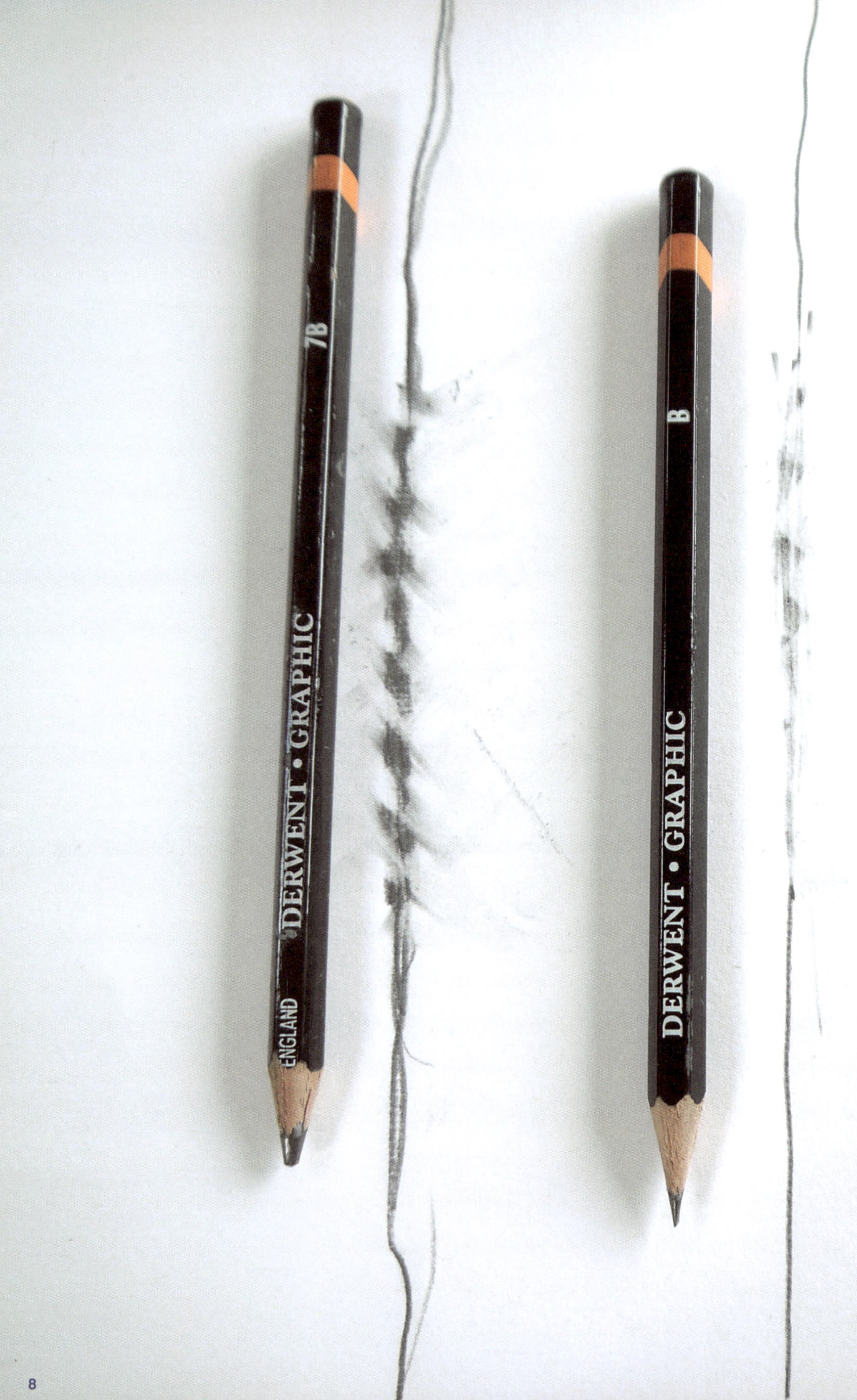

INTRODUCTION

Hello! Welcome to *Drawing Projects for Children*, a book that will give you lots of drawing inspiration, skills and knowledge! In this book are a number of warm ups and projects to take you through drawing all sorts of subject matter, with many different and exciting materials, in lots of new ways.

The warm ups in this book are a great way to gain and practise drawing skills. These short exercises will introduce you to new ways of making marks, or some materials that perhaps you have never drawn with before. Before starting a project, try warming up with one of these tasks.

All of the projects in this book also use a huge range of drawing materials from inks and watercolours to graphite and pastels. Remember, great drawing experiences are not always about the outcome, but often about the things you learn when you experiment. So get ready to try out some new techniques, and make some wonderful creations! You may want to ask an adult to help you with some of the projects.

There are three levels of warm ups and projects in *Drawing Projects for Children*. Why not begin with those in Getting Started, then move on to Have a Go, and finally, to really push yourself, Push it Further. You can see what level a project is, as its title will be underlined by one of these colours:

Getting Started

Have A Go

Push It Further

Have fun!

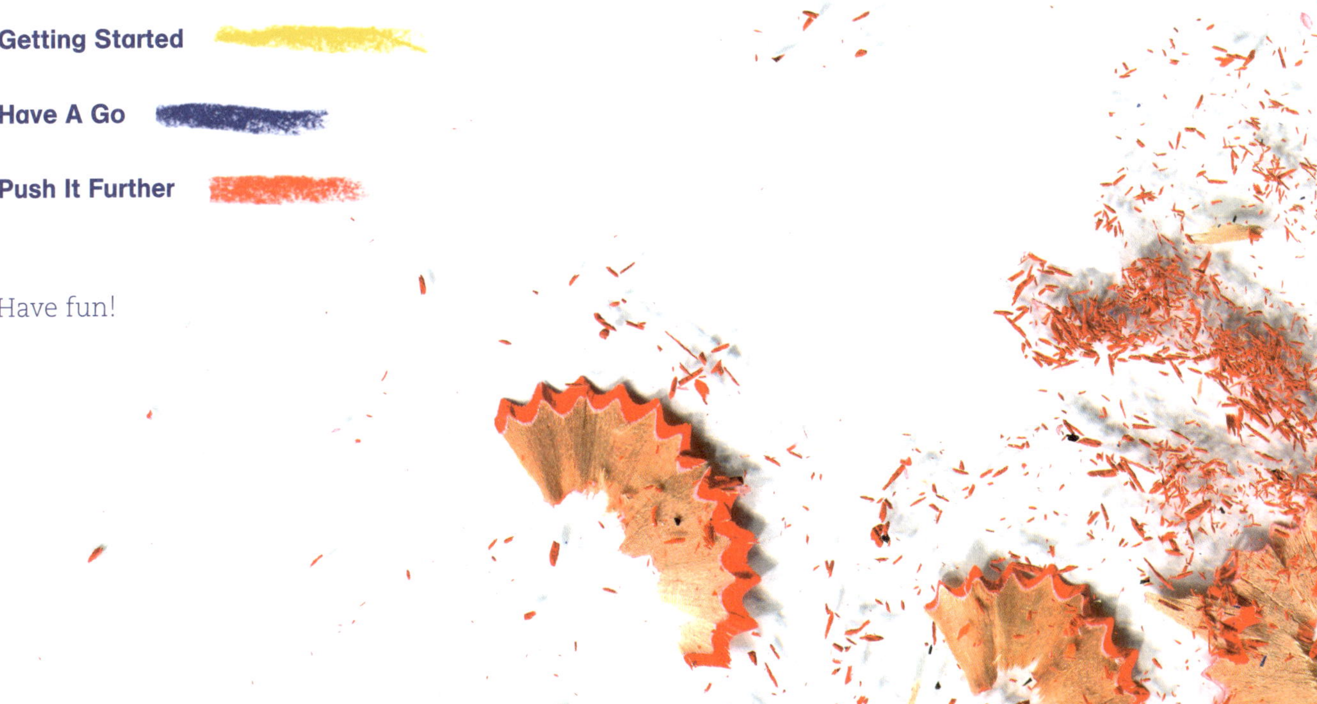

MATERIALS

Pencils

Pencils are the most common drawing tool, but many of us only use a HB pencil, which generally makes grey, uniform marks. But drawing pencils range in 'hardness' or 'blackness' (softness) from 9H to 9B. 9H is the hardest pencil, which makes a hard, light mark. 9B is the blackest pencil and gives a dense, soft and easily produced mark.

Between these grades pencils offer us the opportunity to make all kinds of marks in different densities (how dark or light, thick or thin, gentle or strong the mark is). Whether your pencil is sharp or blunt, the amount of pressure you apply and the way you hold the pencil in your hand will all also affect the marks it makes.

Experiment with where you hold a pencil when you draw: right at the end like you would a handwriting pen, half way up, or at the very top, gripped in your clenched fist. There is no wrong or right way to hold a pencil, only different ways depending on the types of marks you want to make.

Graphite

Graphite sticks are usually graded B to 9B and come in a two main thicknesses (the thickness of a normal pencil, and the thickness of a chunky wax crayon). The graphite in a graphite stick is similar to that in a soft B pencil, without the surrounding wood. The thicker sticks are very useful for making energetic drawings on medium or larger scales. Using graphite with an eraser can also create some interesting marks.

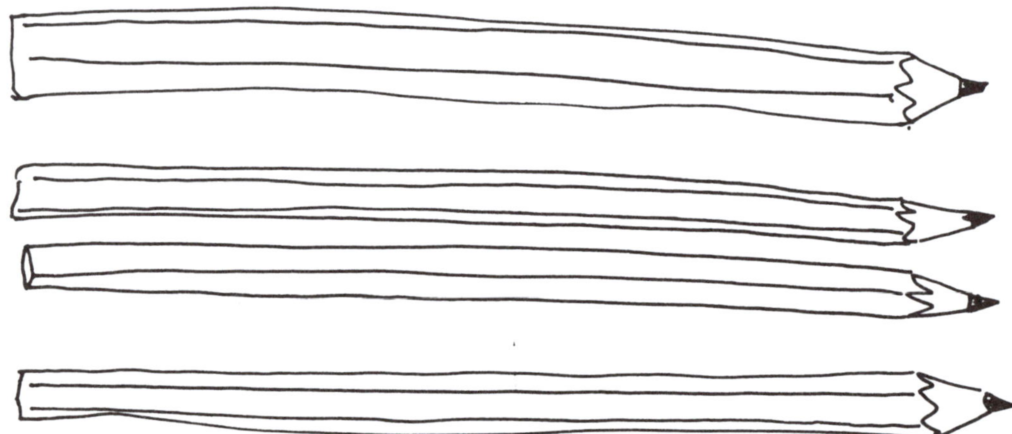

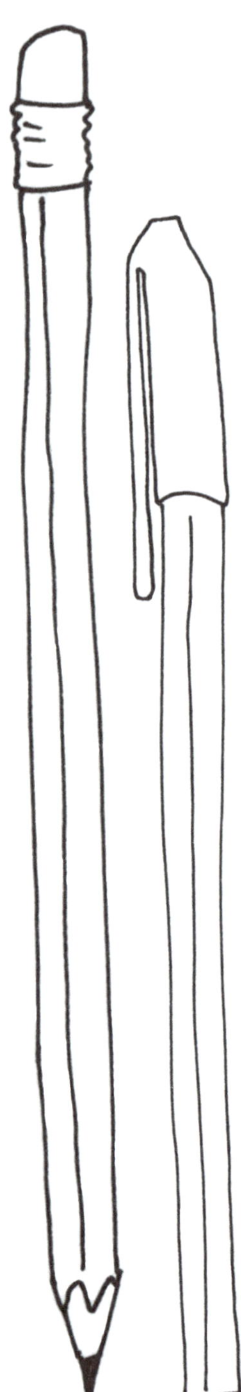

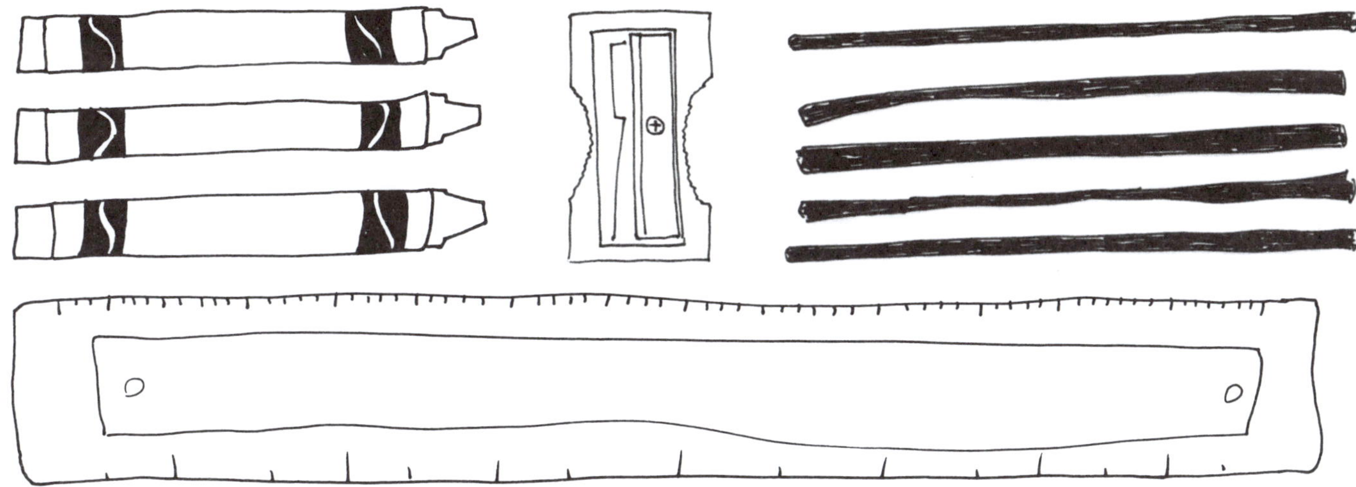

Soluble Graphite

Graphite also comes in 'soluble' form, and there are two main ways that this can be used: you can draw with it as you would with regular graphite, and then use a brush with clean water or diluted watercolours (a small amount of watercolour paint mixed with water) to dissolve the marks across the page, turning the graphite to paint. Marks made in this way will range from very black to watery grey. Or, you can work the opposite way—wet the page first and then make marks with the soluble graphite.

You can also combine soluble graphite with other materials to make more marks. For example, use white wax crayon, white oil pastel or candle wax on a dry sheet of paper before using the soluble graphite and water for a 'resist' effect, where marks made in wax or pastel 'resist' and show through the soluble graphite. Remember not to leave soluble graphite sticks in water or they will dissolve.

Charcoal

Willow charcoal can be bought in different grades and thicknesses (or in mixed boxes) and can create lots of different, fluid marks. The best way to get to know what kinds of marks charcoal can make, is to play with it!

Use the side of the charcoal to cover large areas of your sheet in a light, mid or dark tone. Use the end of the charcoal stick for fine or thick, darker and more controlled lines. Use your hand or your fingers to smudge the charcoal, or use an eraser to remove it and create highlights. Remember you can use all of these methods together and layer your mark making. Once you are finished drawing with charcoal, remember to fix it with a fixative spray in a ventilated area (outside or a room with open windows), or else it may smudge.

As well as bought willow charcoal, you can make your own charcoal by using burnt wood from a fire. Make sure you are very careful and only ever make your own charcoal with an adult, making sure you let the wood cool completely before using it to draw with.

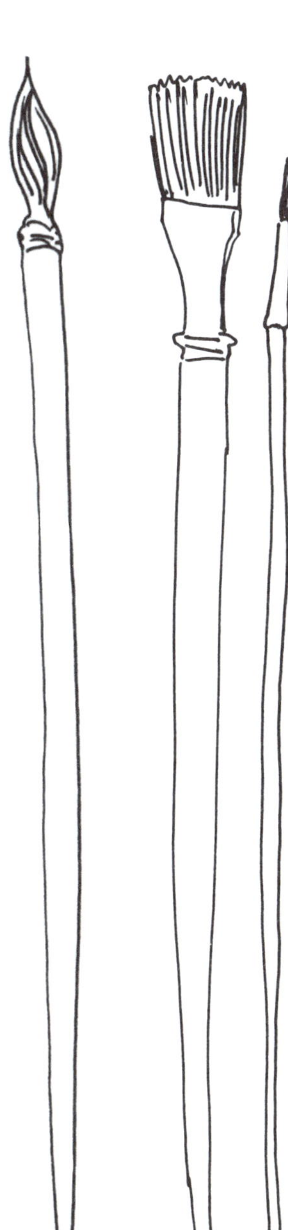

Compressed Charcoal

Compressed charcoal makes a coarser, darker mark than willow charcoal. This is usually used more like a pencil and works best on a large scale.

Erasers

In the warm ups and projects in this book erasers are not used for erasing mistakes. Instead they are used as a mark-making tool. By removing layers of other materials, you can create new, effective marks. This works particularly well with pencils, graphite, erasable coloured pencils and charcoal.

Watercolours

Watercolours are used in this book as a drawing tool, either to add lines of colour, or to add weight or shadow to help show a form. You do not need expensive watercolours, even simple palette (basic colour selection) ones work well.

Oil Pastels

Oil pastels are made from pigment mixed with a non-drying oil and wax binder. They create vivid colour, especially when you apply a bit of pressure.

Oil pastels can be used alone and work very well on a large scale. They also make great partners with graphite (or pencil) and linseed oil. Graphite applied over oil pastel becomes denser and darker as the graphite skids easily over the oily surface, leaving rich marks. Linseed oil can be used to dilute the oil pastel once it is on the page, and if worked in with a brush, can help mix the pastel and leave painterly marks.

Oil pastels are also used in this book with acrylic as a way of creating a sgraffito (scratched) surface.

Chalk Pastels

Chalk pastels make soft marks and are easy to blend. They work well on thick, textured paper—especially if it is slightly coloured—and can be used to draw both highlights and shadows.

Pens

In this book we use three types of pens that may be used to draw: handwriting pens, permanent markers and coloured biros.

Handwriting pens create careful, fluid lines. You do not need to apply much pressure to create a mark, and this means that the pen nibs 'scoot' easily across the paper. Permanent markers create a thicker, heavier line. Coloured biros can come in lots of different colours, which can be used in the same way as coloured pencils to create layered sketches.

Wax Crayons

Light coloured wax crayons can be used as a tool to create a 'resist' effect when working with soluble graphite, ink or watercolours. Other great tools for creating this effect are stubs of candle or oil pastel.

Coloured Pencil Crayons

Coloured pencils can also be used as a sketching tool, and the many different colours they come in can help make interesting layered drawings. Mixing regular coloured pencils with water soluble coloured pencils and erasable coloured pencils in the same work can also create interesting effects.

Inks

Black Indian ink or coloured inks are useful as their colour is richer than that of watercolour. You can use inks with brushes and nibs (you can even make a nib at home using a feather).

When ink is wet, water can be added to it to create a wash, which can create different tones. When the ink dries though, it is no longer soluble. This means ink can be used to create layers too, just by adding more washes of more dilute ink over the top of the original layer.

Homemade Drawing Tools

You can also experiment with making some homemade drawing tools.
For example:

- Create long-handled drawing tools by taping brushes or pencils onto sticks, so that you are further away from your drawing and have less control.

- Tape together a number of graphite sticks or pencils to make one big, chunky drawing tool.

- Apply ink to paper using Plasticine shaped into a drawing tool.

Remember!

- Always be on the look out for how you can use other materials to inspire your drawing.

- Try to choose the right tool for the kind of drawing you want to produce.

- Try out different 'drawing sandwiches'—how might you layer drawing materials within one drawing? For example you might make some marks using graphite, then eraser, then graphite. Each layer of medium adds something to the layer before, and so your drawing is built.

- Match the material you use to the size of your drawing; if you are using a big A1 sheet of paper, for example, you may prefer not to use a hard, fine pencil. Nor would you use a chunky graphite stick if you were drawing on a small sheet of paper.

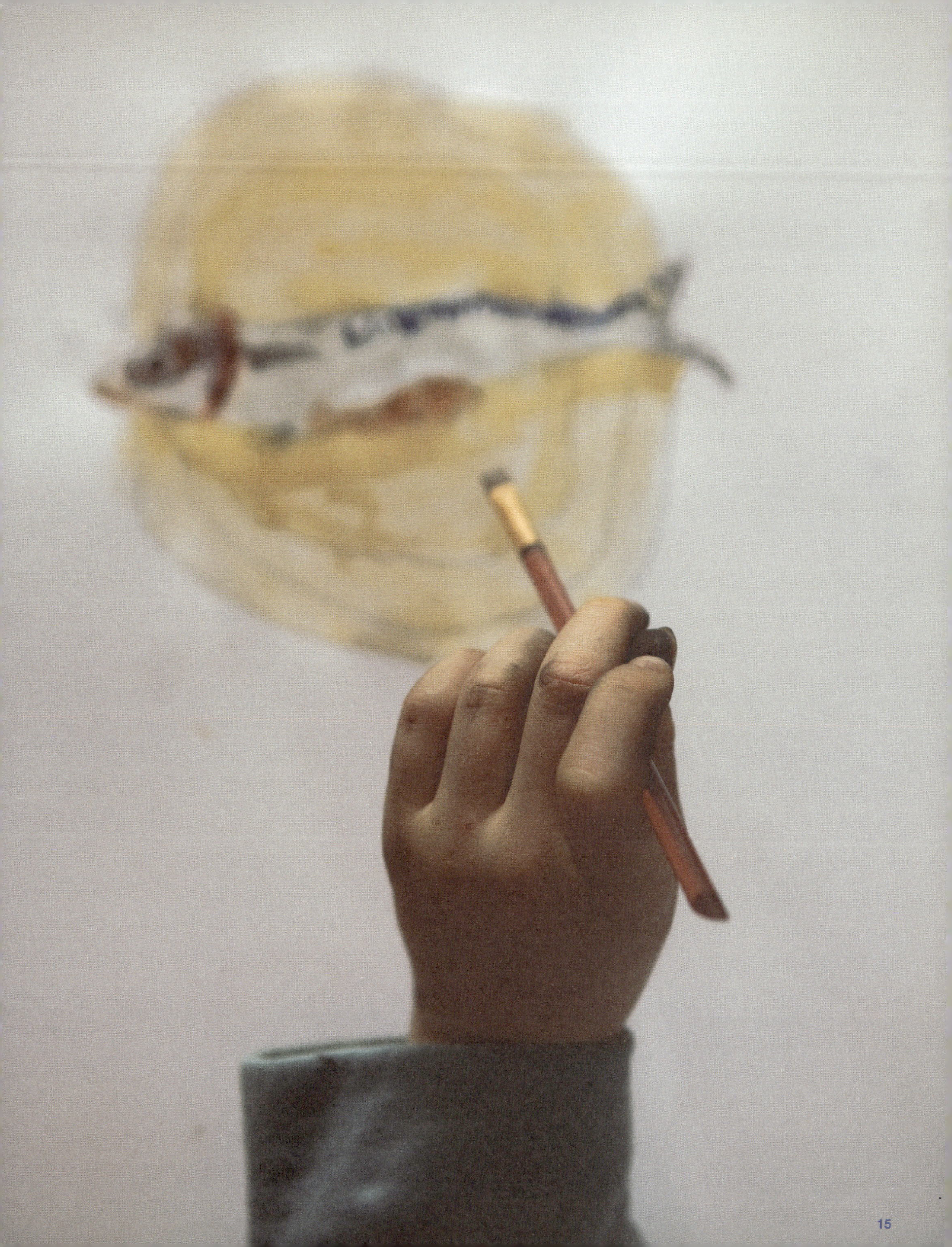

DRAWING SURFACES

While we might think very carefully about the drawing materials we use, sometimes we neglect to consider the surface that we draw on. The warm ups and projects in this book use lots of different drawing surfaces and sizes.

100–140 gsm Drawing or Cartridge Paper

This is a basic drawing paper that works well with most drawing materials. Drawing or cartridge paper is better than ordinary paper because it has more texture, which allows for all sorts of mark making with a pencil or graphite stick.

Sugar Paper

Available in many colours, sugar paper is a cheaper option than drawing or cartridge paper. Sugar paper works well with graphite, chalk and oil pastels, though its texture makes lines appear less sharp or dense. As it is more absorbent than drawing paper, it also soaks up ink and watercolour more quickly.

Newsprint

Newsprint is useful for very quick exercises. It is very thin and absorbent so lines drawn on it are not crisp and it can tear easily. Newsprint is especially useful for placing under sheets of drawing paper to provide protection and for stopping any marks on your desk or workspace showing through your drawing paper.

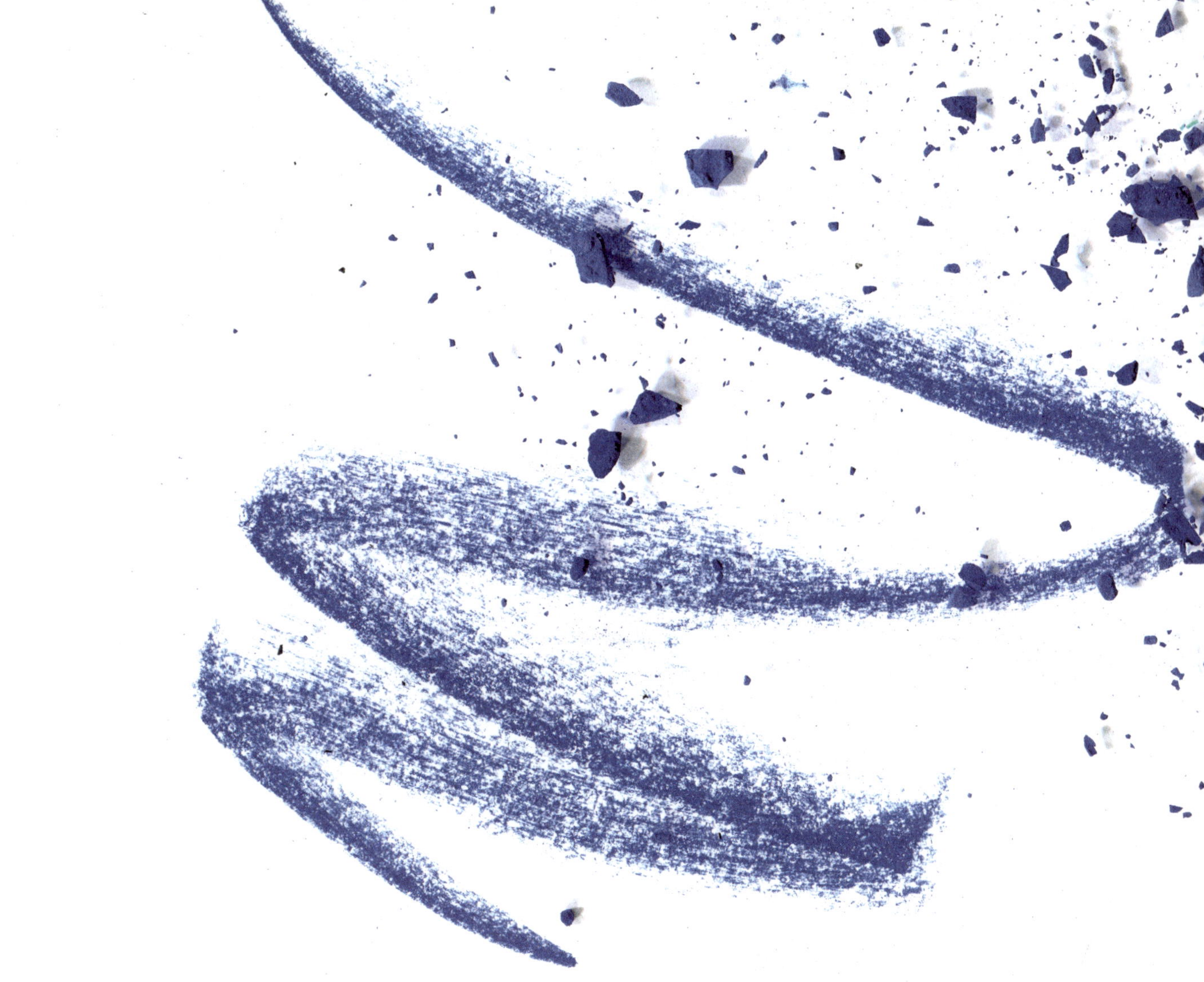

Wallpaper Lining Paper

Some projects in this book use really long sheets of paper. You can make these by joining large sheets of drawing paper together, but a roll of wallpaper lining paper is a great alternative.

Other Surfaces

Be creative when thinking about what can become a drawing surface. Many projects in this book use recycled papers (such as old envelopes) or paper that might not normally be used for drawing (such as graph paper, tracing paper, blotting paper or old maps).

You can also make your own drawing surfaces. For example, casting your own plaster blocks as in Drawing on Plaster (p 100).

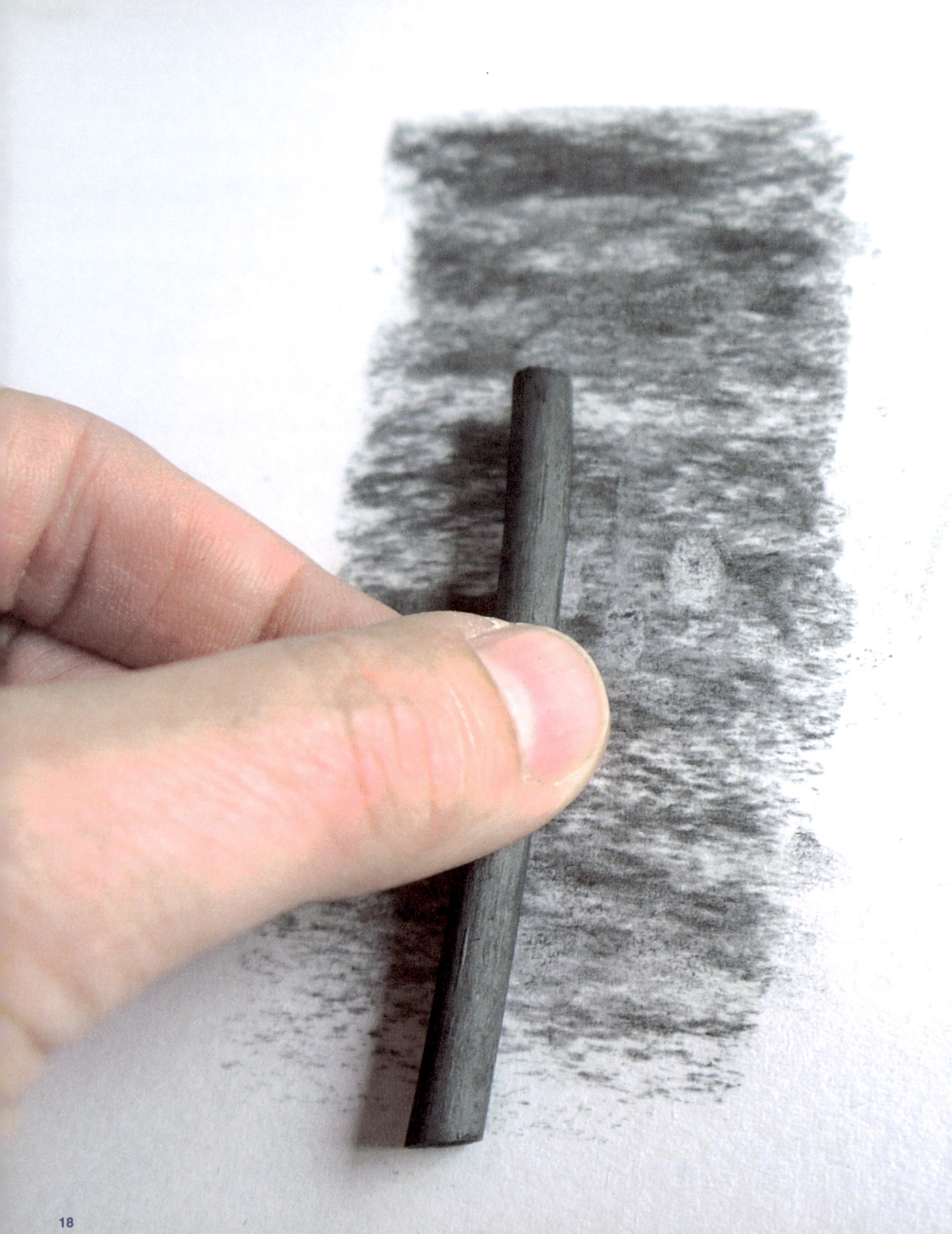

FACILITATOR'S NOTES

While *Drawing Projects for Children* is a compilation of drawing exercises for children to carry out independently, it is also an excellent resource for those who want to help children discover drawing. As a facilitator, you can use the warm ups and projects featured here to help your own child—or children, if you are working in a class or group environment—to get the most they can from drawing, to give them confidence in their abilities, to introduce them to many new drawing materials, and to provide an overarching awareness of how those materials can work for them.

While conducting the warm ups and projects featured in *Drawing Projects for Children*, remember that facilitating drawing is a sensitive business. You must pass on enough knowledge, information and access to materials to inspire and get children started, but you also need to create enough space to allow them to be in control of their own exploration.

The Potential of Materials

Children are naturally attracted to drawing materials—the beauty of a brand new pack of coloured pencil crayons displayed in rainbow order is as attractive to many as sweets in a sweet shop. But understanding the potential of drawing materials is vital if children are to be inspired and energised by the drawing process; by obtaining a level of control over the materials, they will gain confidence in their ability and feel freer to experiment or push themselves.

It is also important to introduce children to the effects available. The projects in *Drawing Projects for Children* use a host of drawing materials, including those that children may encounter everyday as well as many that would usually be considered beyond their reach, from basic soft and hard pencils or watercolour to oil pastels, writing pens and soluble graphite. While the projects featured here give guidance as to what different materials are capable of and how each one can be used, with your help, the children will learn this through their own experimentation.

Playing It Safe And Taking Risks

For children to get the most out of drawing, they need to be encouraged to push beyond what they consider 'safe' ('safe' drawings are those in which we know what the outcome is going to be before we have even started making them) and to take risks. By doing so they will widen their concept of what drawing is and what they are capable of achieving.

Routines of making safe drawings—becoming confident in one style or subject, and repeatedly drawing the same thing until a process is recognisable, predictable and always 'successful'—are easy to fall in to. In one sense this is valuable: drawings made in this way are fully owned by the child creating them. However, it is also important to push beyond this to experience new materials and make drawings in new ways, all of which demonstrate to children skills and abilities they did not know they possessed.

As a facilitator, you should demonstrate that taking risks is not only acceptable, it is desirable. One key way you can do this is by establishing how success might be measured. For example success may be 'an enthusiastic exploration of the medium', rather than 'to produce a beautifully drawn image'.

Though everybody desires excellent outcomes in terms of the drawings produced, it is often true that aesthetically pleasing drawings can hide a less than exciting journey where few risks have been taken and little genuine understanding or experience has been built. Conversely, a fantastically stimulating drawing journey can deliver potentially misunderstood work. Sometimes, a session that has enabled children to learn lots, results in work that is, quite literally, hard work to reflect upon. Balancing the value we place on the journey, with the value we place on outcomes, can help us explore our attitude to risk and many of the projects in this book are designed to try to balance these elements.

Part of enabling this process is being overt with children about when they are playing safe, and when it is appropriate to take more risks. The worst that can happen when we take creative risks, is that we no longer like the outcome. The best that can happen, however, is that the child makes creative leaps, discovers new processes and outcomes, and becomes enthused to explore further.

Warming Up

When used appropriately, warm up exercises can benefit the type of work produced during a drawing session. Positive influences of warm up exercises include: helping to make a clear transition between the rest of the day and a drawing activity; setting the scene for the session, providing a starting point for a later reflection or introducing new materials to be used in a later project; surprising, waking up or settling down a jaded class; helping children follow instructions; boosting children's confidence; and opening their minds, preventing misconceptions and planting seeds for new ideas or ways of working.

Warm ups are also beneficial to you as a facilitator: by thinking through which warm up will be most appropriate for your session, you will be forced to clarify and dissect its aims. You may soon wish to start inventing warm ups to suit your needs. When you do, there are several factors to consider:

- The outcome of the warm up should help create a bridge to the beginning of the main drawing session.

- Plan backwards from where you want to go in the main session ie is it about a material, a technique, a concept?

- Consider potential stumbling blocks both in the main session and in the warm up. Can you split the activities up into smaller stages to help overcome these?

- Think about what new experiences you would like the children to have.

- Keep it simple and short—do not overload a warm up exercise.

- Always try the warm up yourself; what is it really like to do what you are asking of them?

- Finally, leave time at the end for reflection and sharing experiences.

Most of the warm ups featured here will take only five to ten minutes. Like any exercises they can and should be repeated regularly to get the most out of them, and like any skill, the children will quickly improve with practice.

The Projects

The projects in *Drawing Projects for Children* will help you inspire children to discover drawing. They are presented in no particular order, and are designed to last about an hour, but if you are working with a large group of children this could be spread over two hours, or even longer.

When facilitating the projects, there are a number of considerations to bear in mind:

- Try to make each session memorable in some way; you could capture attention from the start by setting up the space in a creative or unexpected way before the children enter, for instance.

- Intersperse drawing with other important and related activities, such as cutting, making, and of course looking and talking.

- If you are working with a group of children, consider how they will be positioned in the room—some activities benefit from having the children work alone and facing away from one another, while others work best with an inward facing circle.

- Do not assume that a drawing class should be any less focused than a maths class. Sometimes the energy of a drawing activity results in noise and movement, but often children need calm and quiet in order to focus.

- Be wary of demonstrations and use them cautiously. A good demonstration will plant seeds and enable exploration. A bad demonstration (or too much of a good demonstration!) will influence the children too strongly.

- If a child becomes stuck, issue a 'challenge'—to use a certain material or to draw to a certain size, for example—to help them move on.

- Finally, listening to intention is vital. Ensure that your mind is as open as the childrens'.

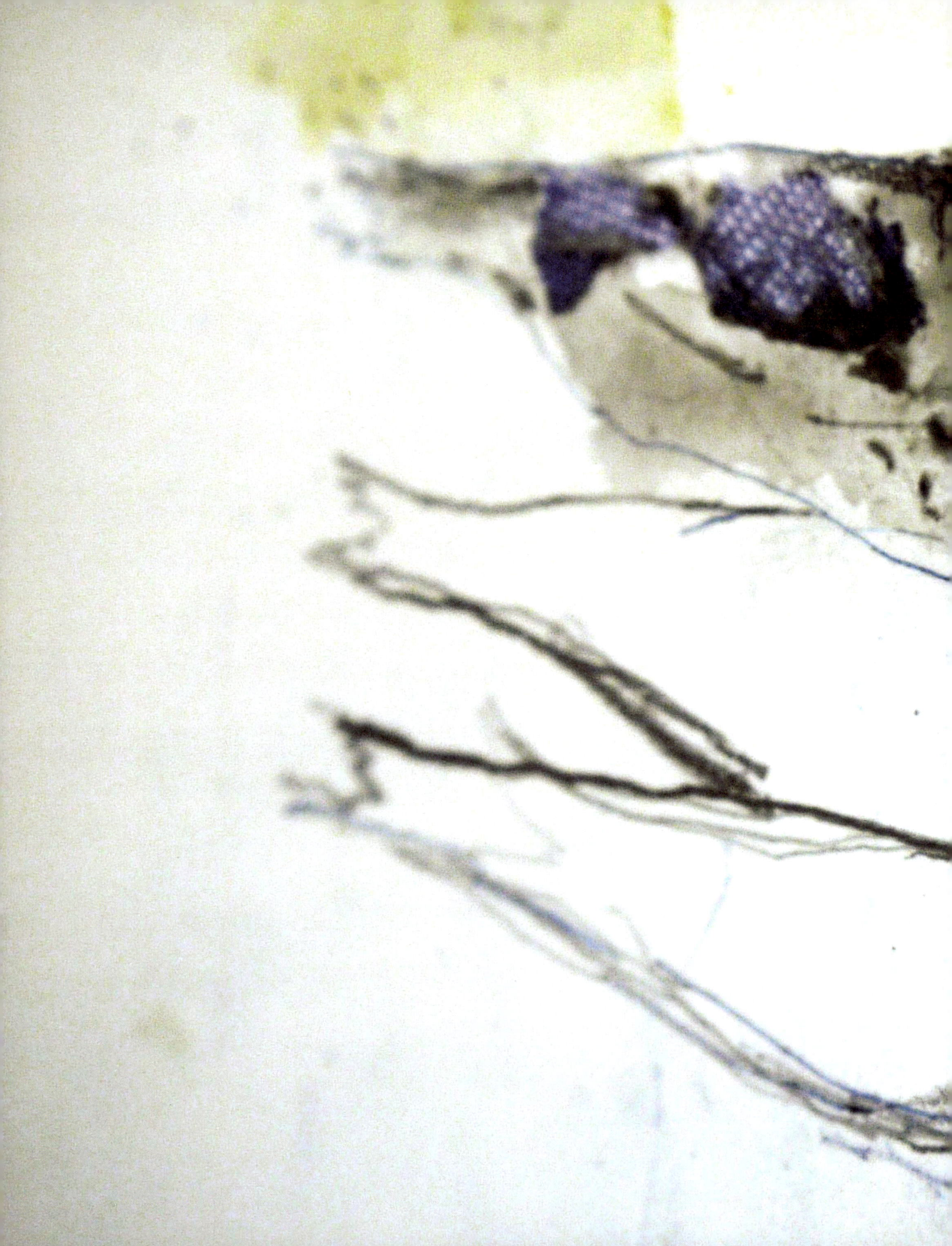

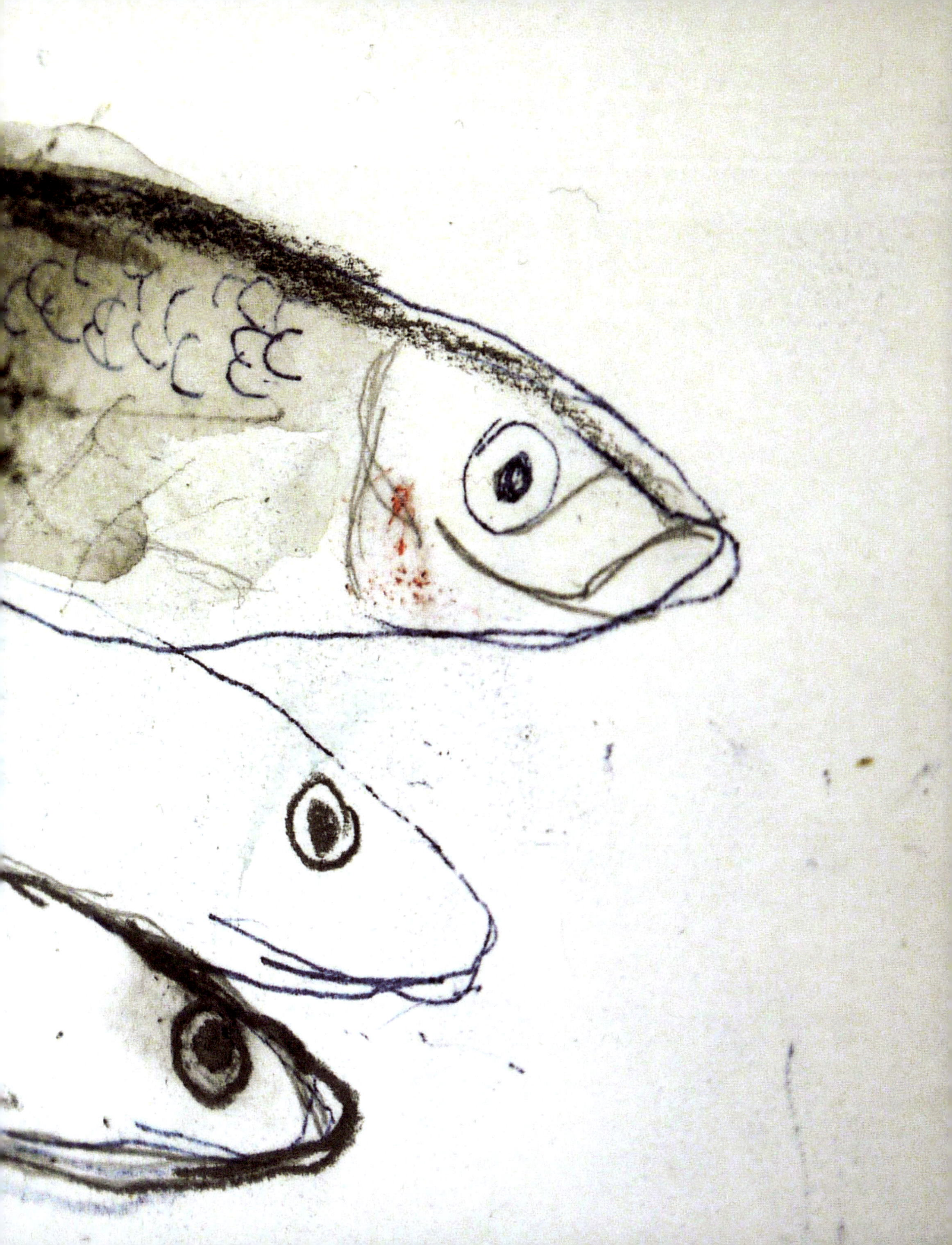

WARM UPS

Continuous Line Drawing

Continuous line drawing is an excellent way to practise your hand-eye coordination. Continuous line drawings are made by never taking the pen or pencil off the paper, and by drawing very slowly—moving your pen or pencil at the same speed that your eye looks at the subject matter. By drawing this slowly you will be able to control the drawing and observe the detail of your subject very carefully.

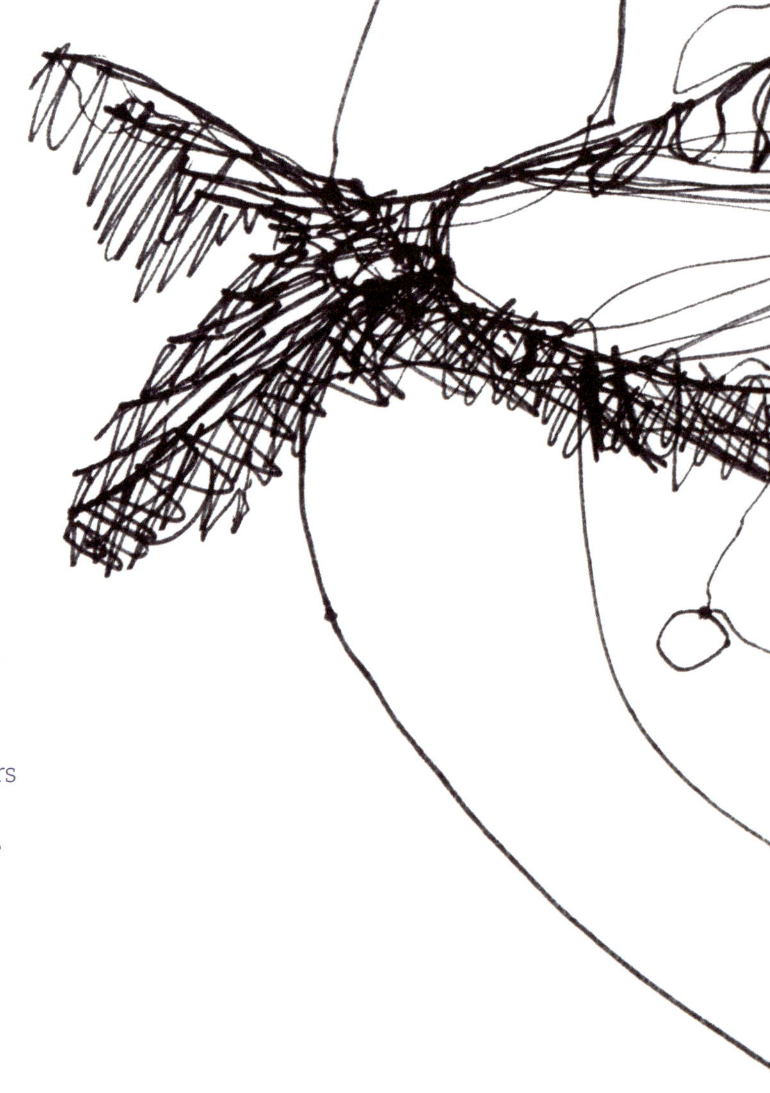

Materials

- Handwriting pens
- Drawing paper

Subject Matter

Choose small objects as subject matter, like keys, cutlery, tools, feathers or coins.

Activity

It is best to do continuous line drawings when you are quiet and concentrating.

1 Make a drawing without taking your pen off the paper. A handwriting pen has less friction than a pencil, so it can 'scoot' more easily across the paper. Your eye should follow details and contours on the object you are drawing, and your hand should draw these details at the same time. The hand wanders wherever the eye sees. To draw some detail in the middle of the object, your pen should stay on the page, travelling to the bit of the paper that you want to draw on.

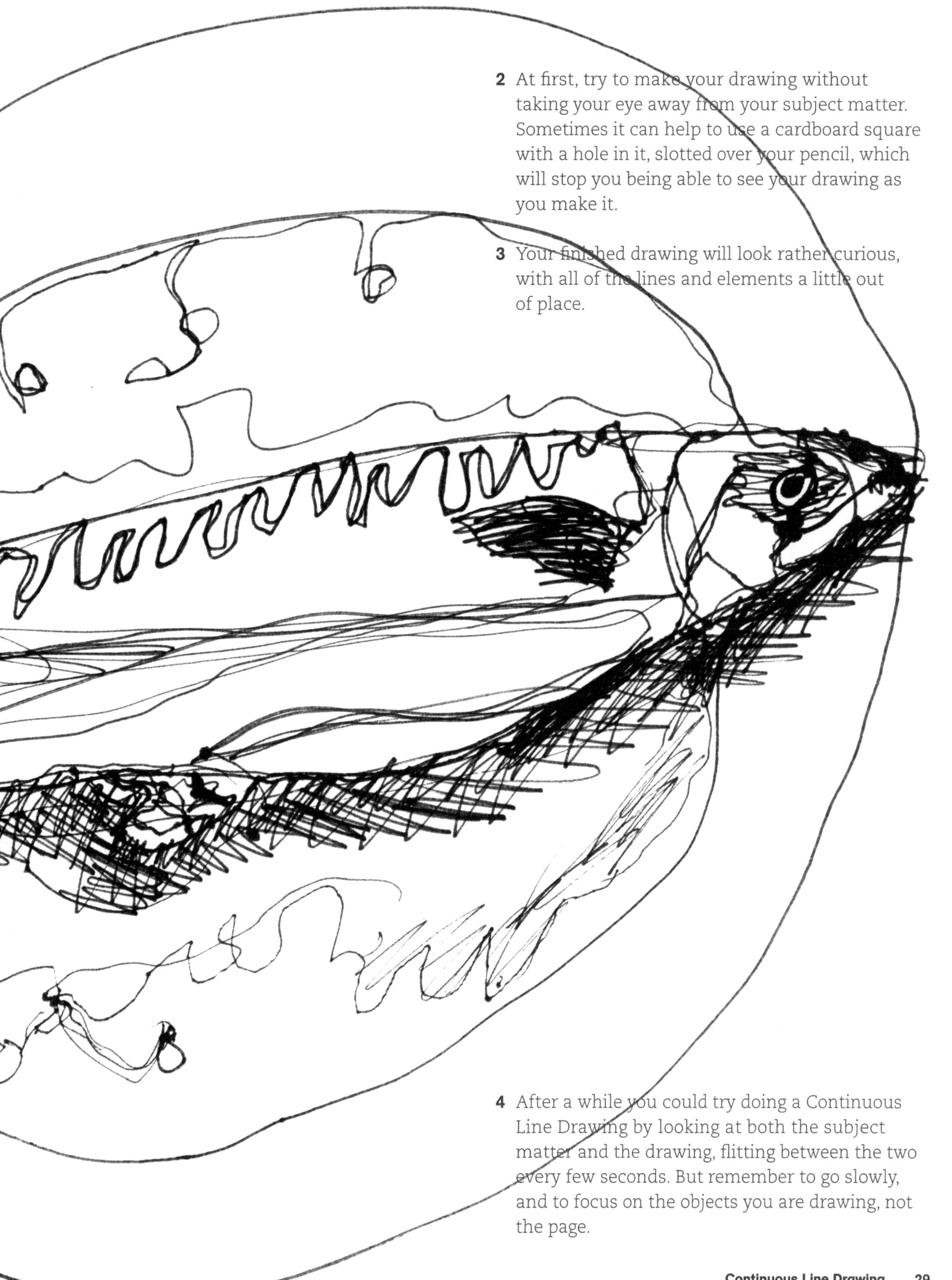

2 At first, try to make your drawing without taking your eye away from your subject matter. Sometimes it can help to use a cardboard square with a hole in it, slotted over your pencil, which will stop you being able to see your drawing as you make it.

3 Your finished drawing will look rather curious, with all of the lines and elements a little out of place.

4 After a while you could try doing a Continuous Line Drawing by looking at both the subject matter and the drawing, flitting between the two every few seconds. But remember to go slowly, and to focus on the objects you are drawing, not the page.

BACKWARDS FORWARDS SKETCHING

Backwards forwards sketching is a simple activity that will help you develop understanding and knowledge of your subject matter through slow, careful observation. It will help you match the speed of looking with the speed of drawing, helping your hand-eye coordination.

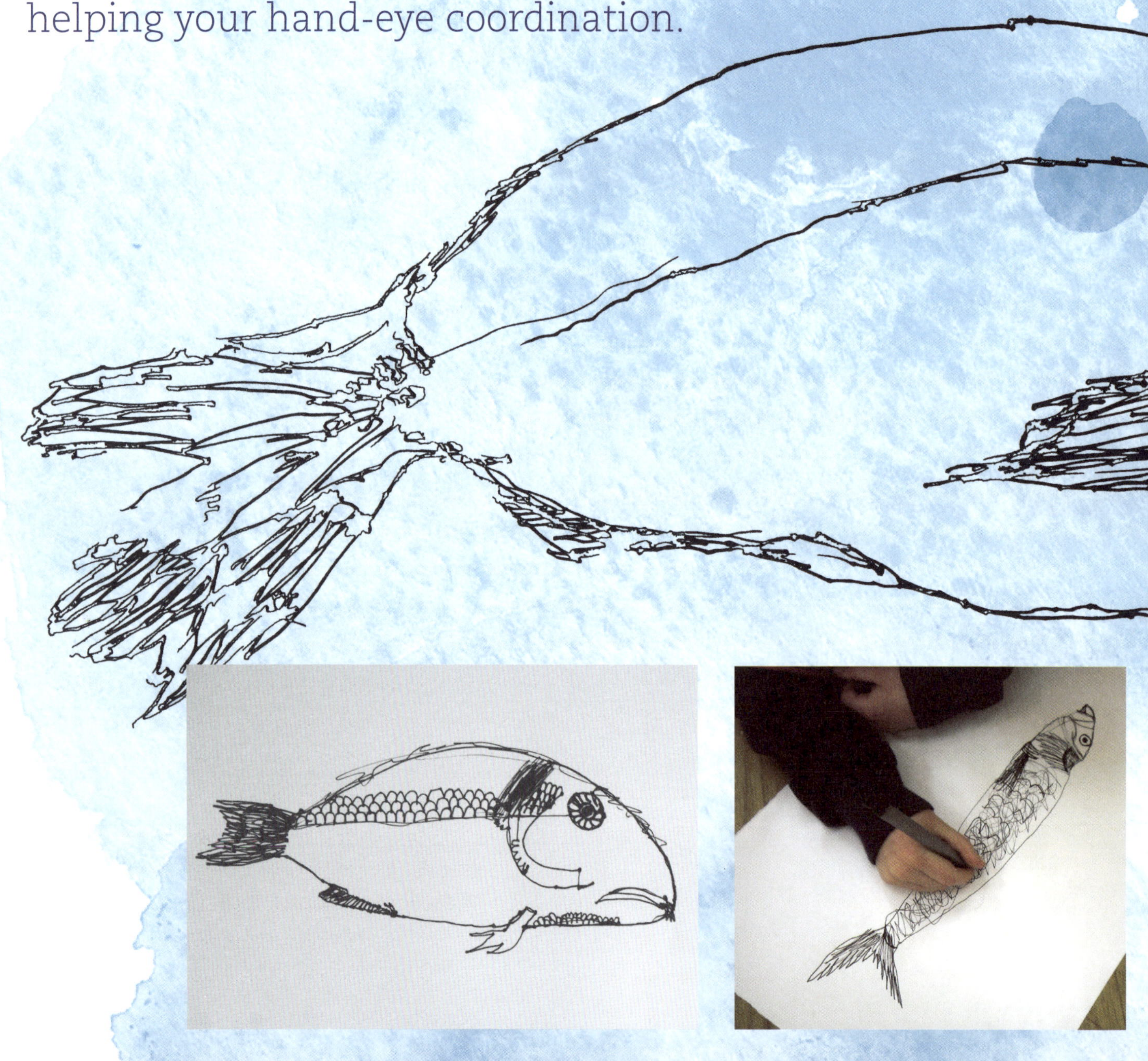

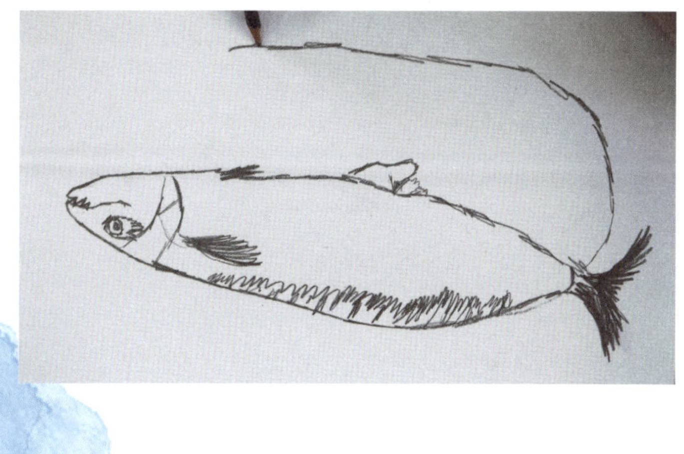

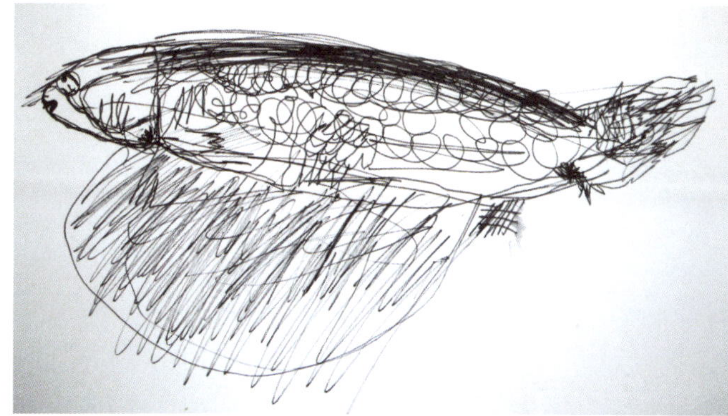

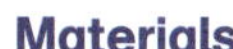

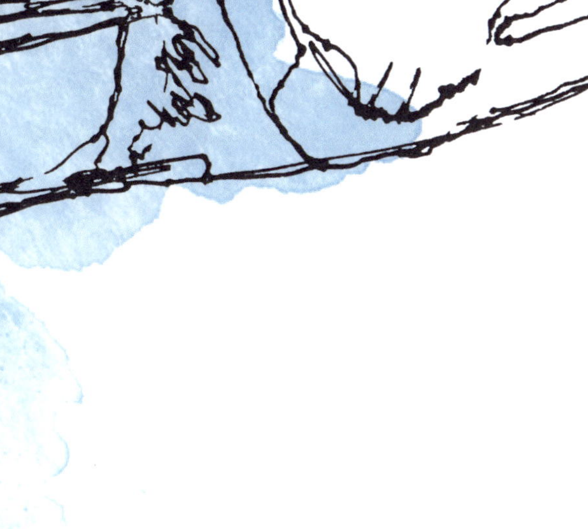

Materials

- Soft (B) and hard (H) pencils
- Drawing paper

Subject Matter

Any small still life object will work well for this warm up.

Activity

1 Make a drawing of your subject matter using only one motion—in backwards forwards sketching you are only allowed to draw from left to right and right to left, from your wrist. This means that the pencil travels forwards, then backwards, forwards, then backwards again. Each line you make in your drawing is repeated as your hand travels backwards and forwards, backwards and forwards.

Facilitator's Note

When children are challenged to only draw using a backwards forwards motion, their mark making is slowed down as the drawing line has to repeat (or reassert) itself. As the mark making is slowed down, the hand is less likely to run away with itself before the eye has really seen. In backwards forwards sketching the hand and eye has to check and check again each line as it is formed, helping to ensure the lines are intentional. This also gives children the opportunity to re-see their lines as they go. By nature, backwards forwards sketches should feel solid and intentional as the pencil 'feels' its way around the image.

COLOURFUL GESTURAL DRAWINGS

Gestural drawings are energetic and fun, and made with lots of quick movements. In gestural drawing, we try to see the whole of a drawing before we look in detail at a single part of it. In this exercise, you will use coloured marker pens to practise gestural drawing, but this type of activity also works well with lots of different drawing materials, including pencils, coloured crayons and graphite.

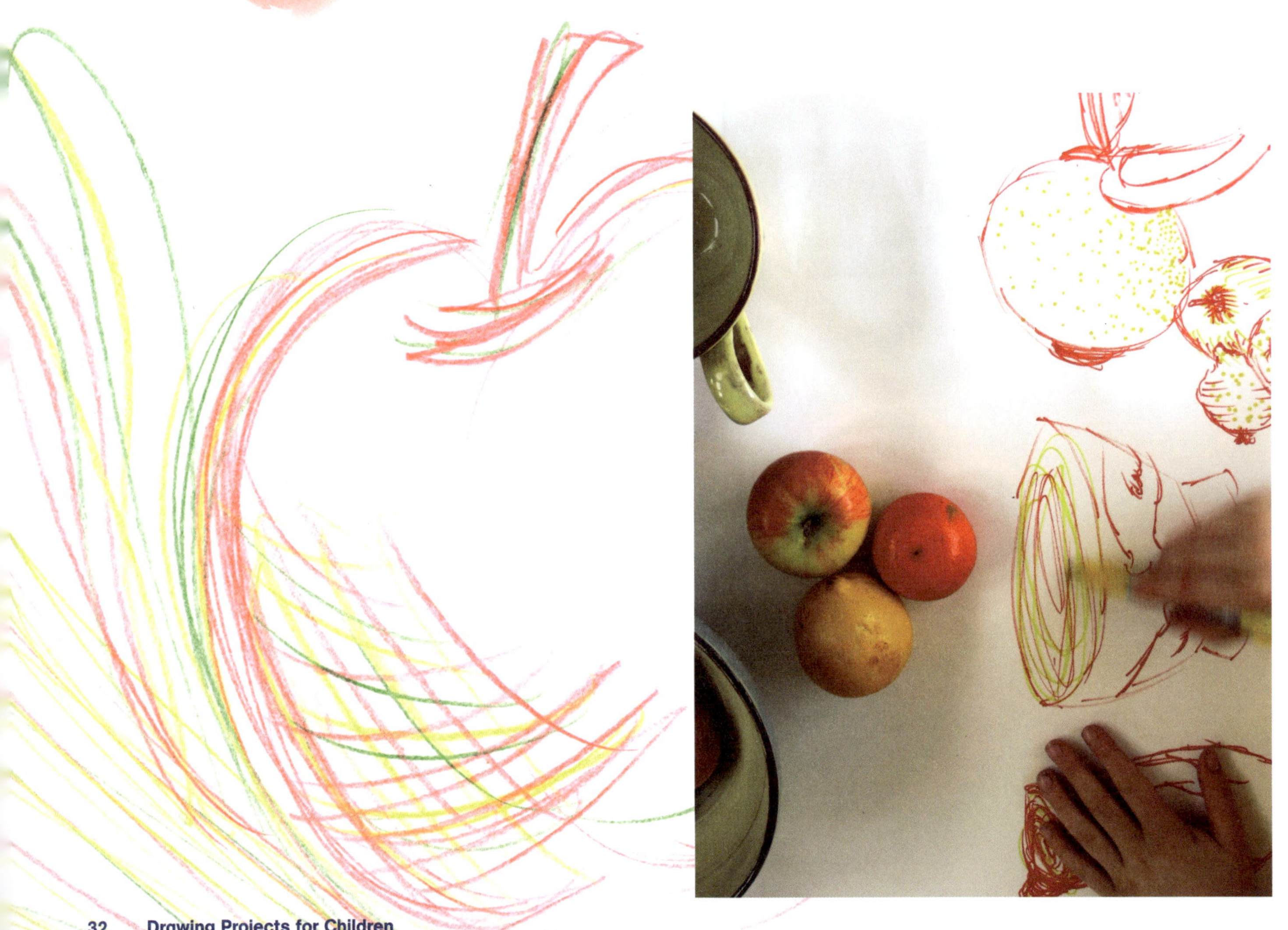

Materials

- Coloured permanent marker pens

Subject Matter

Simple still life objects, such as fruit or vegetables.

Activity

Gestural drawings are about using fast actions to make quick marks on the paper. But, just because they are about speed and motion, this does not mean they should be careless!

It is also important to work on all parts of the drawing at once. This means trying to see and draw the whole thing—you should get a quick impression of composition (how all the objects sit on the page), form, negative space (the space between two objects), line, dark and shadow, all at once. This sounds tricky, but it is fun to do.

1 Set up a still life with various objects and begin drawing the arrangement with a pale colour.

2 Start by making a series of simple marks to show where a certain colour will go, or where a particular object will sit, etc. By doing this, you will be considering the whole picture, using the whole sheet of paper in a rough, sketchy way.

   Add layers of these sorts of marks, building up your picture. You should follow a pattern of looking, then drawing, then looking, then drawing. Gestural drawings are full of mistakes! No eraser allowed—just keep making new marks on top of old ones until you like what you see.

3 After a few minutes, change to a second colour. Try to make these second marks different to the first ones, varying your marks and working on all different areas of the drawing at once.

   For each layer of coloured marks you might: re-draw an element correctly, add a shadow or highlight, add a texture, capture a negative space, or make something feel 3D.

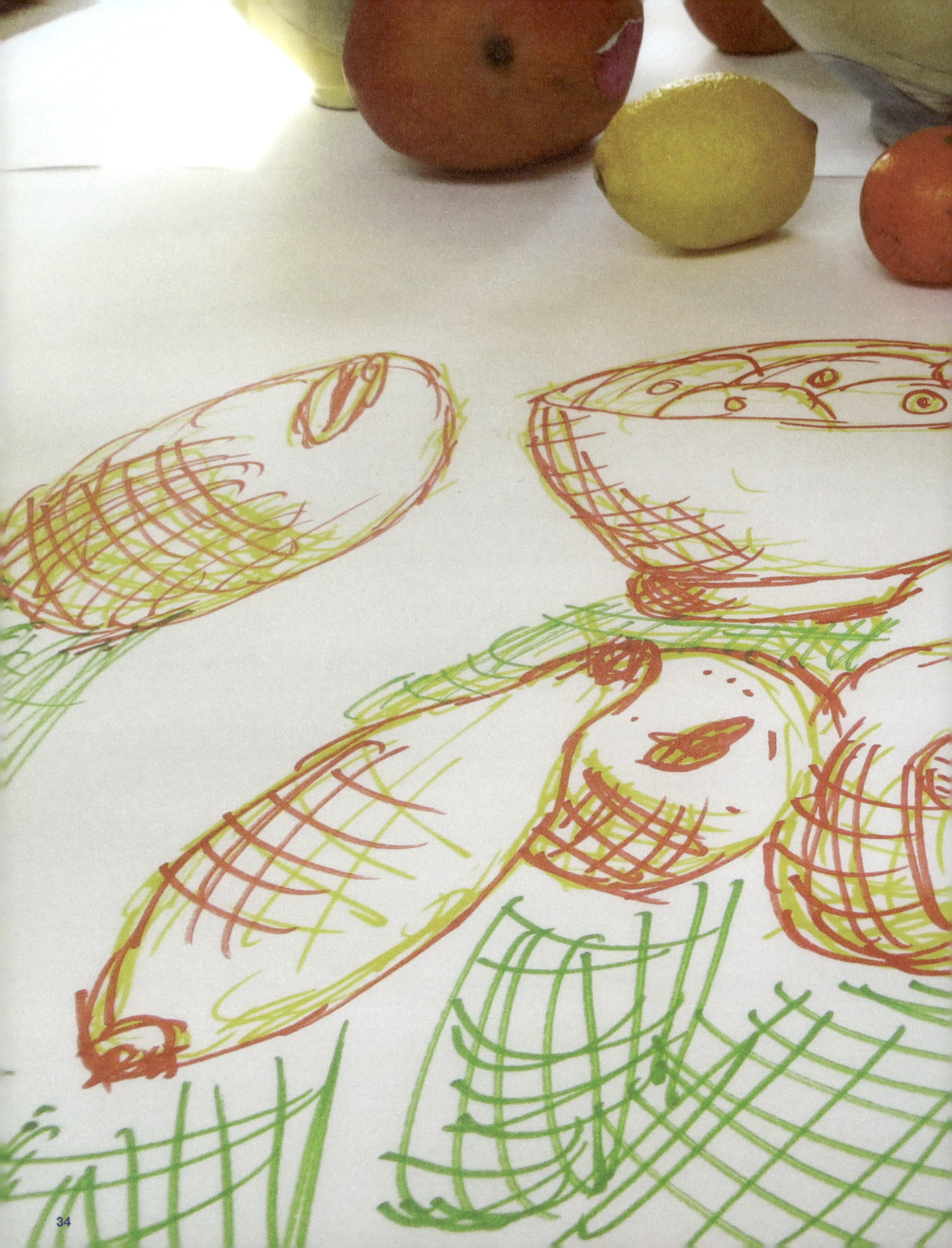

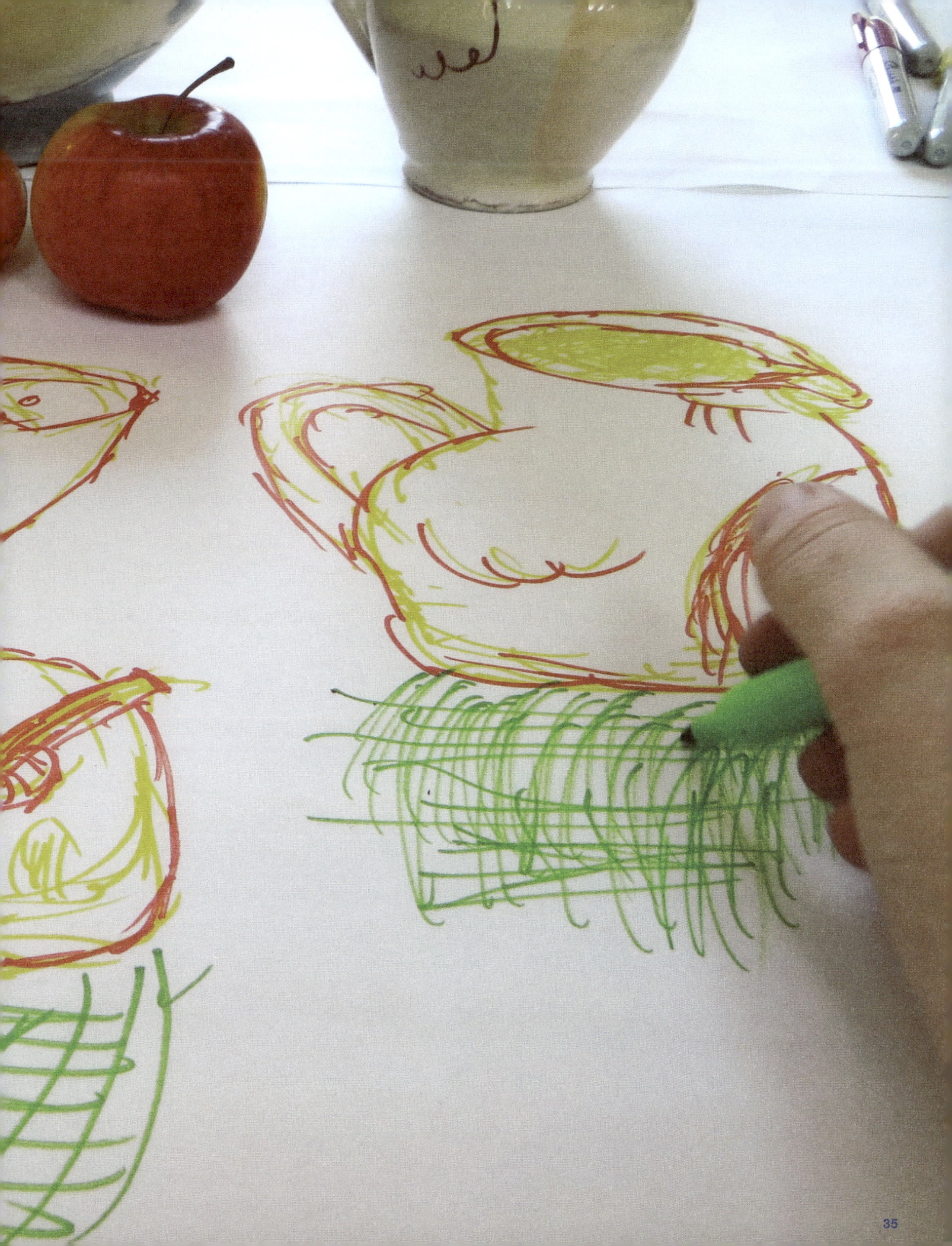

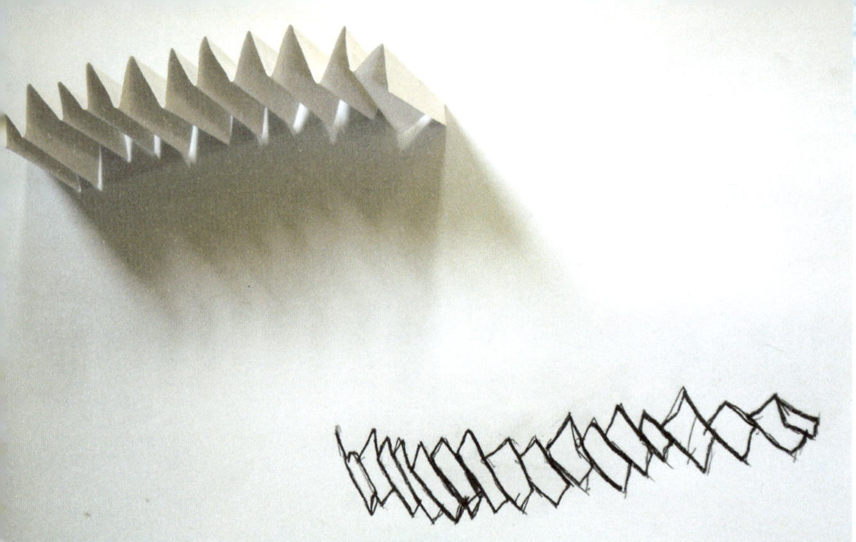

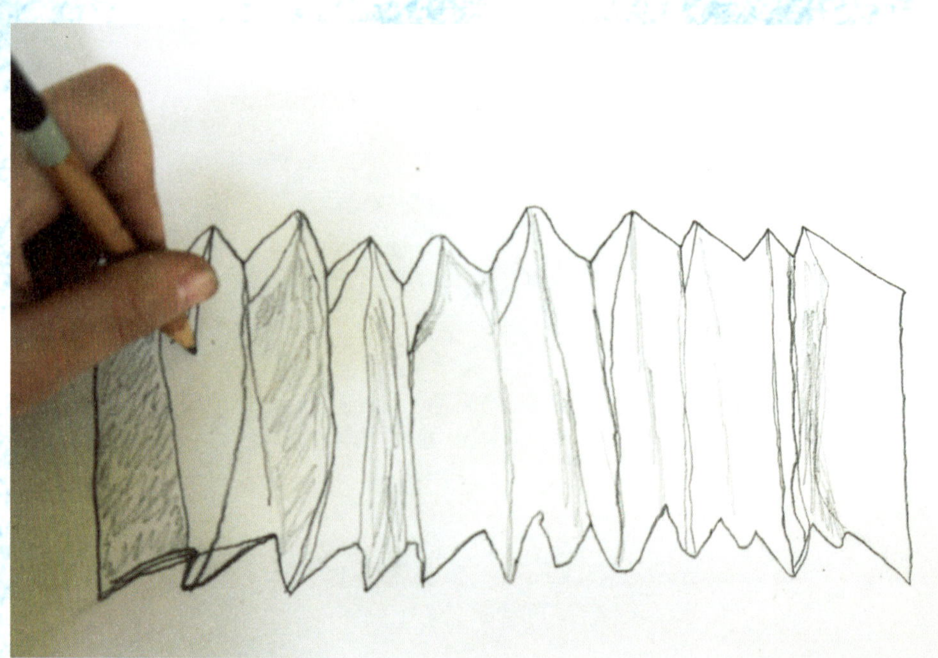

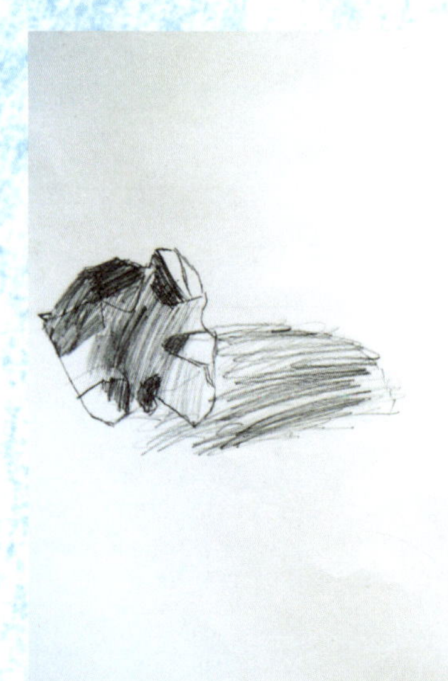

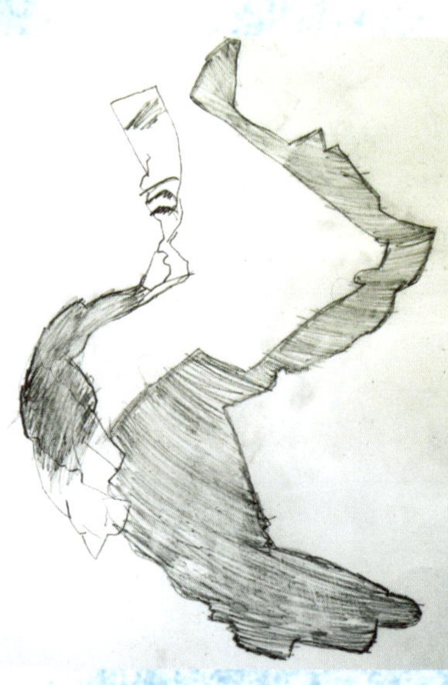

DRAWING TO A SLOW RHYTHM

Sometimes making calm, slow drawings can be very enjoyable. Drawing slowly helps you to look more carefully at your subject matter, and this helps you gather lots of information to help with the drawing. In this warm up, you will use a metronome to create a steady rhythm to make slow drawings to.

Materials

- Soft (B) pencils
- Hard (H) pencils
- Handwriting pens
- A4 drawing paper
- Metronome or a metronome app on a smart phone

Subject Matter

Create a variety of paper shapes out of torn, cut, folded, twisted or shaped pieces of paper, and arrange these with a collection of paper items, such as toilet roll, a paper fan or a folded newspaper.

Activity

1 Before starting this project, you will need to set up a metronome, or a metronome app on a smart phone. Set this to two beats per second.

2 While the metronome beats, make a slow, careful drawing of your chosen paper object or shape with a sharp pencil or a pen.

3 Keep focused and work to the rhythm for ten minutes.

Facilitator's Note

There is something very meditative about a slow drawing session and surprisingly children seem to enjoy them too.

In this session a metronome provides a background rhythmical sound which acts as an aural reminder of the passing of time. The steady rhythm helps the children to settle and draw at a prescribed pace. Encourage children to remain quiet in this process, for the full effect.

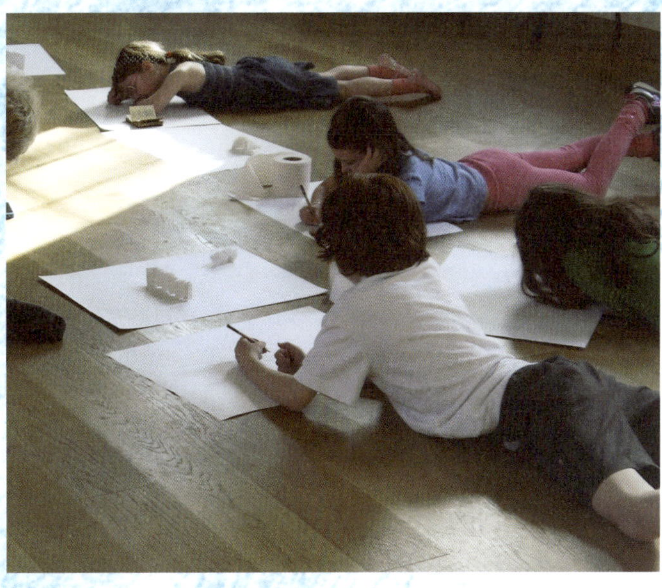

DRAWING BY TOUCH

Before we can make a drawing, we need to begin to collect information about what it is we want to draw. We do that by looking, or sometimes imagining. In this exercise you are going to gather information using your sense of touch! You will then make a drawing based upon what you can feel instead of what you can see.

Materials

- Soft (B) pencils
- A4 drawing paper

Subject Matter

The subject matter in this exercise needs to be something small enough to fit very comfortably in the palm of your hand, and something that is tactile but not too complex. Pruned twigs—no more than 5 cm long, and the stubbier the better—work perfectly. If possible, ask an adult to keep the subject matter in a bag so that you cannot see it!

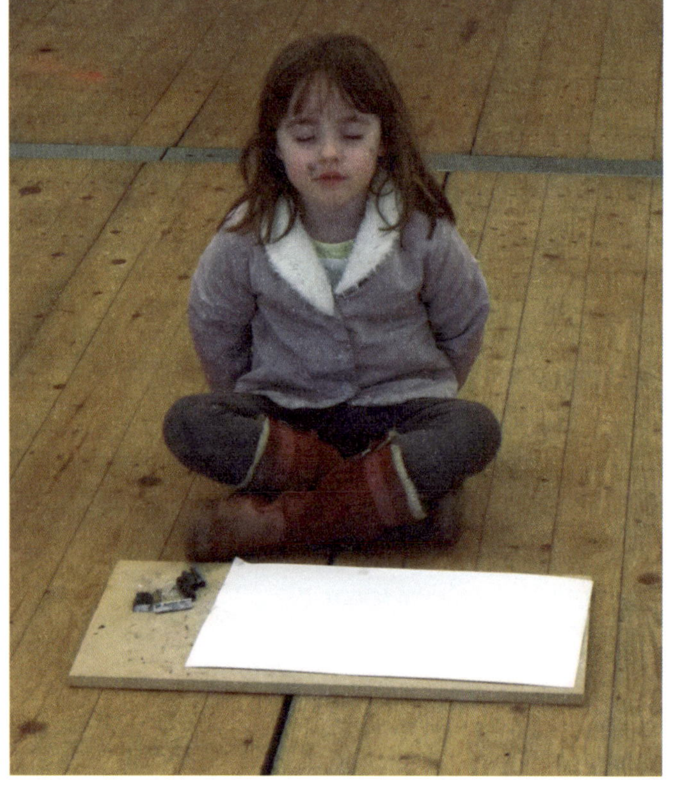

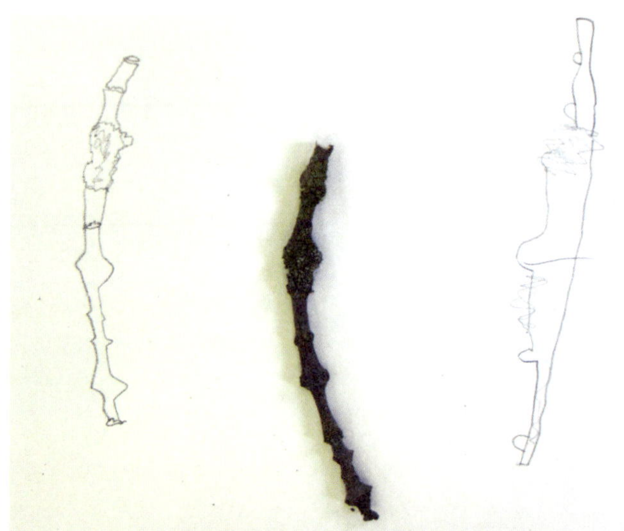

You are going to make a drawing based upon the information you get from your fingers, by feeling an object. While you will not be able to see your subject matter, you will be able to see your drawing.

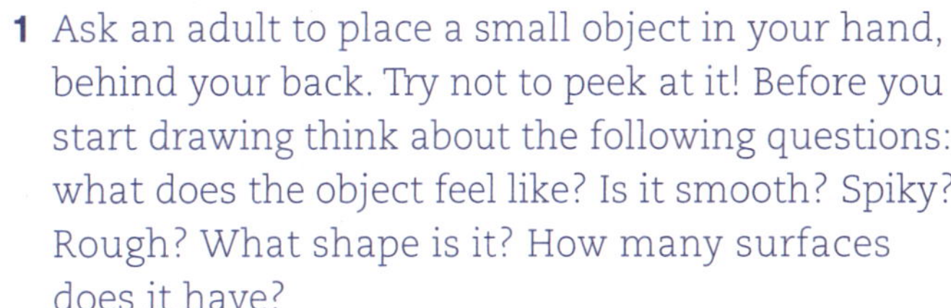

1 Ask an adult to place a small object in your hand, behind your back. Try not to peek at it! Before you start drawing think about the following questions: what does the object feel like? Is it smooth? Spiky? Rough? What shape is it? How many surfaces does it have?

2 When you are ready, make a drawing with your dominant hand (your writing hand) and hold the object in your non-dominant hand behind your back, and, as you draw, ask yourself the questions again, and this time add: how can I make marks that help show what I feel? How can I show the form and shapes?

Facilitator's Note

The objects you choose should have characteristics that children recognise easily, so they can build a picture in their mind before they start to draw.

Keep the drawing session short, and give the children plenty of opportunity to share the results and their thoughts on drawing by sense of touch.

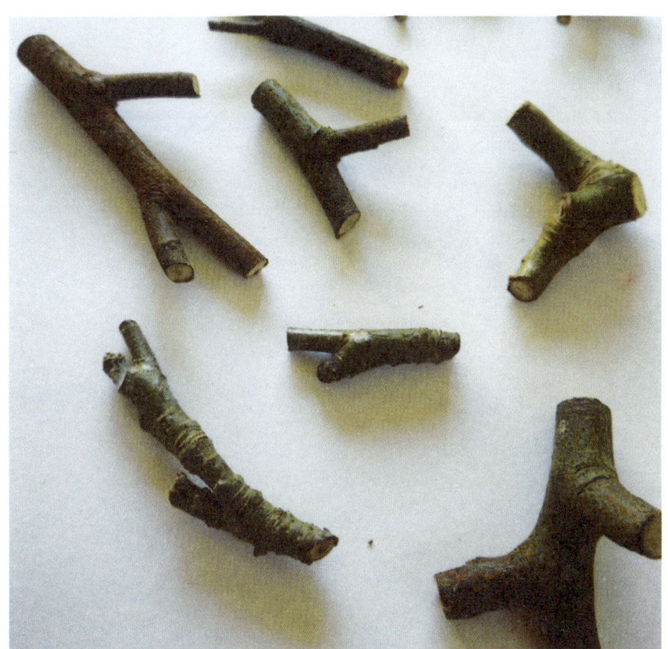

SEE THREE SHAPES

This exercise splits looking and drawing into three simple stages and shows how one drawing material can be used in different ways to create different effects. In this warm up you will make a drawing with a wonderful, sculptural feel, using only three marks!

Materials

- Indian ink (pour the ink into some small cups, one with only ink (undiluted), and one with half ink and half water (diluted)
- Feathers cut at an angle to use as nibs
- Brushes
- A4 drawing paper

Subject Matter

Choose a subject matter with a strong but simple shape that will cast a simple shadow on the paper. Eggs, apples and lemons work well, but keep away from perfect spheres like balls. Placing the subject matter on white paper helps their shadow stand out.

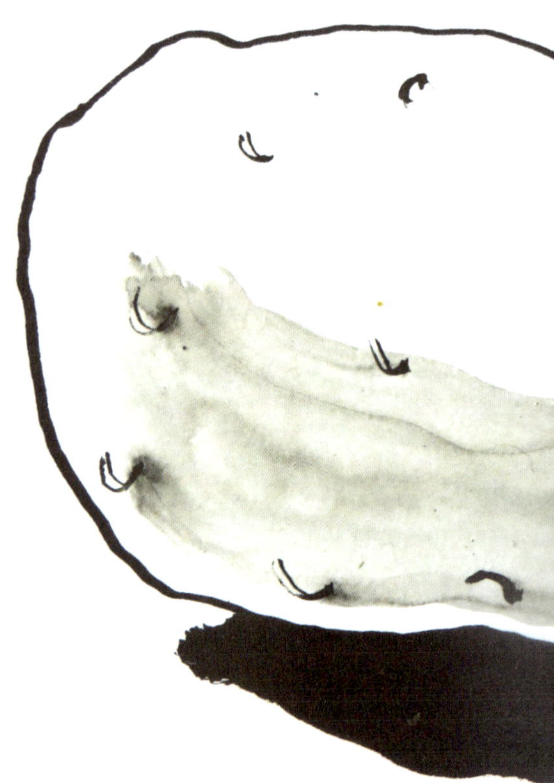

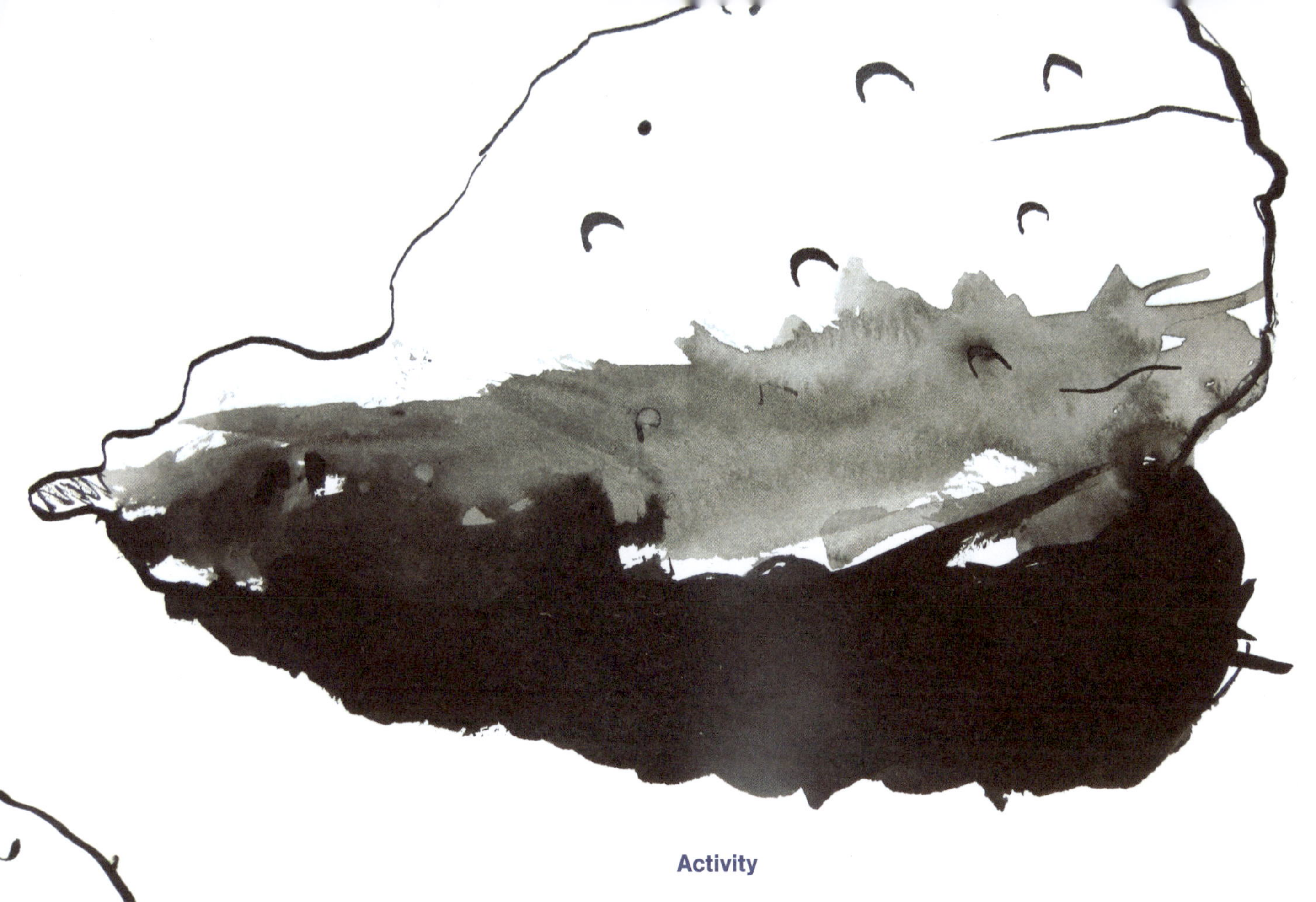

Activity

You can make a simple study of the subject matter by seeing, and drawing, in three shapes.

1 Starting with the undiluted ink and using a feather nib, make a simple line drawing of the outside of the object. If the feather holds plenty of ink, add a few lines of detail inside the line drawing to show some texture.

2 Take a moment to squint at the subject matter and observe where its shadows lies. Using the undiluted ink again, this time work with a brush, and make a single brush mark to show this shadow.

3 Finally make a third mark for the shape of the shading on the subject matter itself. This time use the diluted ink to provide a lighter mark. Try to use a single stroke.

4 Remember that if you apply water over wet ink the ink will run. If you wait until the ink has dried, the water can be used to create a wash that will stay as a separate layer.

MAKING LARGER DRAWINGS

It is a useful skill to be able to draw on all different scales. This really simple exercise will help you to expand your drawings to fill the page, whatever the size.

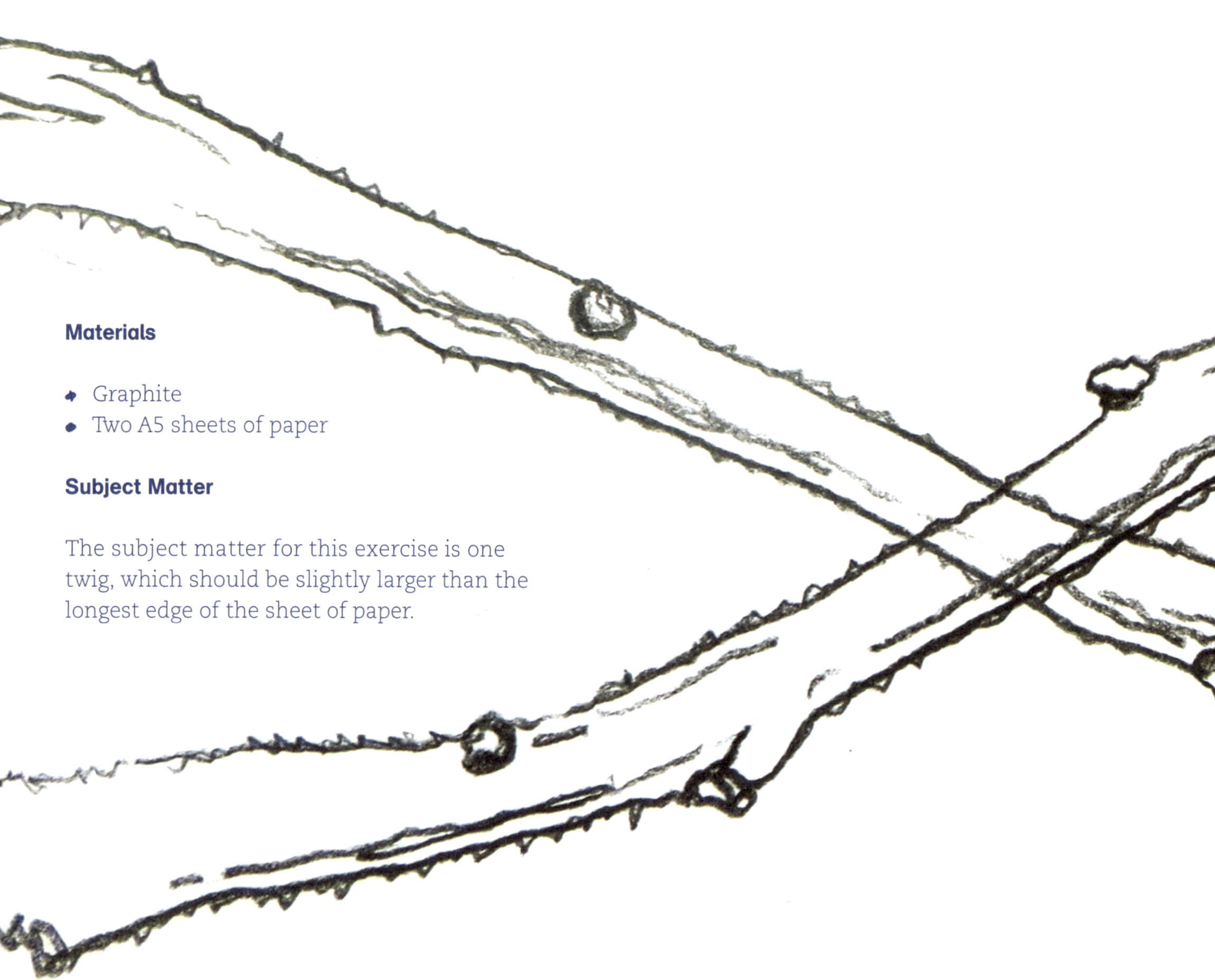

Materials

- Graphite
- Two A5 sheets of paper

Subject Matter

The subject matter for this exercise is one twig, which should be slightly larger than the longest edge of the sheet of paper.

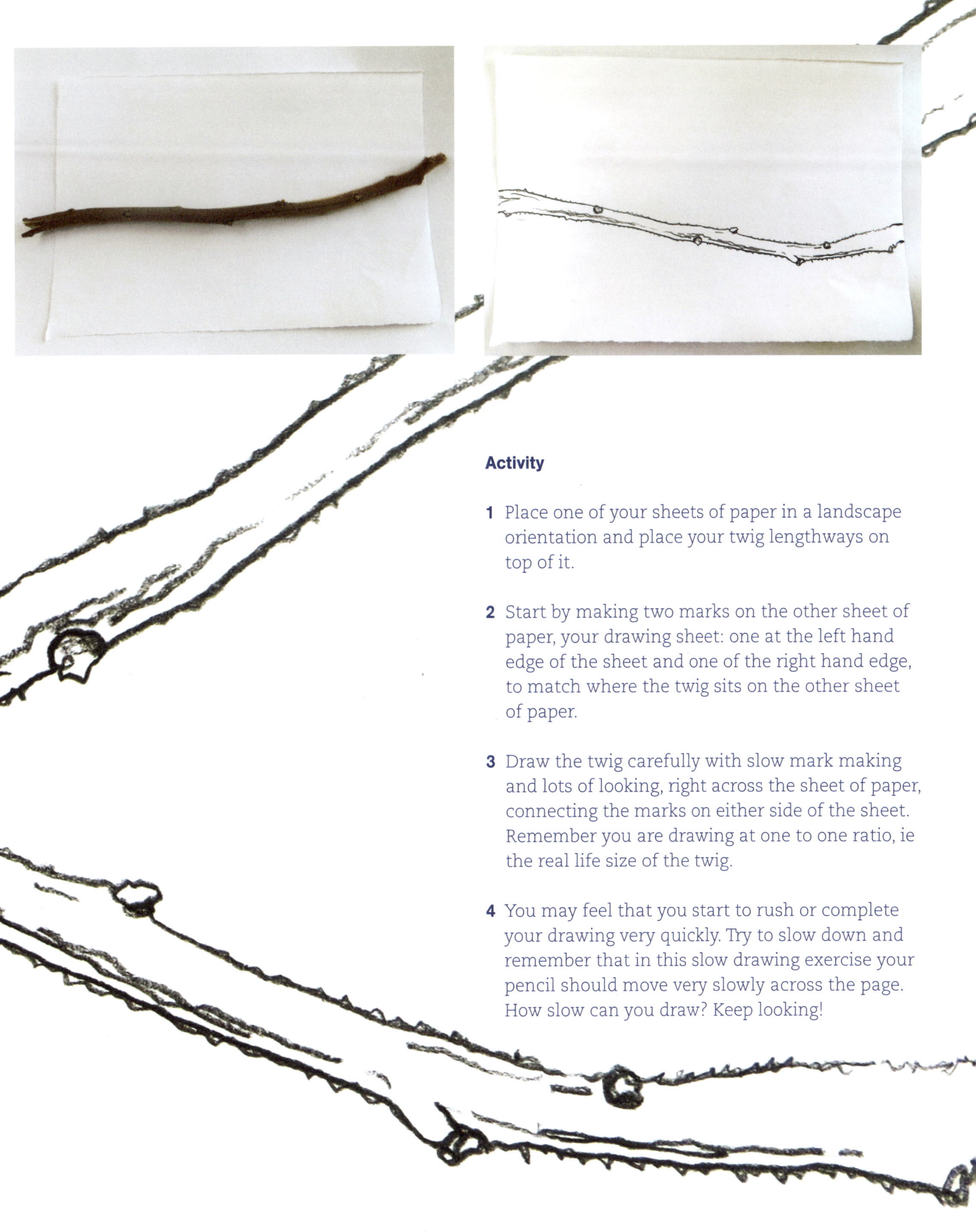

Activity

1 Place one of your sheets of paper in a landscape orientation and place your twig lengthways on top of it.

2 Start by making two marks on the other sheet of paper, your drawing sheet: one at the left hand edge of the sheet and one of the right hand edge, to match where the twig sits on the other sheet of paper.

3 Draw the twig carefully with slow mark making and lots of looking, right across the sheet of paper, connecting the marks on either side of the sheet. Remember you are drawing at one to one ratio, ie the real life size of the twig.

4 You may feel that you start to rush or complete your drawing very quickly. Try to slow down and remember that in this slow drawing exercise your pencil should move very slowly across the page. How slow can you draw? Keep looking!

MAKING STRONGER DRAWINGS

Soft pencils, such as a 4, 6 or 8 B, can be used to make marks from the very palest, softest marks to the heaviest, darkest black line. This exercise will show you how to use soft pencils to make all of these marks, and create very strong and bold pencil drawings.

Materials

- Soft B pencils (2B to 9B would be ideal)
- A selection of old maps (You can find old maps in charity shops or jumble sales). Try to avoid road atlases that are on shiny paper, as these will not hold the pencil marks as well as a matt paper. If you cannot find enough old maps, try photocopying some maps instead.

Subject Matter

Choose small objects such as a bundle of keys, feathers, pebbles, or a selection of cutlery as the subject matter for this warm up.

Activity

1 Cut or tear the maps into A5 or A4 sized pieces.

2 Using a soft pencil, make a drawing of one of the objects directly onto a piece of map paper. Imagine that the marks you make are in competition with the lines of the map. Make sure your drawing wins! But remember that you must still make careful, considered marks and look at your object carefully. Experiment with pressure to discover how dark your lines need to be so they can be seen over the map. Are there areas of the map where you can use a relatively light mark?

3 Test the strength of your drawing by viewing it from a distance. How well does the drawing carry? Can you see the object over the map?

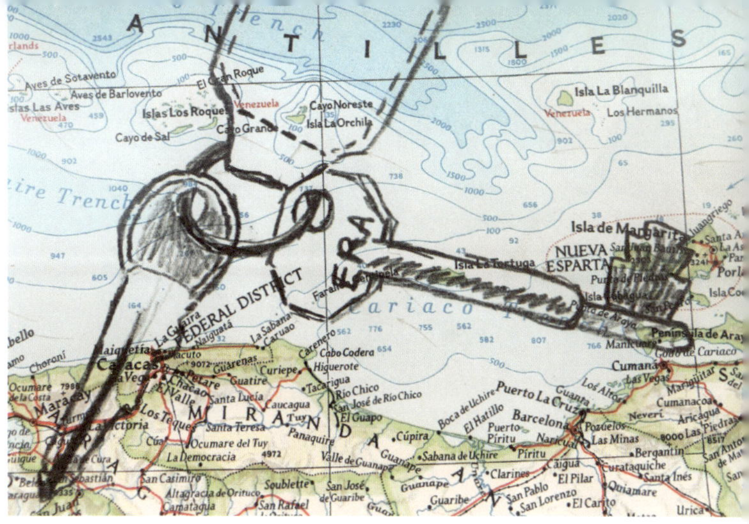

Facilitator's Note

Typically when children are given a pencil it is a HB, which creates a very uniform line with little tonal variety, and they are not often encouraged to experiment with pressure. When children are then given a soft pencil like a 4, 6 or 8 B, they carry their experience of using HB pencils with them, failing to realise the amazing tonal range that a softer pencil is capable of.

Added to this, many children have a natural tendency to make quite tentative drawings. This exercise was developed as a way to demonstrate to children the full potential of working with soft B pencils, and to encourage more cautious children to make strong, bold drawings.

This can be used as a warm up exercise before specific drawing tasks or it can be used as an intervention or challenge if a particular child would benefit from being encouraged to have more belief in their drawings.

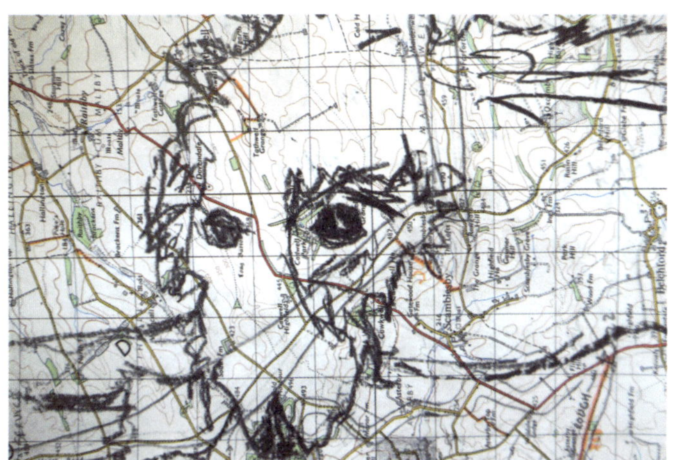

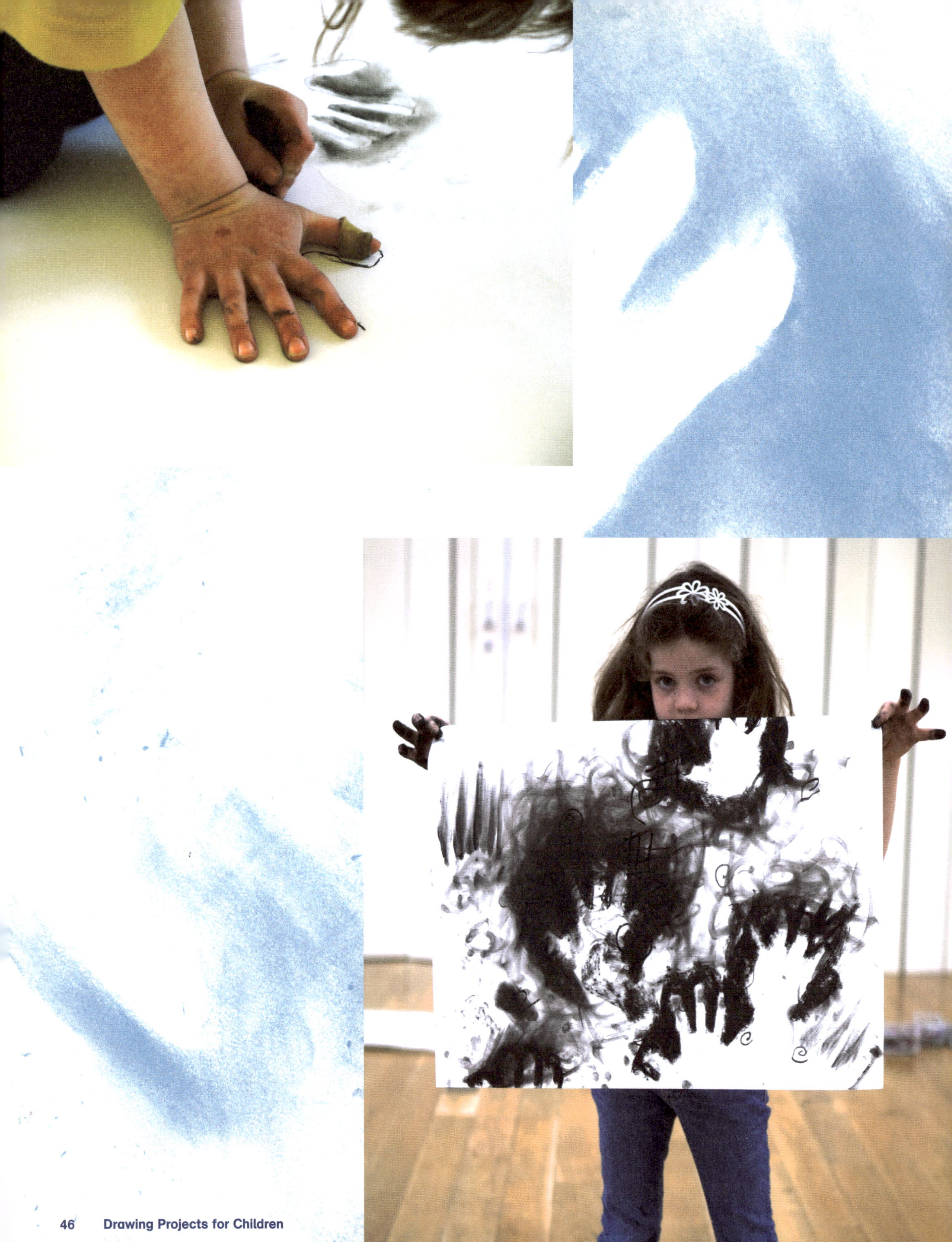

DRAWING LIKE A CAVEMAN

There are so many wonderful drawing materials to use that it can be easy to forget where drawing started. This exercise is a reminder of how simple and natural drawing can be.

Materials

- Charcoal
- A2 and A3 drawing paper

Activity

1 First, make a simple drawing on the large A2 sheet of paper by tracing around your hands with the piece of charcoal. Try to imagine that your hand is a stencil, and once you have drawn around it with the charcoal, use the fingers of your other hand to smudge the charcoal. When you take your hand off the paper, you will have a negative image of it!

2 You can create a palette by rubbing a piece of charcoal on the A3 piece of paper until the surface becomes dark grey or black, and covered in charcoal dust. Then, run your fingers, thumbs and the side of your hand over the charcoal palette to pick up the dust, and use your fingers as a drawing tool to make a new kind of mark around the negative space hand print you made earlier.

3 You can experiment with how hard to press to create very dark or light marks. Try pushing the charcoal dust around the drawing until the whole page is covered and notice how the charcoal leaves an echo of the journey your fingers make.

Facilitator's Note

This exercise can be used to introduce children to cave drawings and charcoal; what charcoal is and how it is made. Help them imagine how prehistoric man might have reached for a burnt piece of wood from the fire to use as a mark making tool and wonder why they might have made the marks they did. It may also be interesting to talk about the universality of the handprint as a symbol.

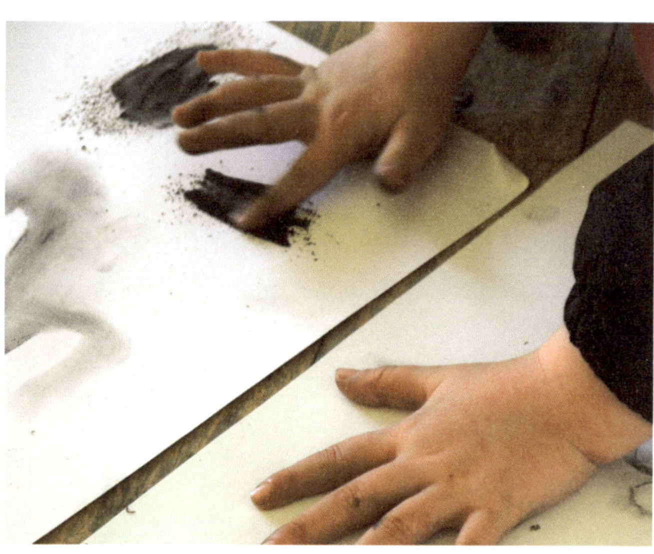

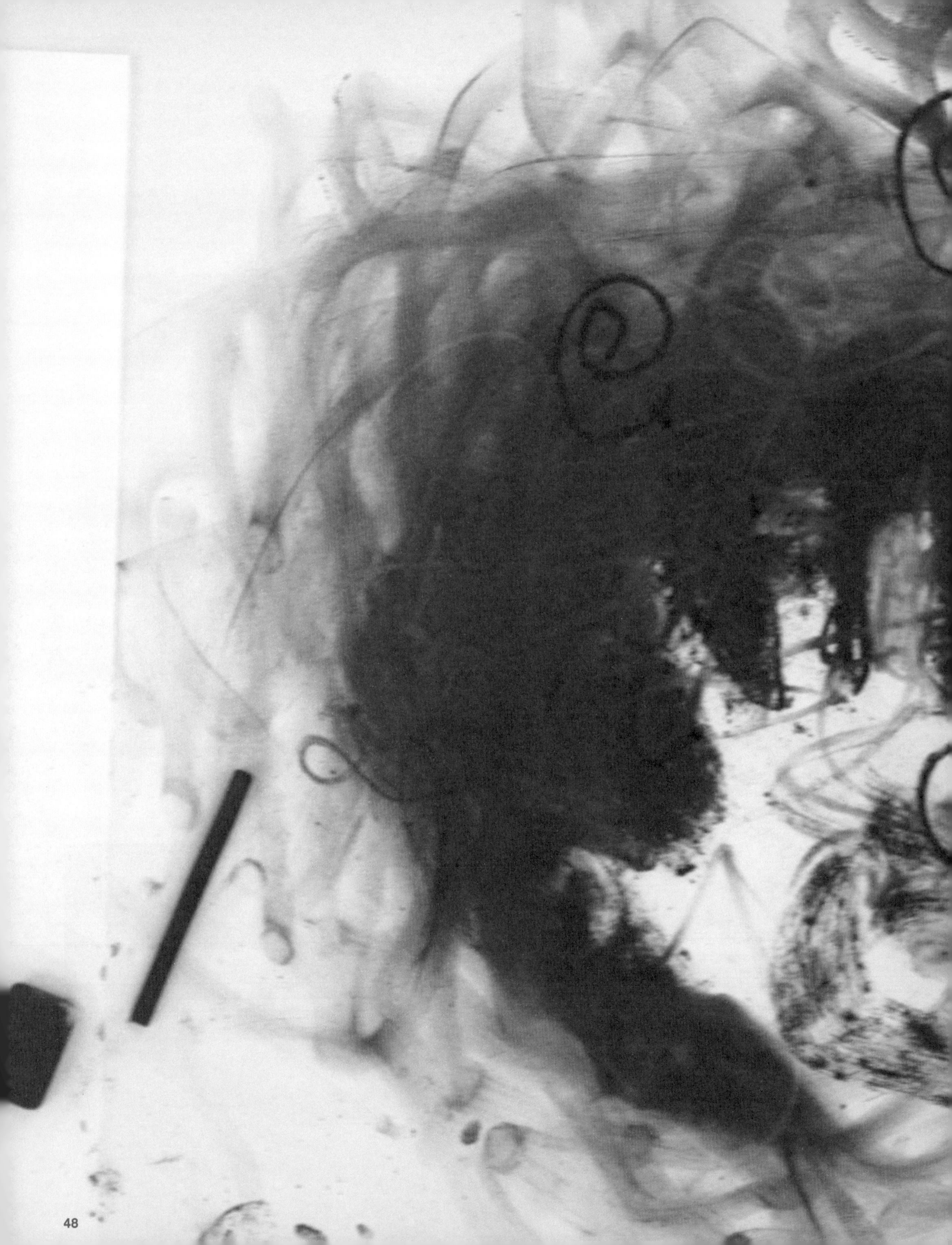

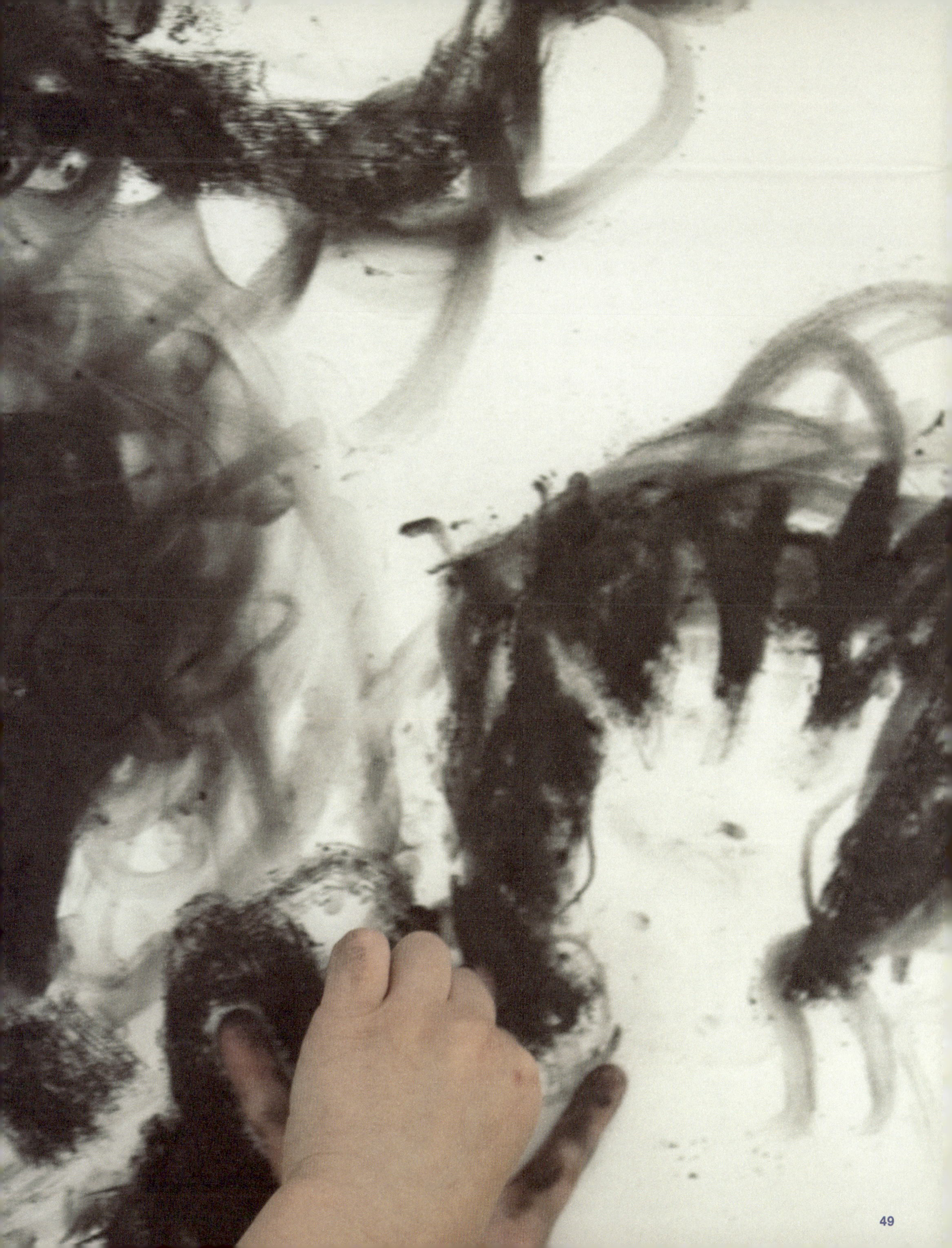

THOUGHTFUL MARK MAKING

Have you ever wondered how you might make your drawings more *interesting*? Varying the types of lines you use in your drawing can really help make your work sing. In this guided exercise, you will work with an adult to explore how you can create wonderfully varied marks.

For this warm up we took our inspiration from some wonderful fossils that provided the opportunity to make drawings that contained lots of observational detail. You will be able to explore how you can build a drawing through a series of guided, mark making acts.

Materials

- Handwriting pens
- A4 drawing paper

Subject Matter

Make sure you are near enough to the subject matter to easily observe small details. Choose small items such as rocks, fossils, brushes or feathers.

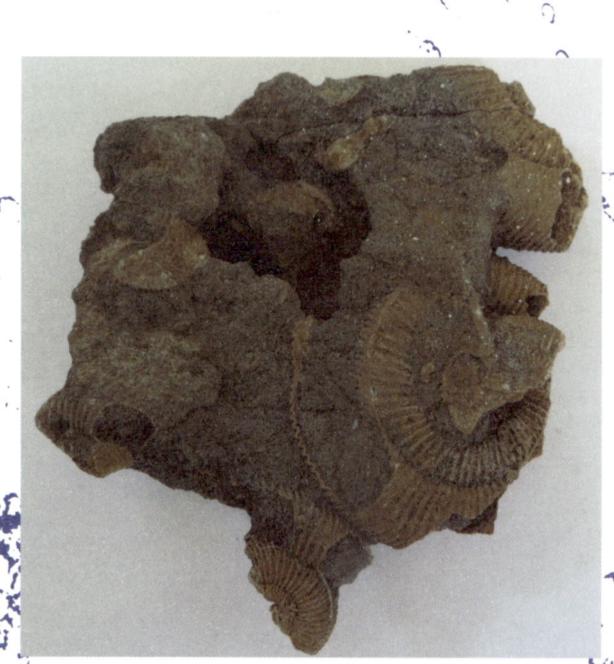

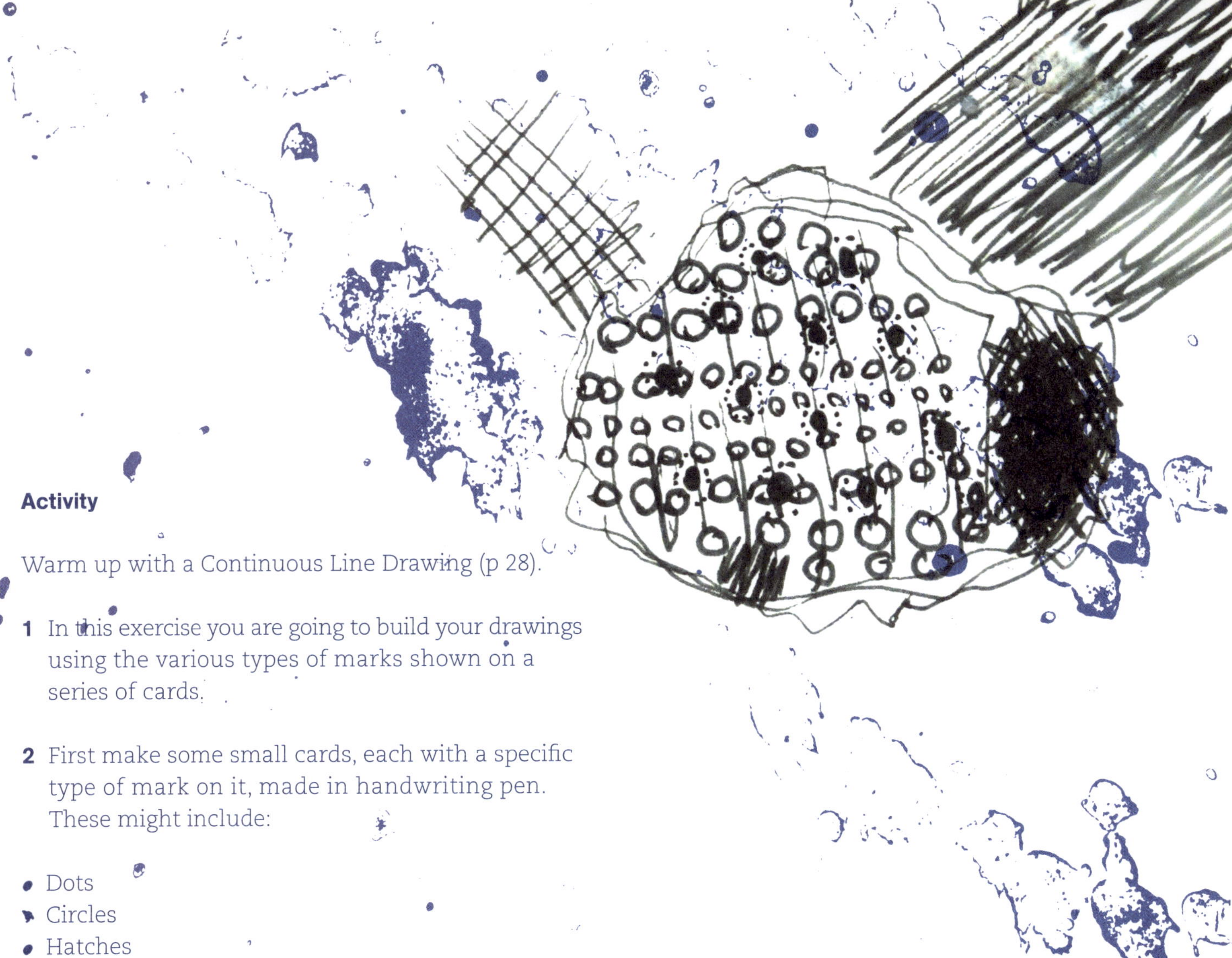

Activity

Warm up with a Continuous Line Drawing (p 28).

1 In this exercise you are going to build your drawings using the various types of marks shown on a series of cards.

2 First make some small cards, each with a specific type of mark on it, made in handwriting pen. These might include:

- Dots
- Circles
- Hatches
- Cross hatches
- Dashes
- Dotted lines

3 Randomly pick a card, and think where that type of mark would work best in your drawing. If an adult is helping you then they can choose the card for you and hold it up for you to see. When you make your drawing, make sure you use careful looking and drawing, but add in an extra step: thinking.

It might help to make the first mark very lightly by holding the pen loosely—to help ease you into your drawing.

4 For the last card, pick whichever mark you feel you need to use to finish your drawings. Your drawing should take no longer than ten minutes to make.

Facilitator's Note

Children are usually most concerned with the act of making a drawing, but it is important to encourage them to talk about the act of looking, and to think about a drawing as a means of communication. This warm up exercise helps children think about how we can make our drawings more interesting by using a variety of marks within an image. Even using a single mark making tool such as a handwriting pen can produce drawings which the eye likes to linger over.

Sometimes when we draw we do so intuitively —other times we work more thoughtfully. This exercise also helps children to understand the importance of looking, thinking and acting when making a drawing.

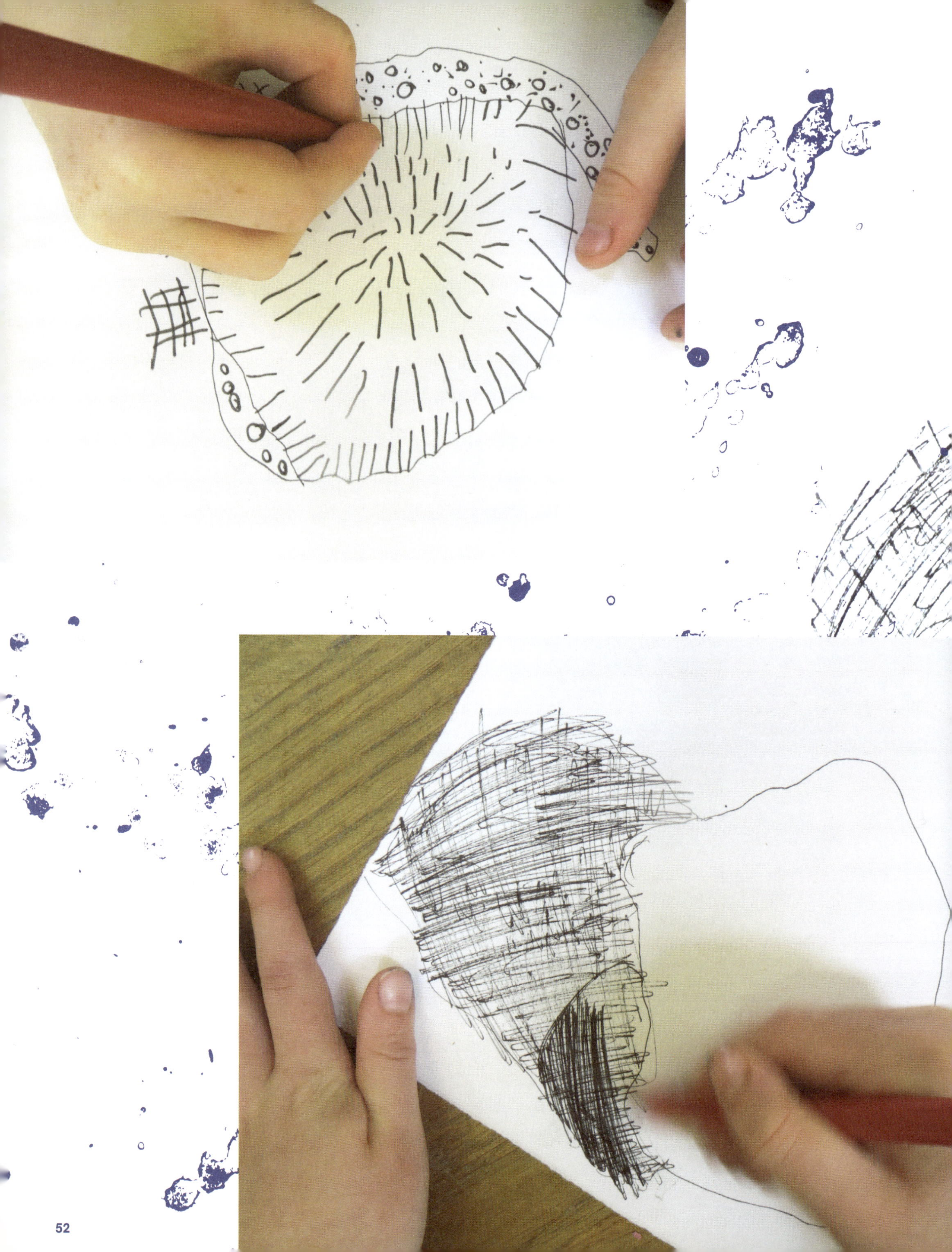

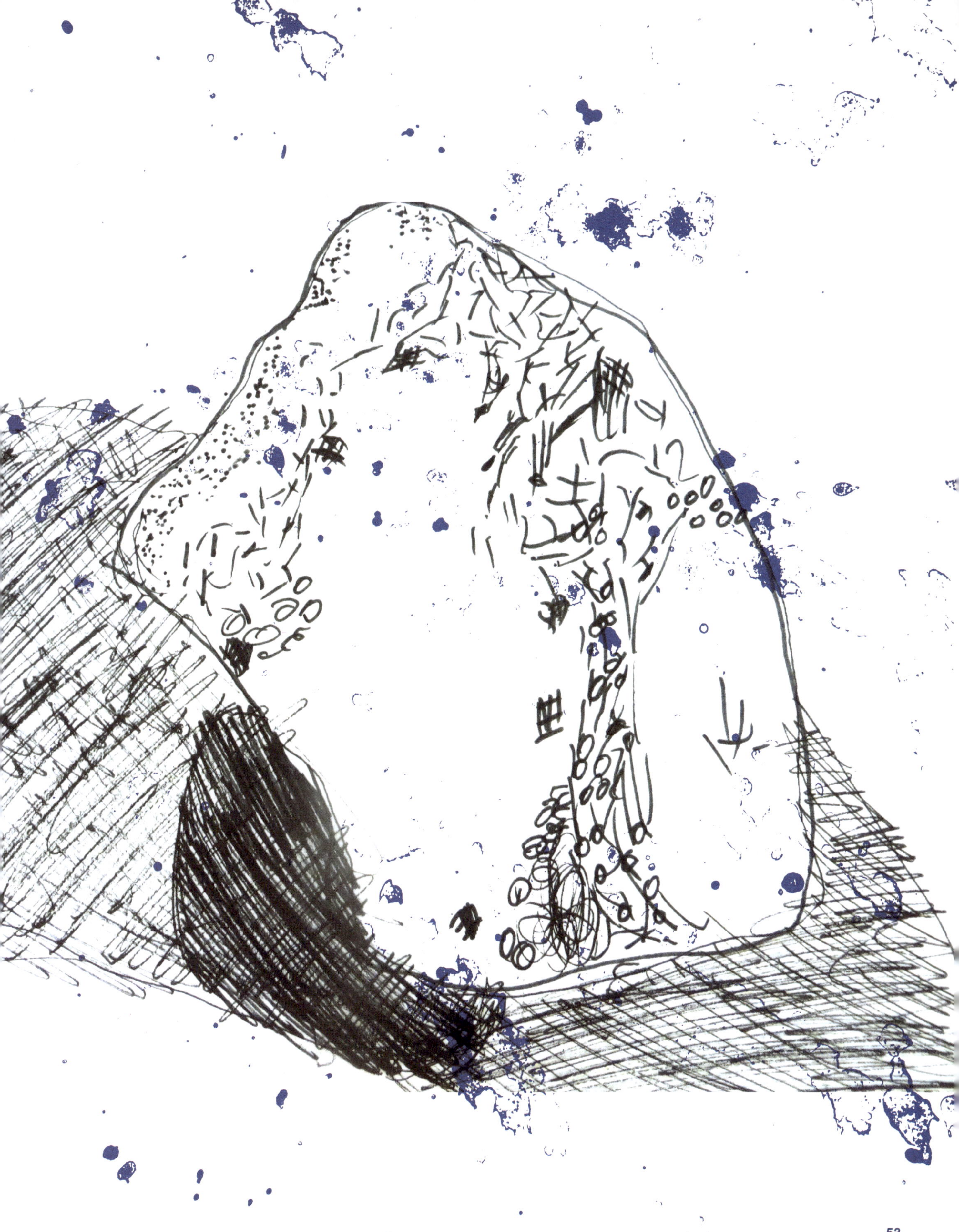

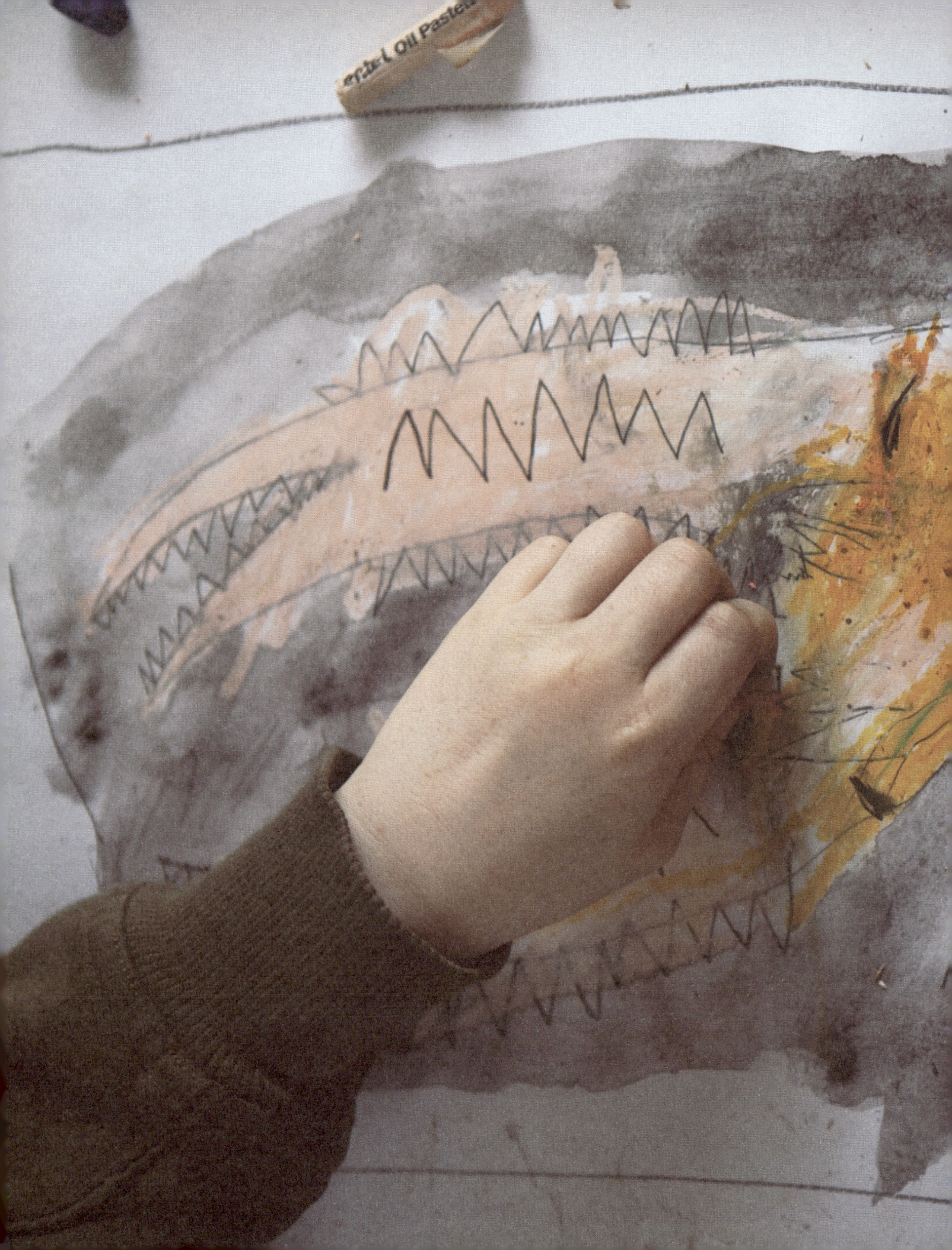

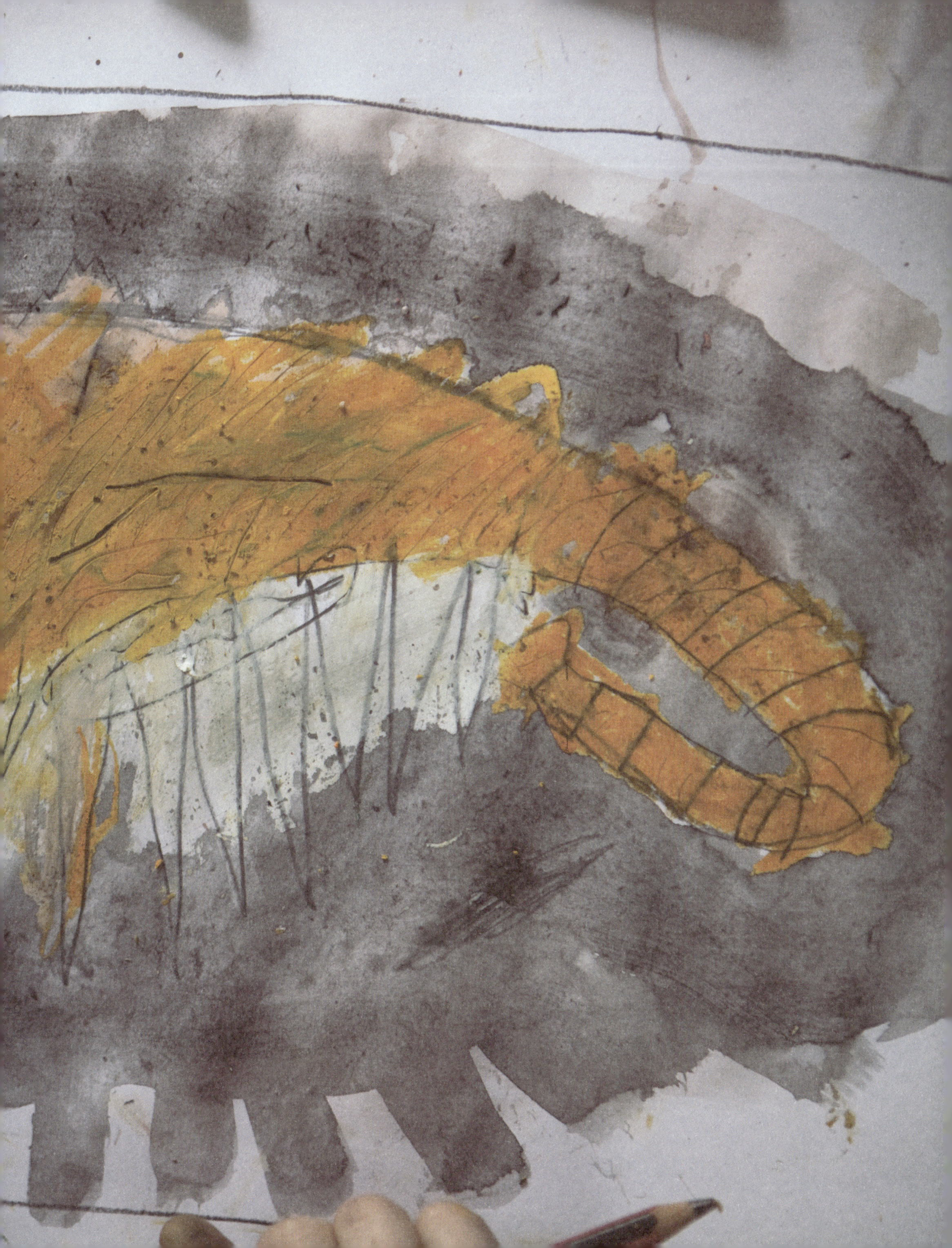

PROJECTS

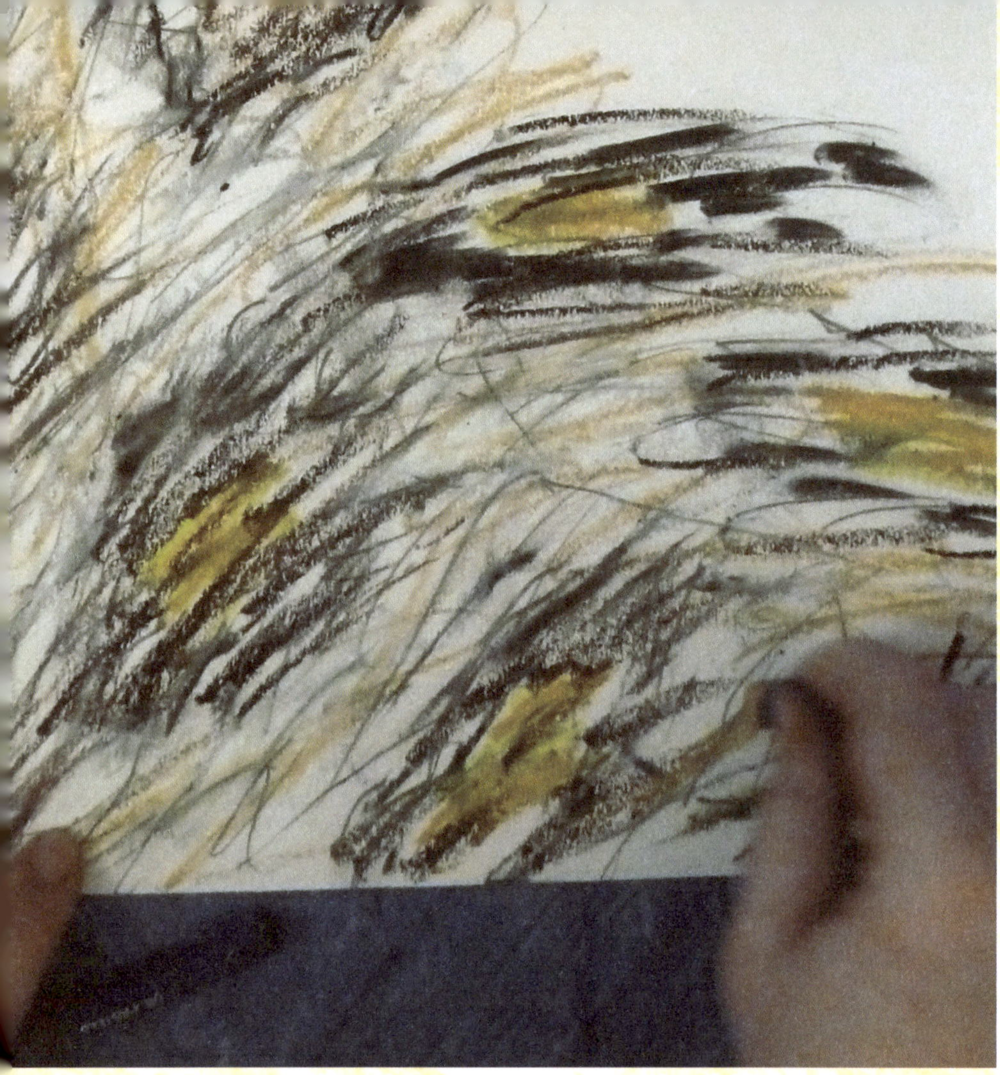

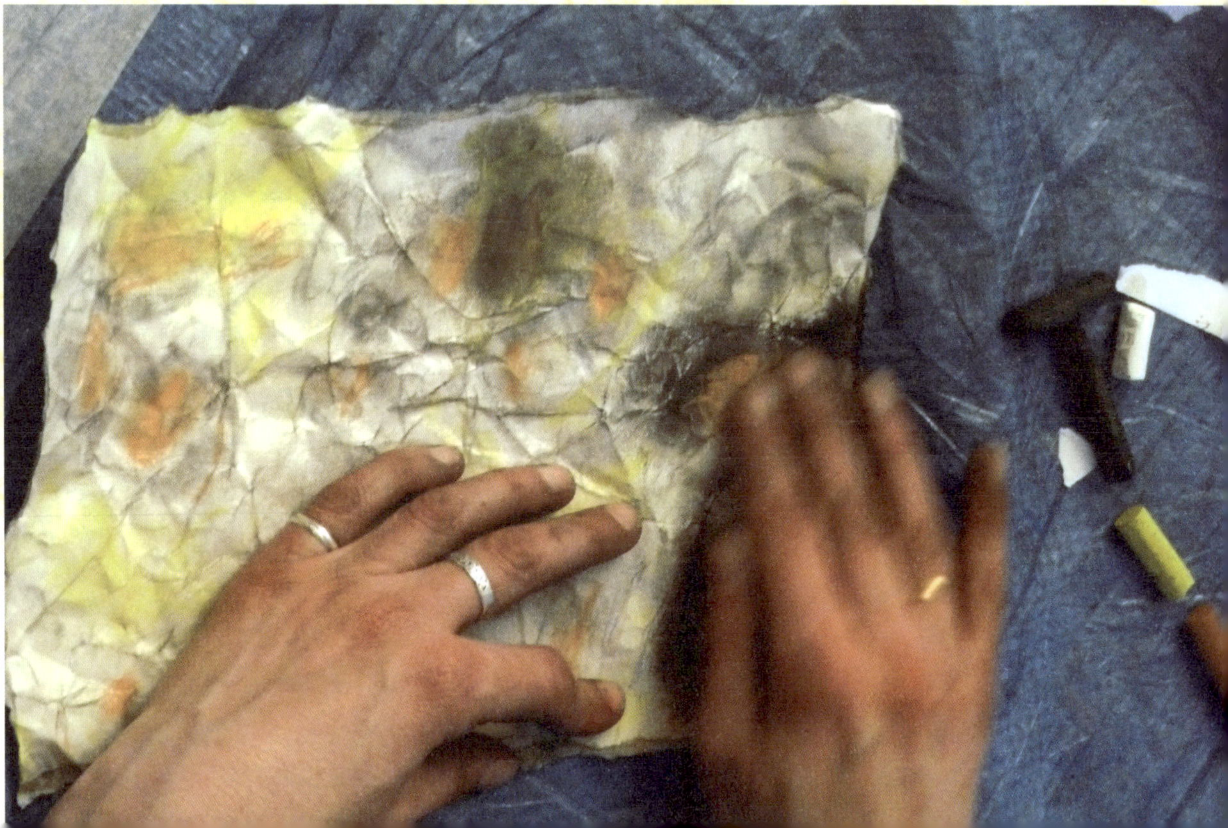

TURNING PAPER INTO FUR

This project's challenge is simple: to turn a piece of paper into a piece of fur (or a piece of sponge, a plank of wood or some knitted wool…).

We often forget that drawings can transform paper. When we look at a drawing, we no longer see the paper—we see what is *on* the paper. In this activity you will transform your own paper by drawing on it!

Materials

- Soft (B) and hard (H) pencils
- Graphite
- Chalk pastels
- Oil pastels
- Erasers
- A3 drawing paper or sugar paper

Subject Matter

Any material with an interesting texture will work well as subject matter for this activity. We have used fur.

Activity

1 Before you start your drawing, take some time to explore your subject matter. What does it look like? Which colours can you see? What does it feel like? What happens when you balance it on your finger—if it is fabric, how does the weight of the material make it act?

2 Examine your drawing paper in the same way as your subject matter. How do they compare? How are they different?

3 Now try to turn your paper into the fur by tearing, scrunching, creasing, and drawing on it. You can transform the look of the paper by covering the entire sheet, rather than just drawing on a part of the page. Be confident! Really push your drawing and the paper to the limits!

DRAWING FEATHERS

Drawing feathers is a great way to explore making marks with lots of different materials. You can keep these as pictures in themselves, or you could use them as collage materials for the Drawn and Collaged Birds project (p 122).

Materials

- A2 drawing paper
- Soft (B) and hard (H) pencils
- Oil pastels
- Watercolours
- Erasers
- Handwriting pens
- Charcoal
- Graphite
- Chalk pastels
- Brushes and water

Subject Matter

For this project you will need a selection of feathers (you can buy these online or in craft shops, or collect your own).

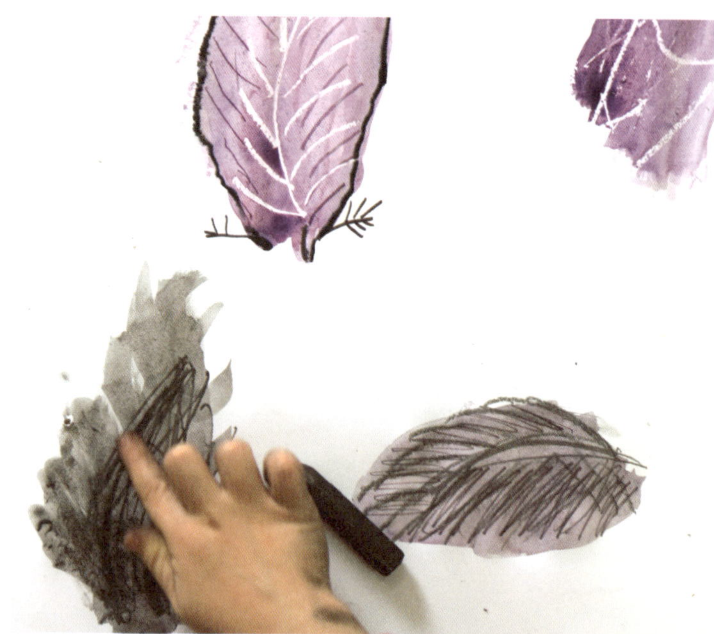

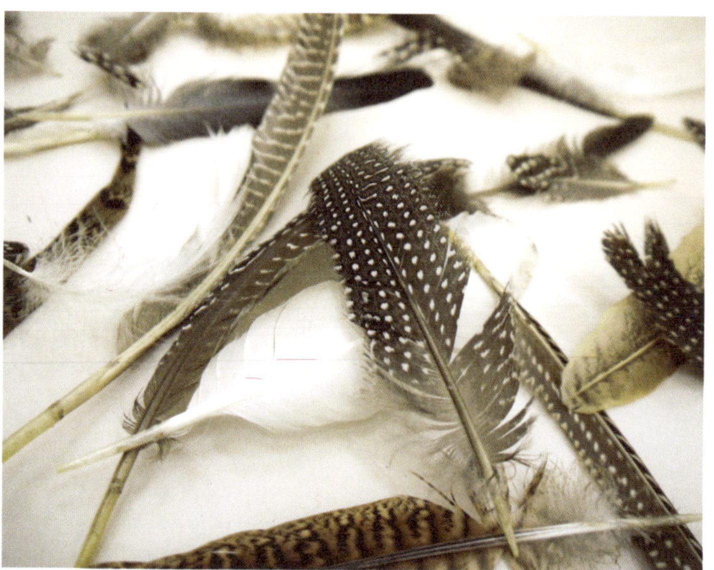

Activity

1 Working on A2 sheets of paper, make a series
of drawings of the feathers, capturing their
'featheriness' with lots of different textures. You
may want to make lots of different drawings on
one sheet—see it as a sort of sketchbook page.

2 Try using your materials in layers on top of one
another, to make 'drawing material sandwiches'.
For example, you could try using graphite, then
oil pastel, then more graphite, or pencil, eraser,
pencil, or pen, watercolour, pen.

3 Try changing the size and strength of the marks
you make: use a sharp pencil or a handwriting
pen to make accurate, detailed marks, and chalk
or oil pastels to make bigger smudges. This will
make your drawing very rich in texture.

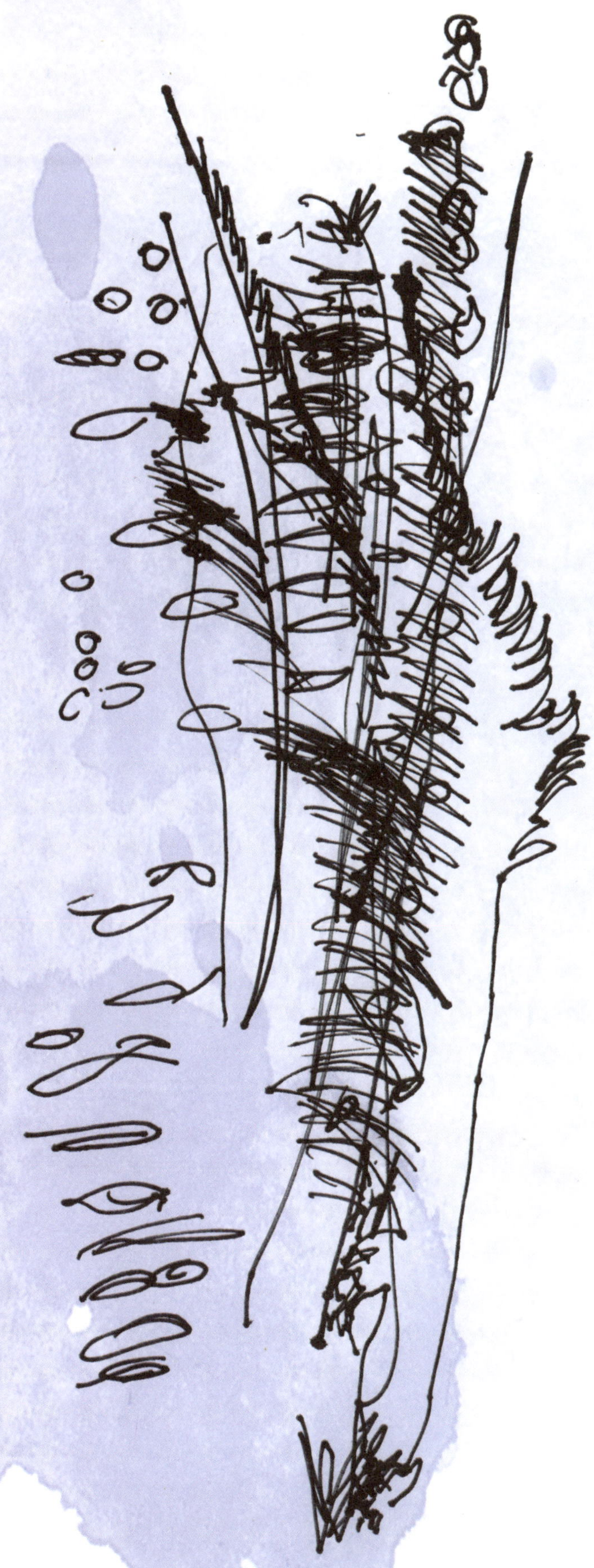

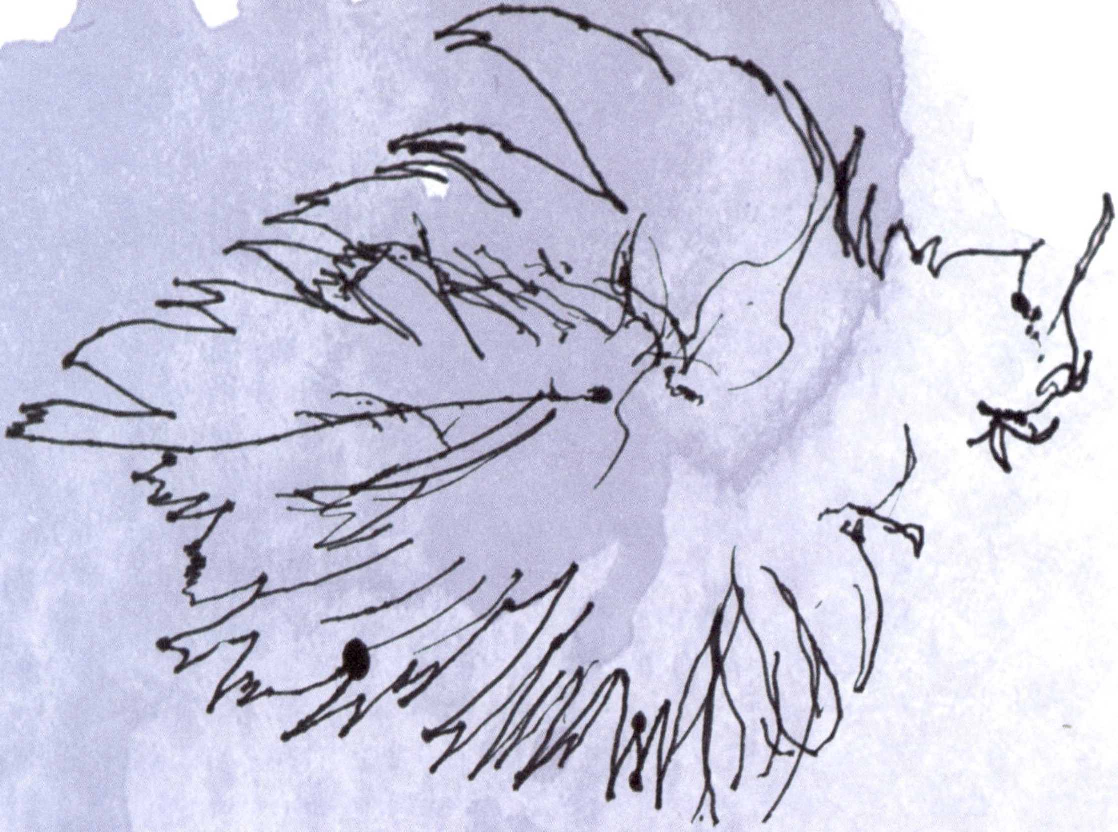

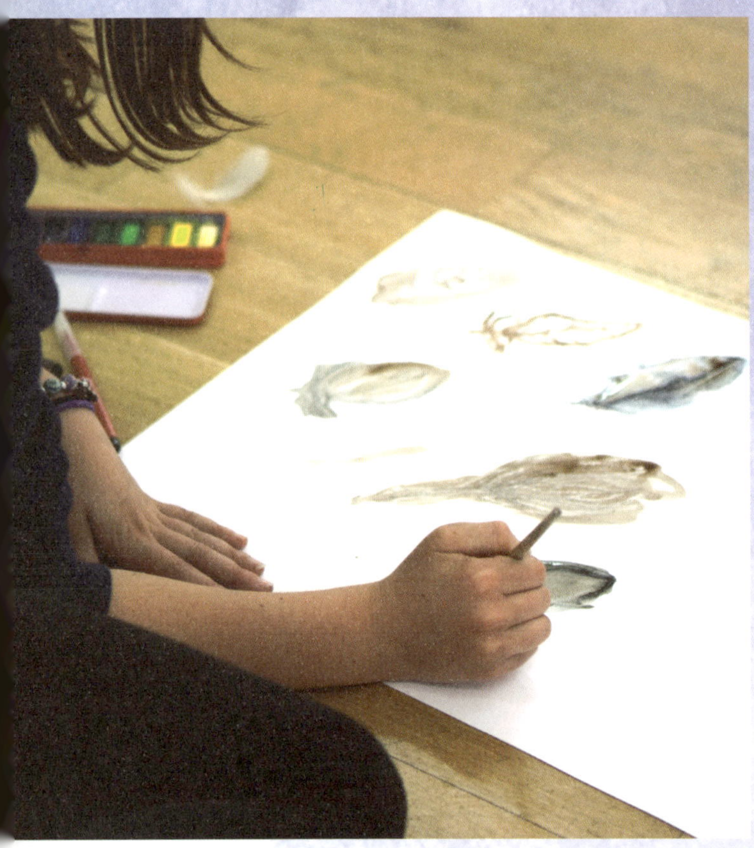

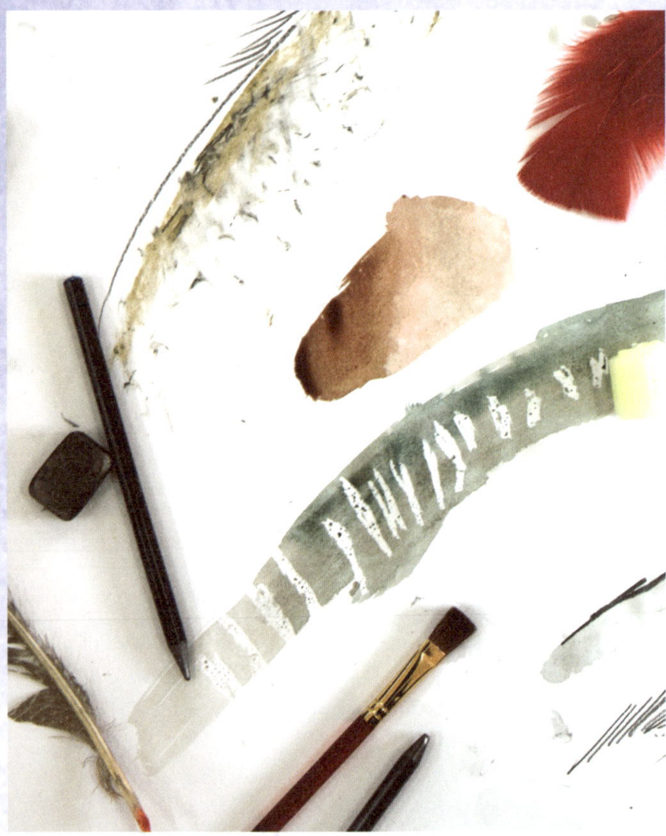

Facilitator's Note

Drawing feathers provides a great opportunity to explore material-based mark making. It is relatively easy for children to achieve some degree of 'featheriness' in their work, which will boost their confidence.

Start the session with a Continuous Line Drawing (p 28) to encourage children to focus and look closely at their subject matter. This helps in gathering the information they need, before they go on to explore materials and mark making. If they are not familiar with the materials, demonstrate the potential of each one, and of materials used in combination.

It is interesting to note that many children often make their biggest leaps and discoveries near the very end of sessions like these, so it is worth pushing on. Energy levels often increase towards the end of a session, rather than decrease, which highlights the importance of giving children the space and time in which to develop and discover. At the very end of the session, leave time for the children to share their favourite discoveries and successes.

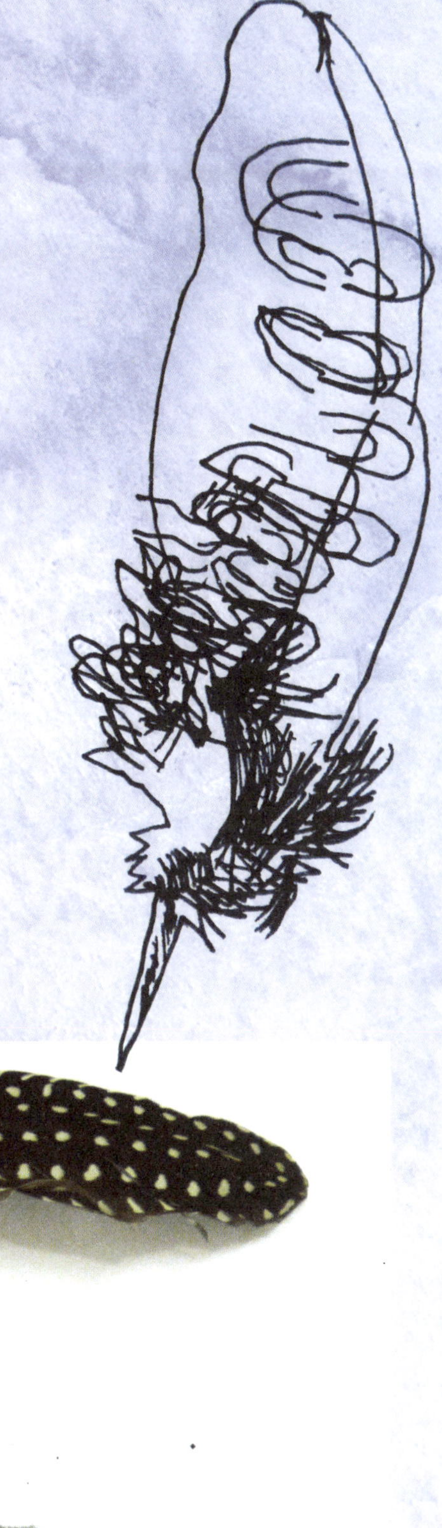

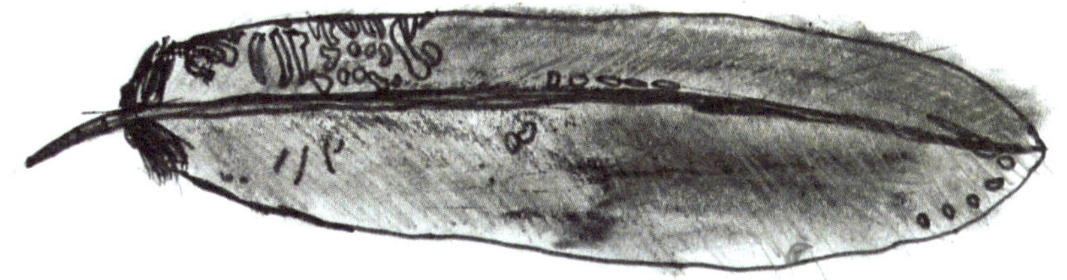

CAPTURING TEXTURE

Clothes that are pegged out on a washing line or folded into new forms provide the inspiration for this drawing session. Use chalk and oil pastels, graphite and handwriting pens to recreate the texture of the clothes.

Preparation and Materials

- Oil pastels
- Chalk pastels
- Soft (B) pencils
- Erasers
- Water soluble graphite
- Handwriting pens
- A2 drawing paper

Subject Matter

Create a temporary washing line on which to hang some soft, thin items of clothing, which should drape nicely. These might include items made of slinky silk, lace or thin cotton. You could also choose some textured knitted or denim items to put on sheets of white paper, or fold some items into big, boxy shapes.

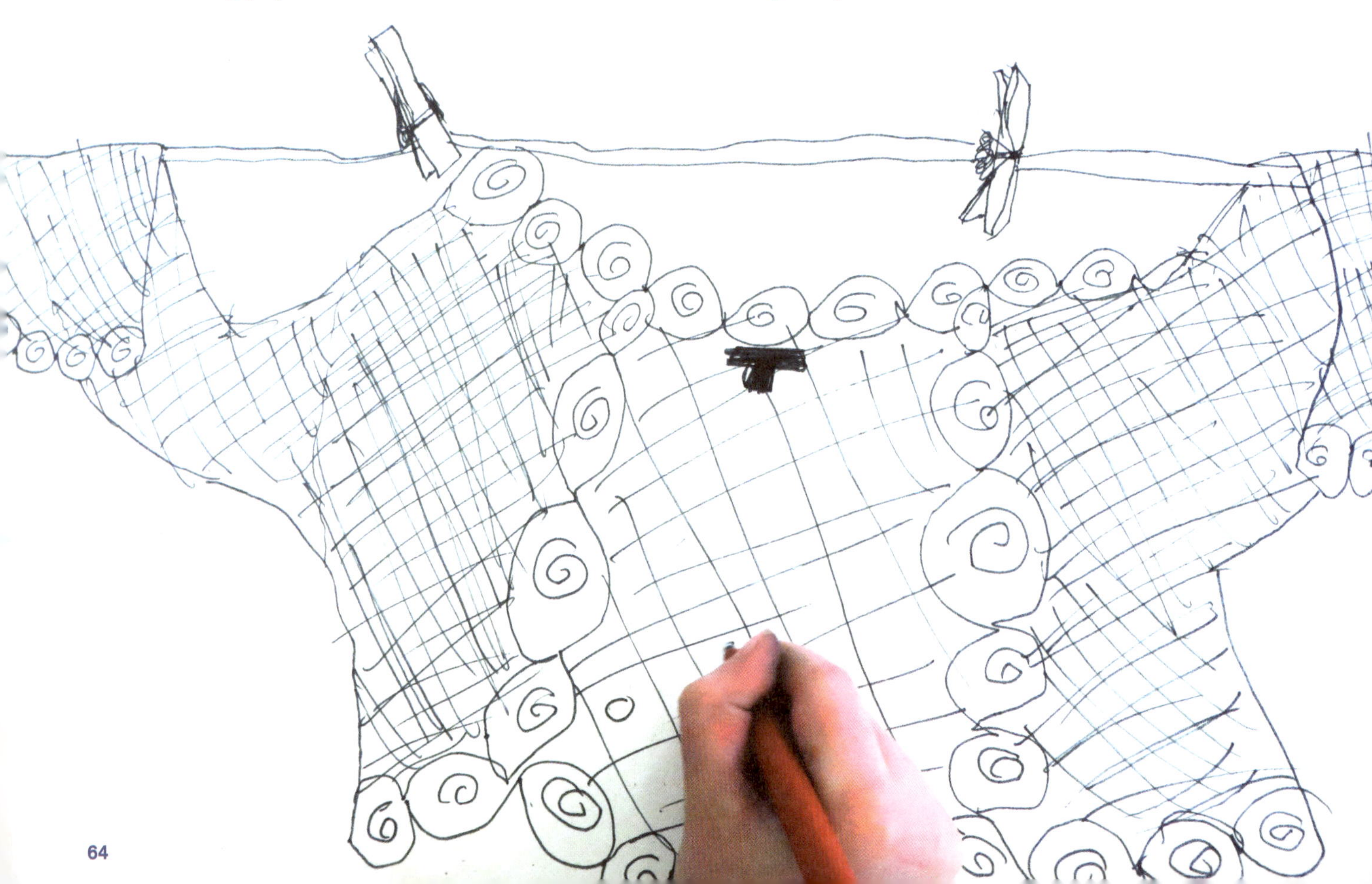

1 The purpose of this project is not to draw a recognisable garment, but to make drawings that capture the texture of different fabrics and to discover how you can use chalk and oil pastels, graphite or pen to do so. Try to capture a sense of the garment, to get an impression of its textures and colours.

2 Choose a large sheet of paper so that you can work on a large scale. This will allow you to use the materials freely. First put down a general colour on the paper, the main colour of the garment, perhaps. Then use graphite over the top of the pastel to help create the garment's texture, detail or form. Alternatively work in pen to capture lacy textures.

3 Try to capture a sense of the weight of the object pulling on the line, or the creases of the folded clothes. What sort of marks might you use with each medium to show all of the textures?

4 When your drawing is completely finished, use fixative, in a ventilated area, to stop them from smudging.

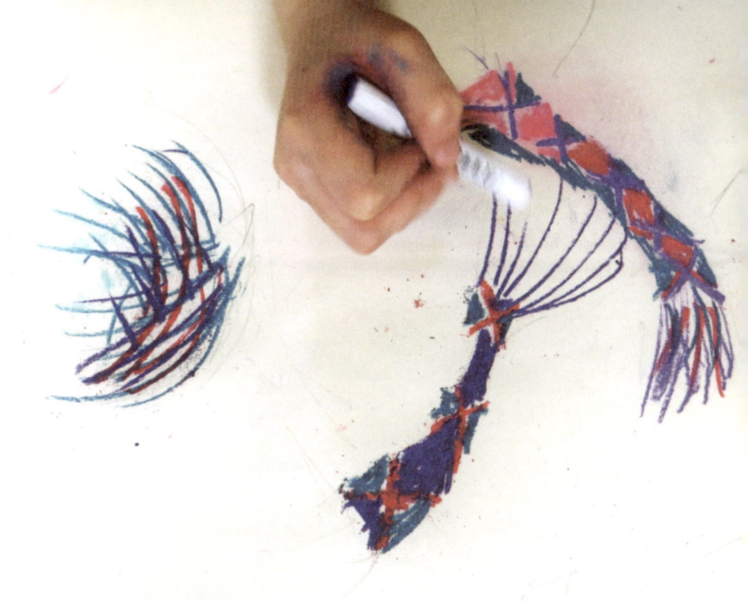

Facilitator's Note

Provide inspiration by placing the drawing materials next to the objects to be drawn in ways that will encourage the children to explore materials and textures. For instance you might place handwriting pens next to a lacy top, or selected colours of pastel next to a particular jumper.

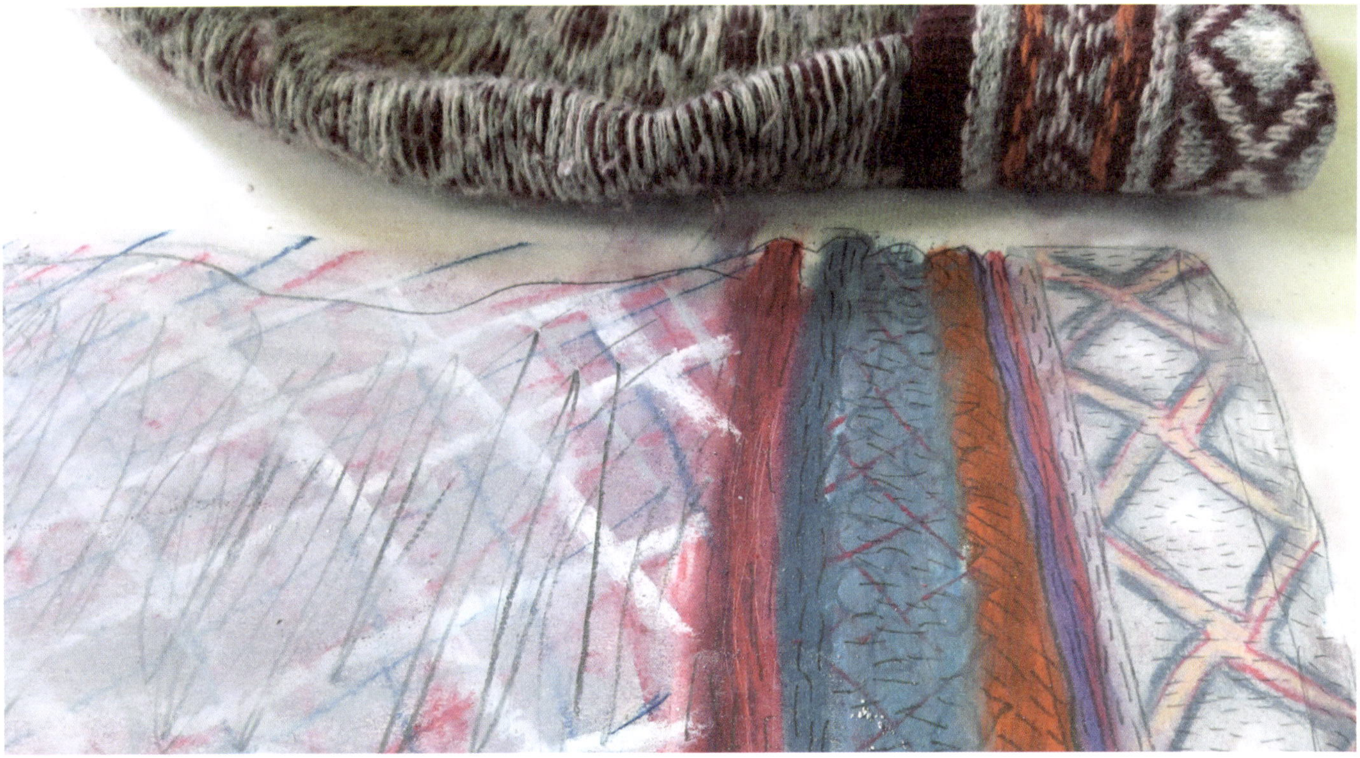

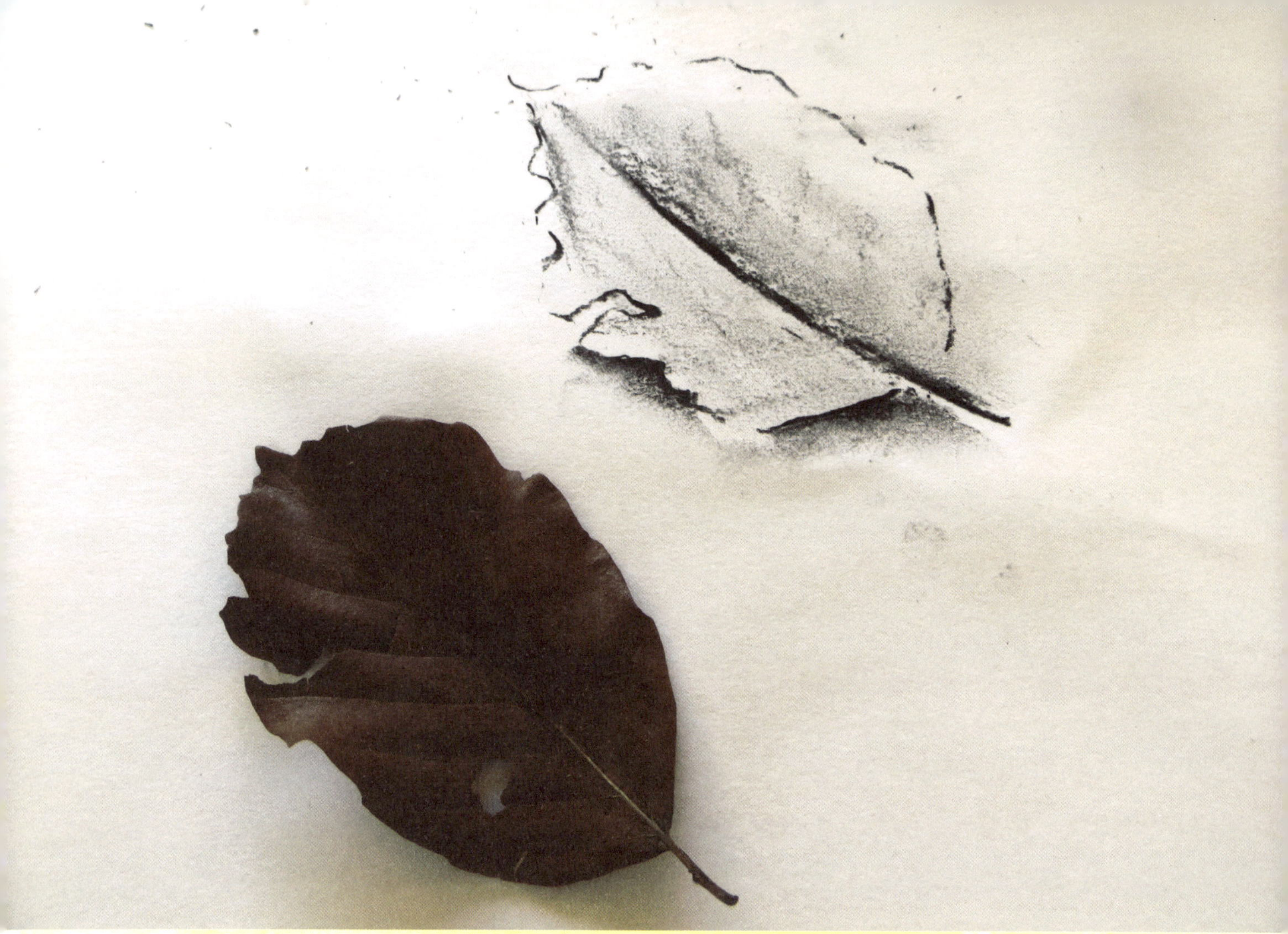

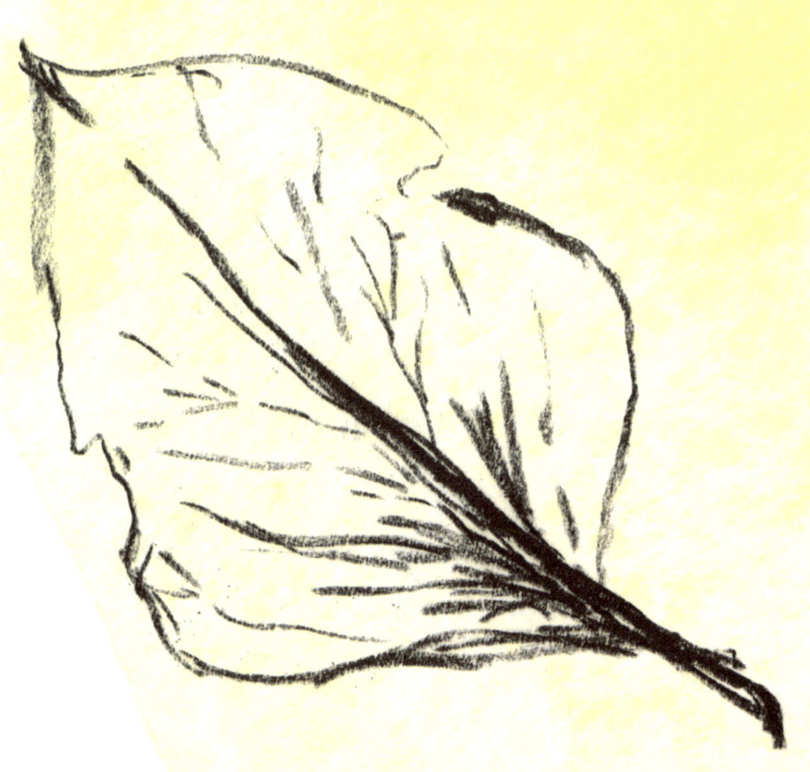

AUTUMN FLOOR DRAWINGS

In this exercise, you will experiment with composition, material and technique, making a drawing with no 'top' or 'bottom'.

Materials

- Graphite
- Soft (B) and hard (H) pencils
- Erasers
- Charcoal
- Handwriting pens
- A3 drawing paper or neutral colours of sugar paper

Subject Matter

You will need a collection of 'autumn debris' from the pavements and footpaths: leaves, twigs, small branches, conkers (buckeyes), pine cones, stones, feathers, etc.

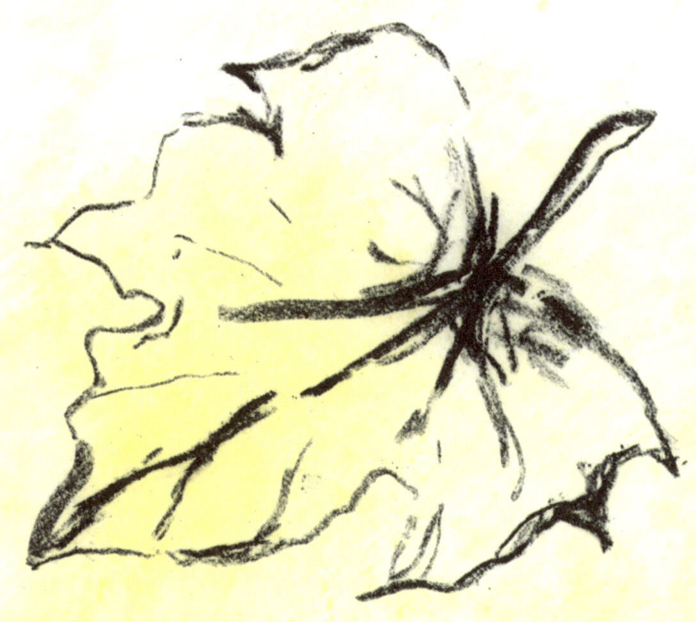

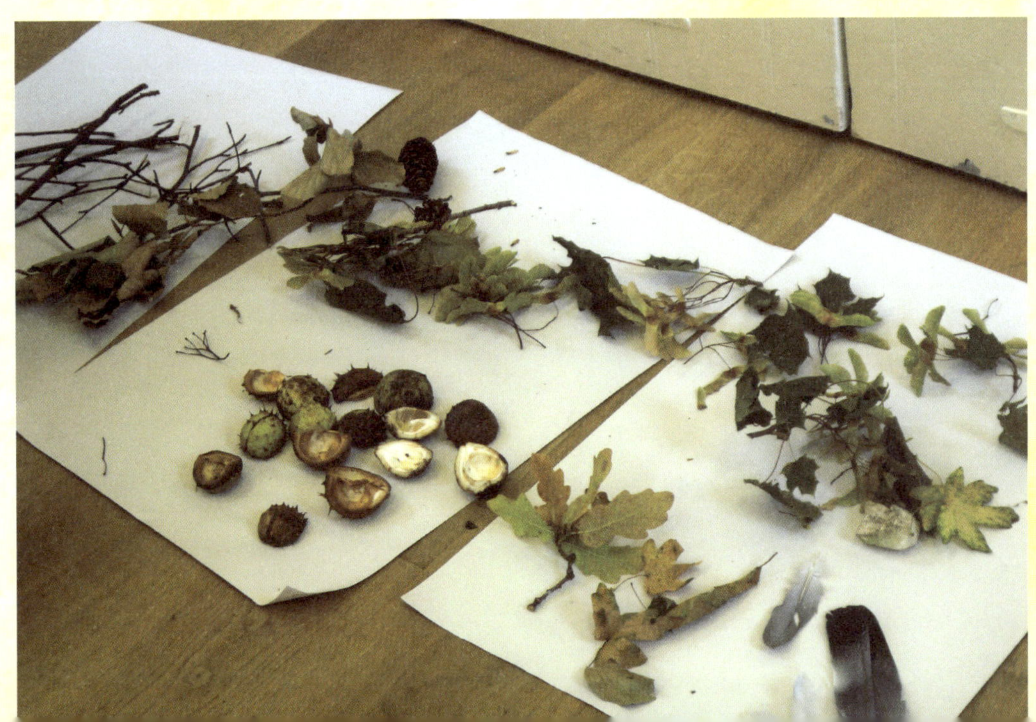

1 Imagine your drawing or sugar paper is a paving slab, covered in autumn debris. Choose an item from your subject matter and a drawing material that you think would suit the object.

2 Place the object on the sugar paper and make a drawing of it on the same paper. You will have to draw the object at its real life size, and you will have to look very carefully at the object as you go. Once you have finished the object, you can take it away from your sheet and pick another.

3 Keep choosing new objects, materials, and ways of drawing them, and each time you pick a new item, think carefully about where you want to place it on your paving slab. Why not turn your paper around each time you pick a new object? This will help you create a drawing that looks like the items are scattered on your paving slab, just as they would be on an autumn floor.

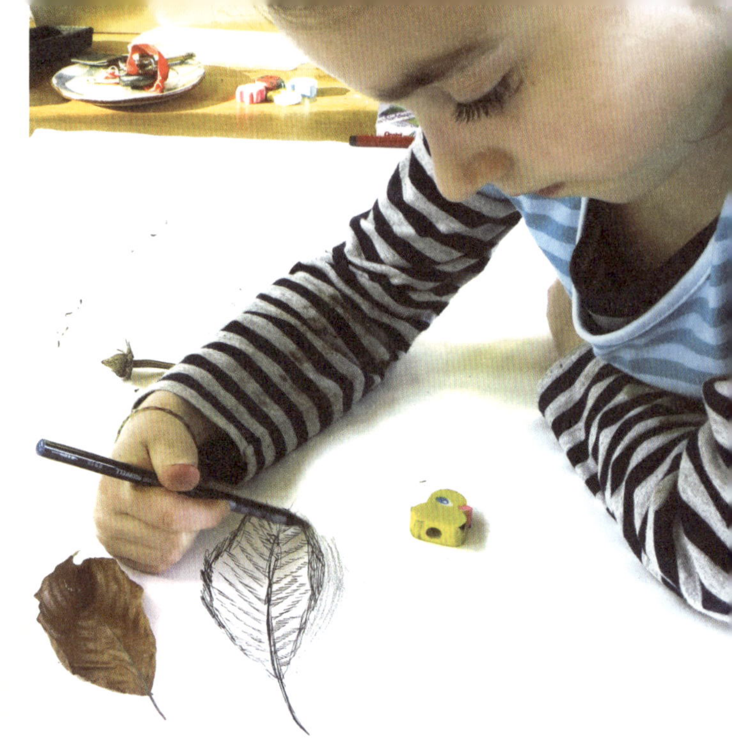

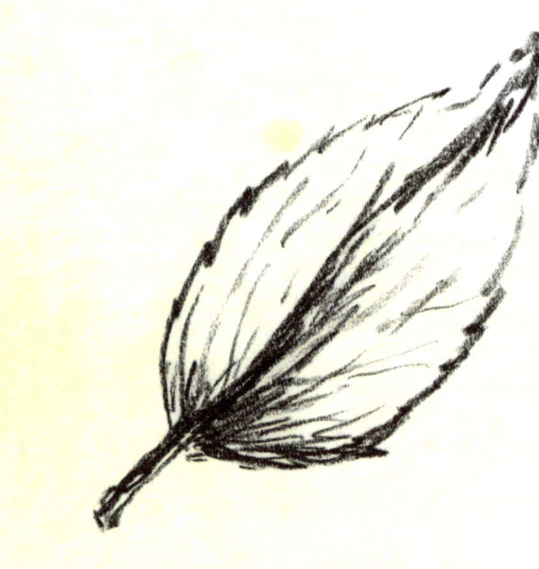

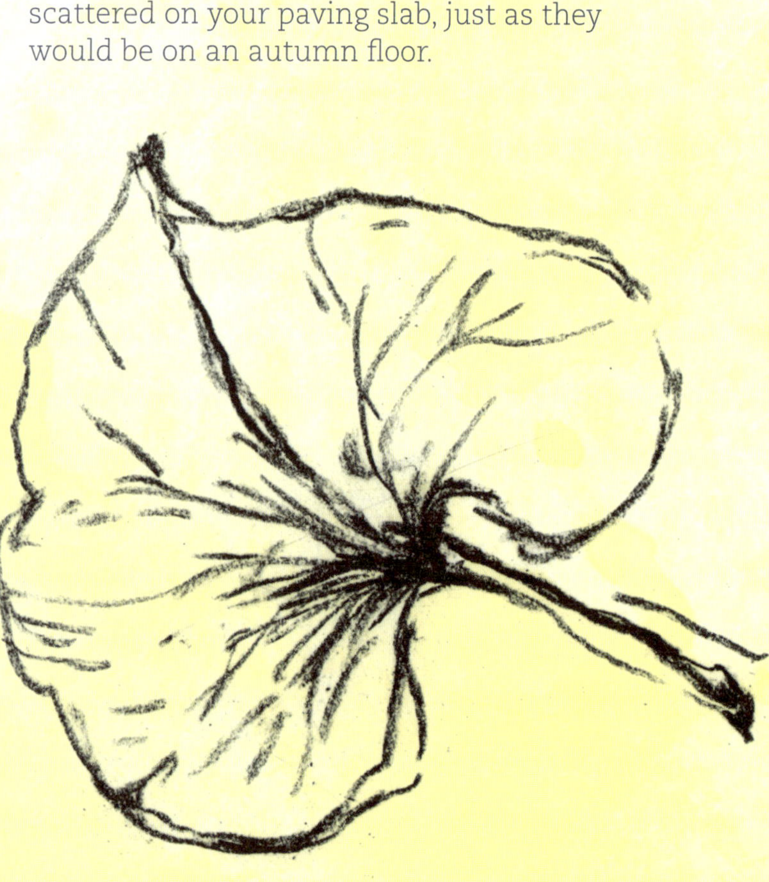

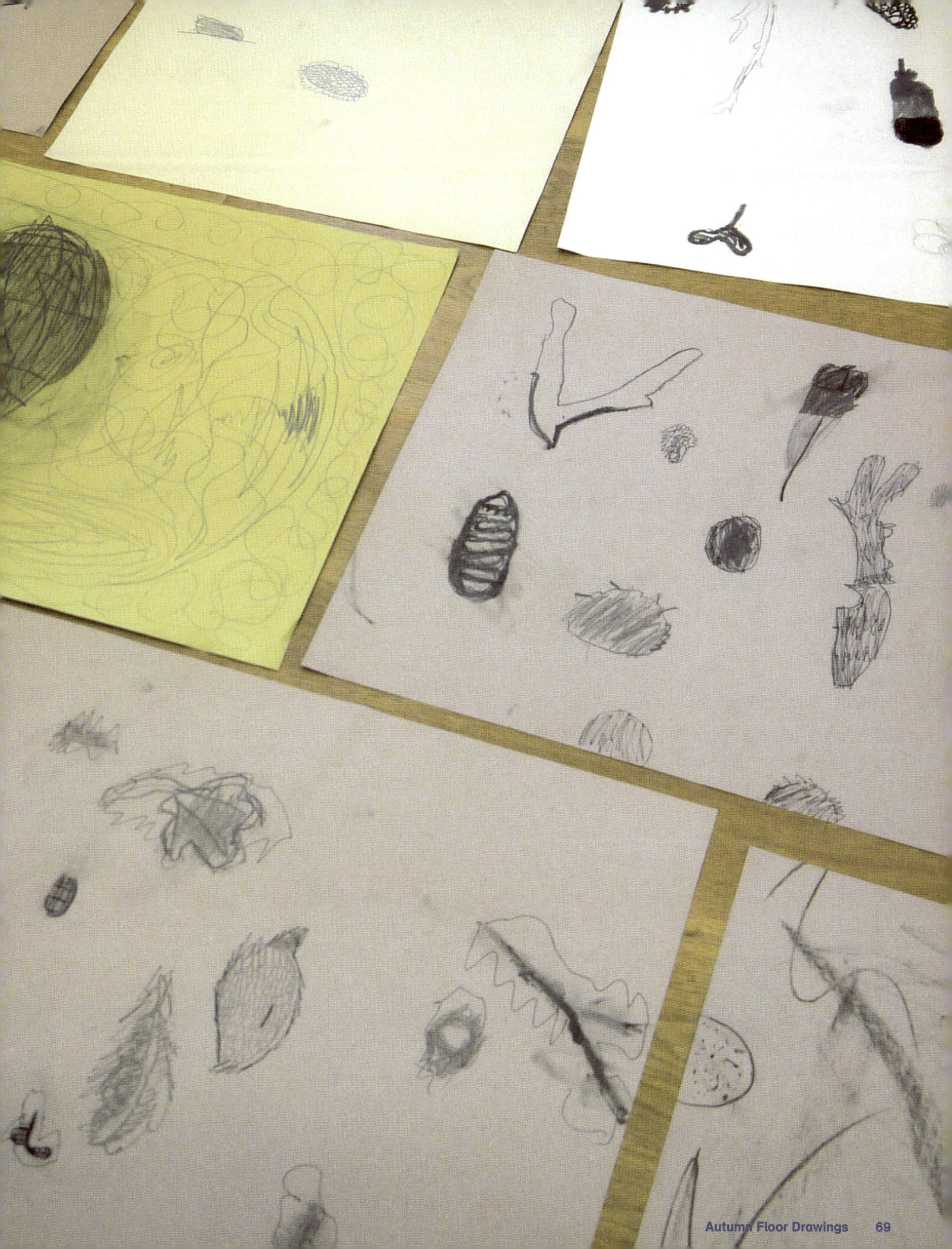

DRAWING POURING WATER

When drawing a moving subject matter, there is no time to worry about making your drawing look exactly right. Instead, drawing something that is moving becomes about showing its essence or personality. In this exercise you will try to draw the essence of moving water. You may need somebody to help you by pouring water for you to draw.

Materials

- Soft (B) and hard (H) pencils
- Graphite
- Water soluble graphite
- Handwriting pens
- Erasers
- Brushes
- Plastic bowls and plastic jugs
- A2 and A3 drawing paper

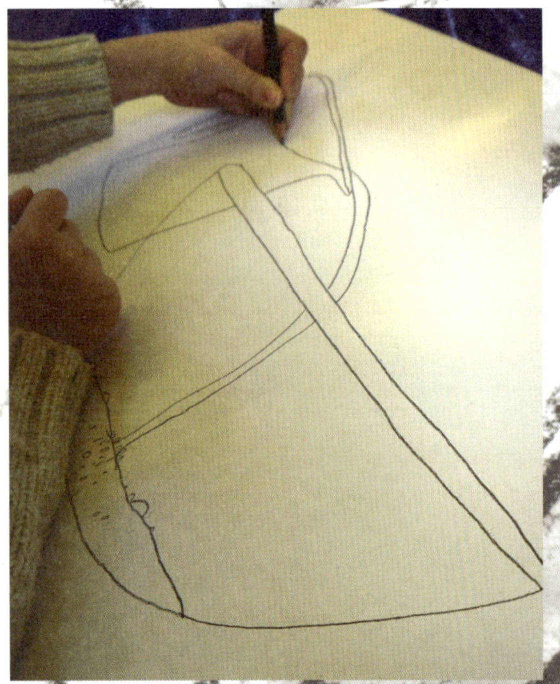

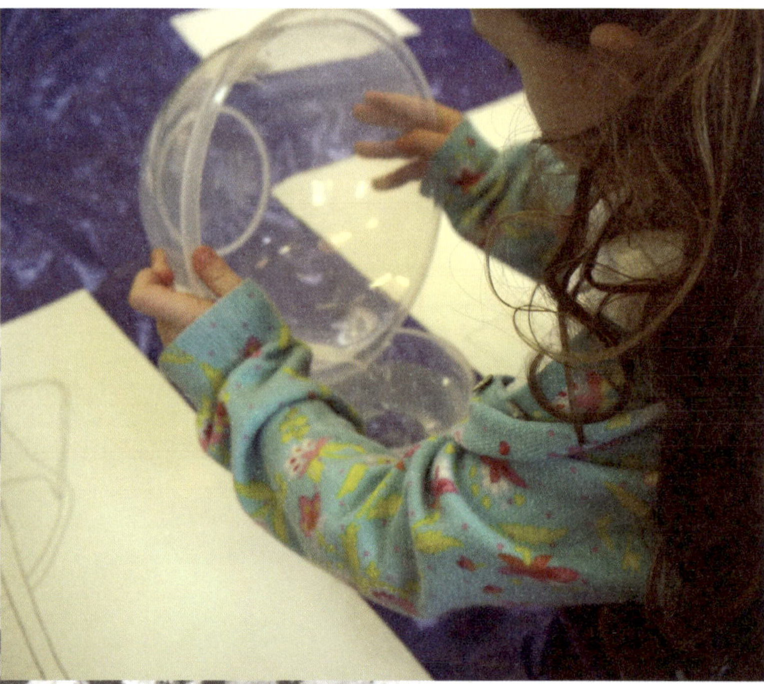

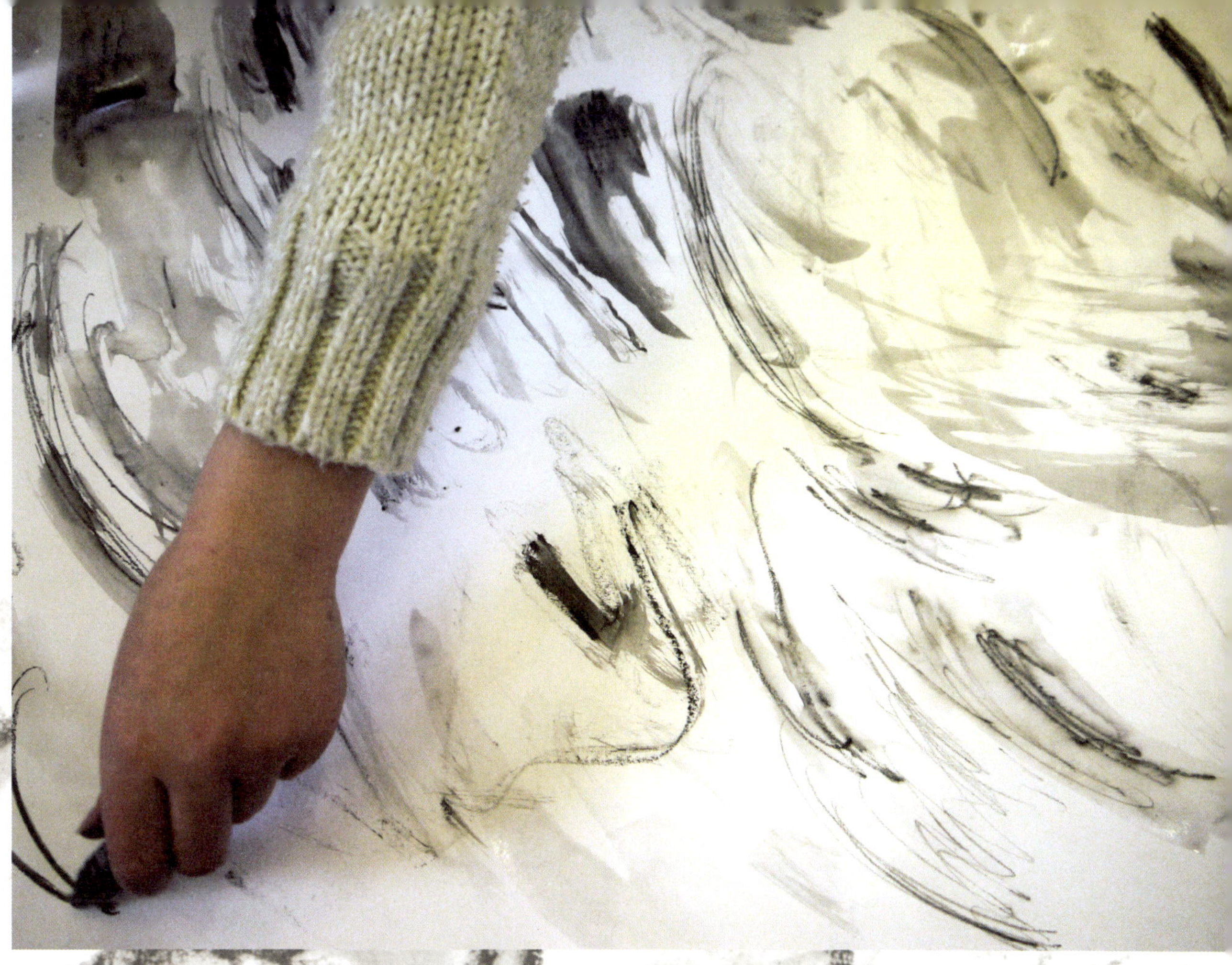

Activity

1 Try looking at some real running water, for example the water that flows out of the tap and into the sink. Try to look at the energy of the water. How might you capture the water's personality?

2 Your partner could pour water slowly from a jug into a bowl. While the water pours into the bowl, try to observe the patterns that it makes.

3 Make three drawings of the pouring water. First, use pencil to make a study of the water flowing. Then, use erasers over graphite to make some watery marks to capture some of the water's properties. Finally, use soluble graphite, water and brushes to make even more watery marks. Allow each drawing you make to become freer and more inventive in terms of the marks you make.

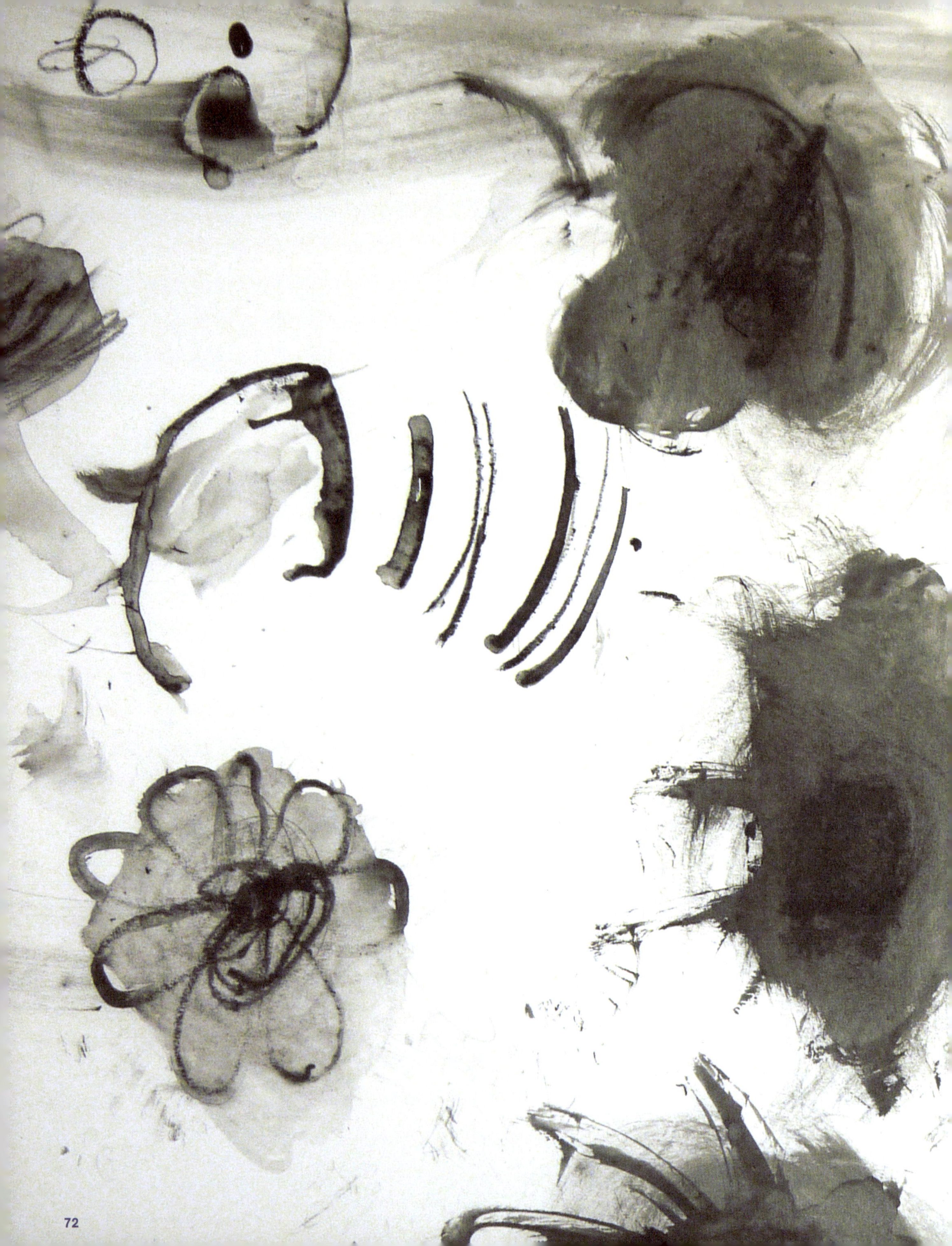

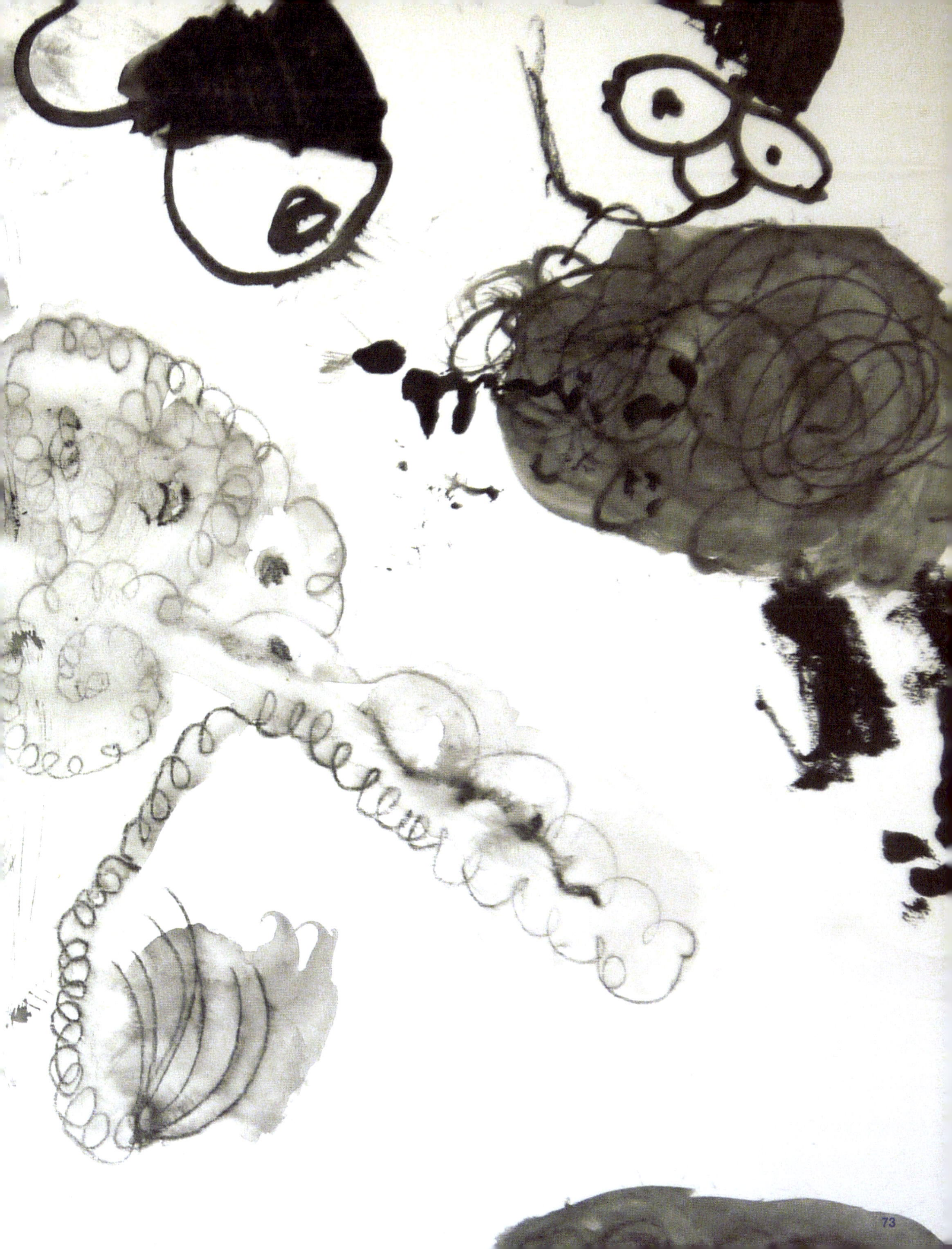

COLOUR AND LINE

We have all used colour to colour in between lines. In this exercise, you will push your use of line and colour further by making two drawings, one on top of the other.

Materials

- Soft (B) pencils
- Graphite
- Chalk pastels
- Erasers
- White paper
- Brown paper

Subject Matter

You will need a variety of objects as subject matter: balls of string or wool, tape, paintbrushes, tape measures, etc. Arrange these on some sheets of white paper.

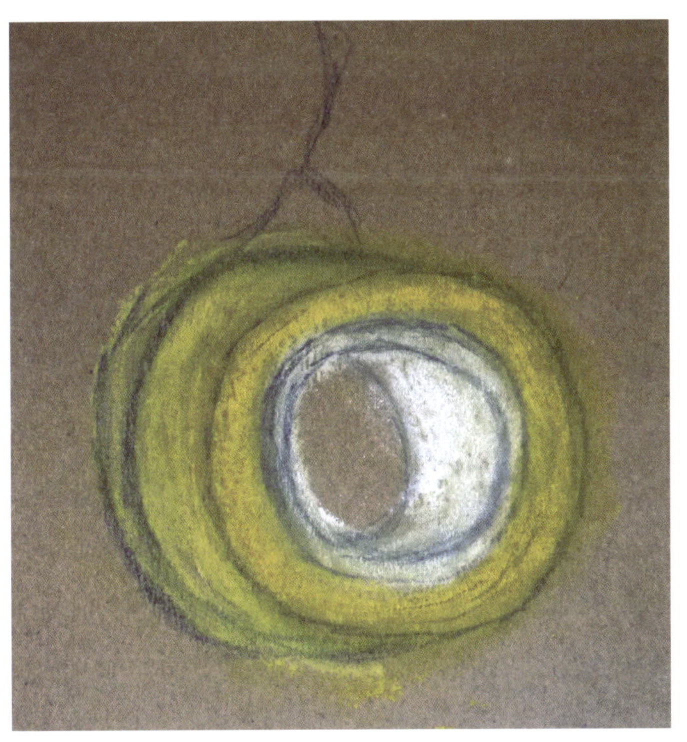

Activity

1 Tear up the brown paper into A4 sized or larger sheets.

2 Make a series of drawings in two stages. First, use coloured pastels to put down blocks of colour onto the paper, inspired by the objects you are drawing. Secondly, use graphite to make a line drawing, over the top of the blocks of colour. Remember, the aim is not to rush and complete the drawing as fast as you can or to make as many as you can, the aim is to look carefully and make thoughtful drawings.

3 When you are ready, move on to draw another object. You will find your own drawing pace.

Facilitator's Note

This simple project has two aims: to let children explore how colour and form can exist as two distinct yet complementary elements within a drawing; and to enable children to find their own momentum or pace in creating a series of drawings. If you are working with more than one child, encourage them to create at their own pace; some will work quickly and some will work slowly.

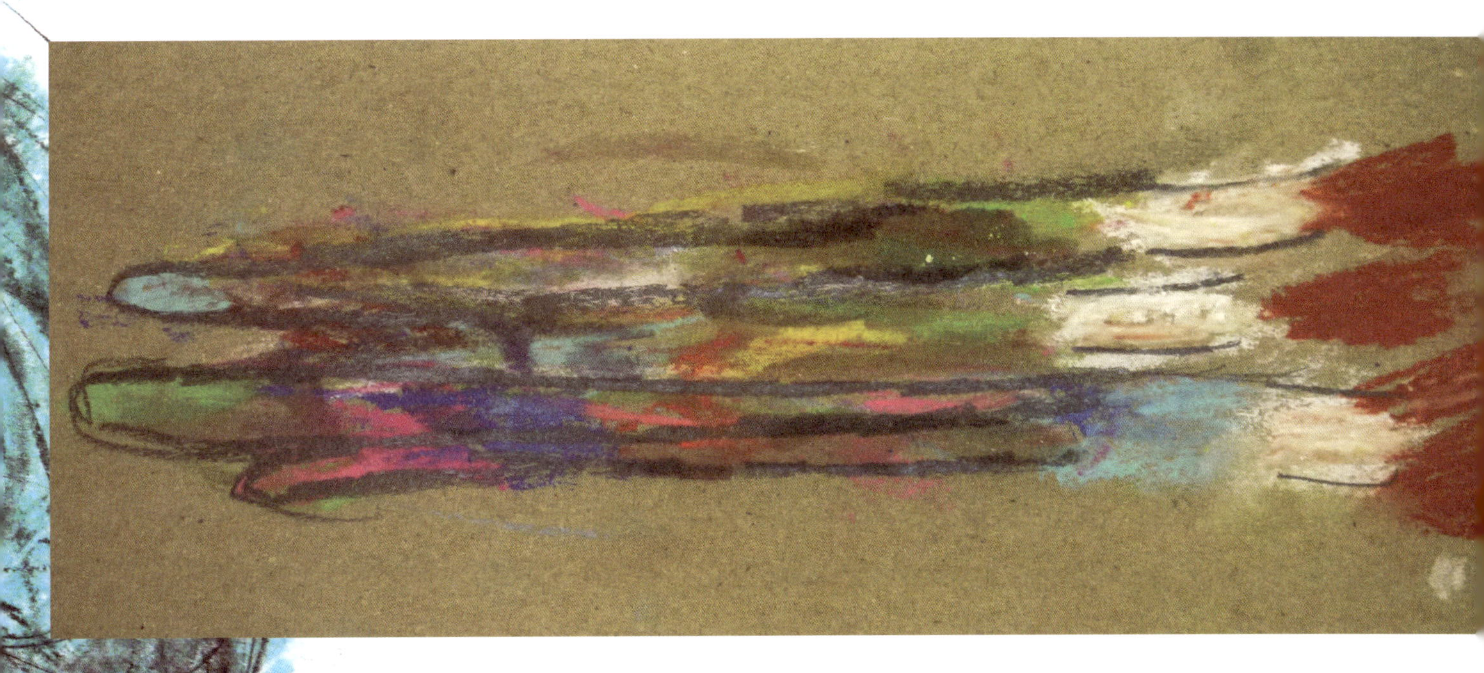

ANIMAL CARTOON CHARACTERS

In this project you will create your own animal cartoon characters and learn how mark making can build the personality of your cartoons.

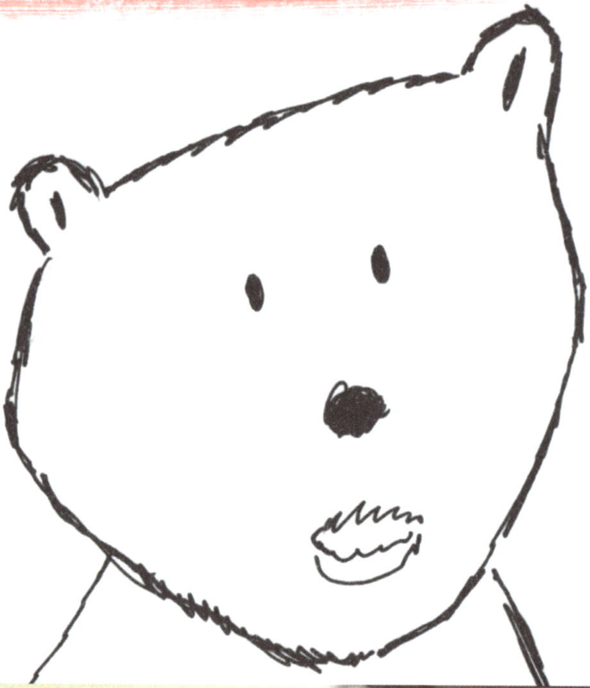

Materials

- Soft (B) and hard (H) pencils
- Handwriting pens
- Graphite
- Charcoal
- Erasers
- A2 drawing paper

Subject Matter

You will need a photograph of an animal of your choice—this must be a photograph, rather than a drawing or painting (or cartoon).

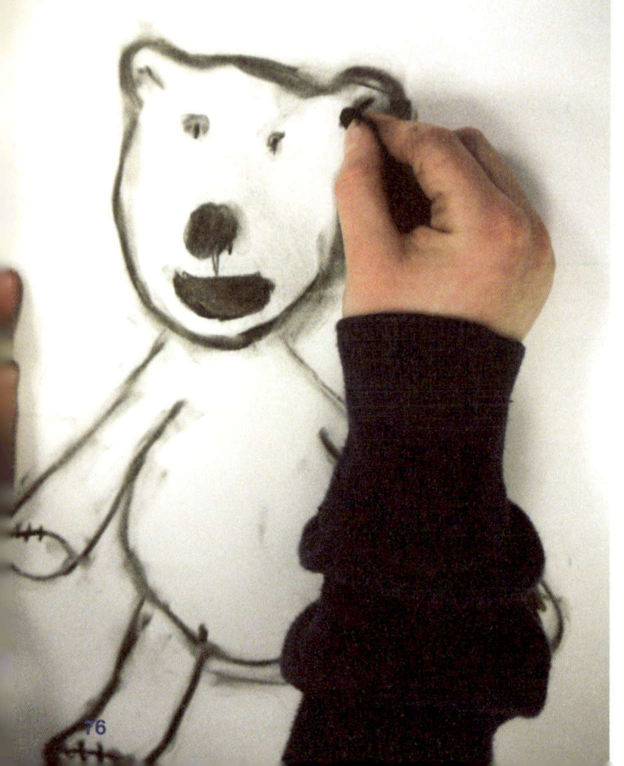

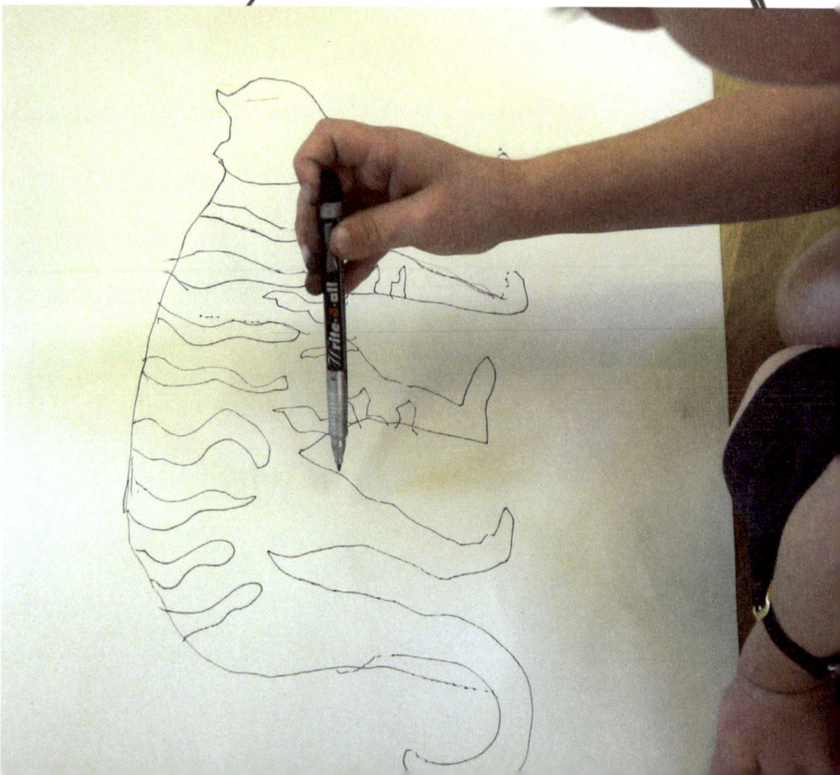

Activity

1 Before you make your cartoon, think about what makes a good cartoon character drawing. How might an artist capture an animal's personality, or draw its features to show that personality?

2 Look at the photograph of your chosen animal and the way the animal looks (and acts). You might even watch a film or video of the animal. Building knowledge is a crucial part of developing a cartoon-like character. To familiarise yourself with the character of the animal, you could try some different drawing exercises. For example, you could create some Backwards Forwards Sketches (p 30), or try a light pencil drawing (where the pen or pencil is held lightly, at the top of the pencil, and movements are made from your shoulder, rather than your hand), or a side of pencil gestural drawing (use the side of a piece of graphite or charcoal to try to capture the strong shapes and mass of the animals).

3 After you have tried a selection of drawing exercises and become more familiar with your animal, start to think about what makes a cartoon different from a normal drawing. Think about the use of human qualities (standing on two feet, expressive face and eyes), exaggeration, personality, action and even if the animal will wear clothes.

4 Using the images, start to draw your cartoon animal! Remember all the information you have gathered through your warm up sketches and research, and let this feed into the creation of your cartoon creature. Once you have drawn your cartoon animal in one position, challenge yourself to draw it in other positions, so that you can begin to build up a storyboard, comic strip or even animation.

Facilitator's Note

Children are often encouraged to draw cartoons by building a series of shapes that relate in a simplistic way to a particular portrayal of an animal. Circles, squares, triangles and cones are often used to help build and describe a cartoon through a series of steps, and details are prescribed and didactic. Through this method children are enabled to replicate a known end result of a cartoon in a particular pose, but it does not help them develop their drawing skills.

In this project children build an understanding of their subject matter together with an awareness of how mark making can help portray personality and intention. Cartoon-like characters emerge which are completely original. In this way children can develop their visual vocabulary and learn the drawing skills needed to make their cartoon drawings truly their own.

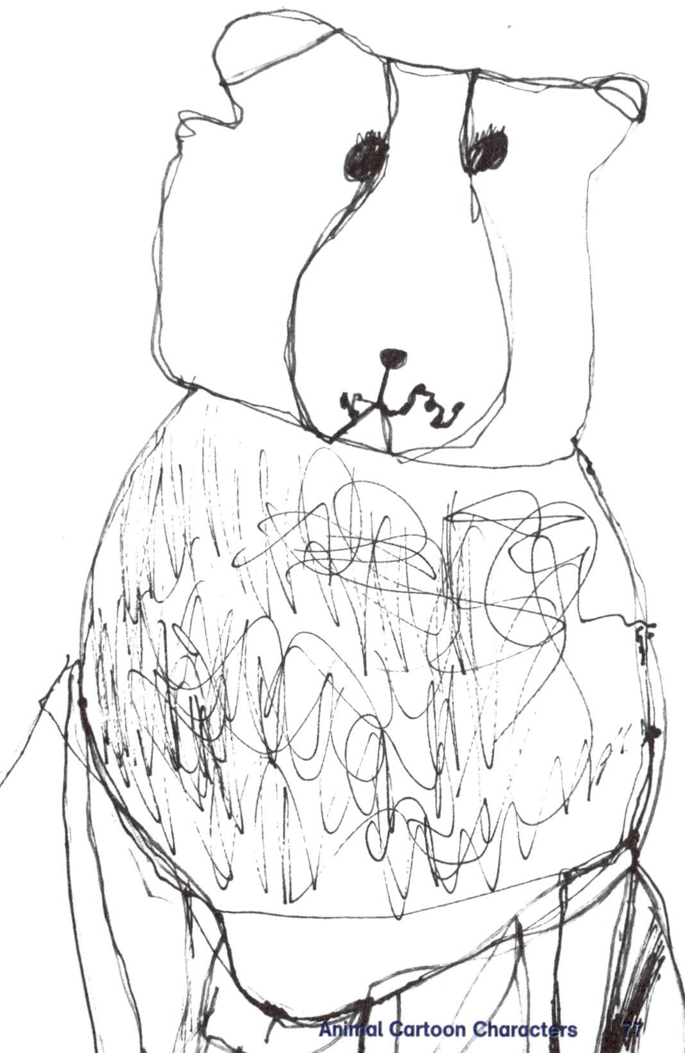

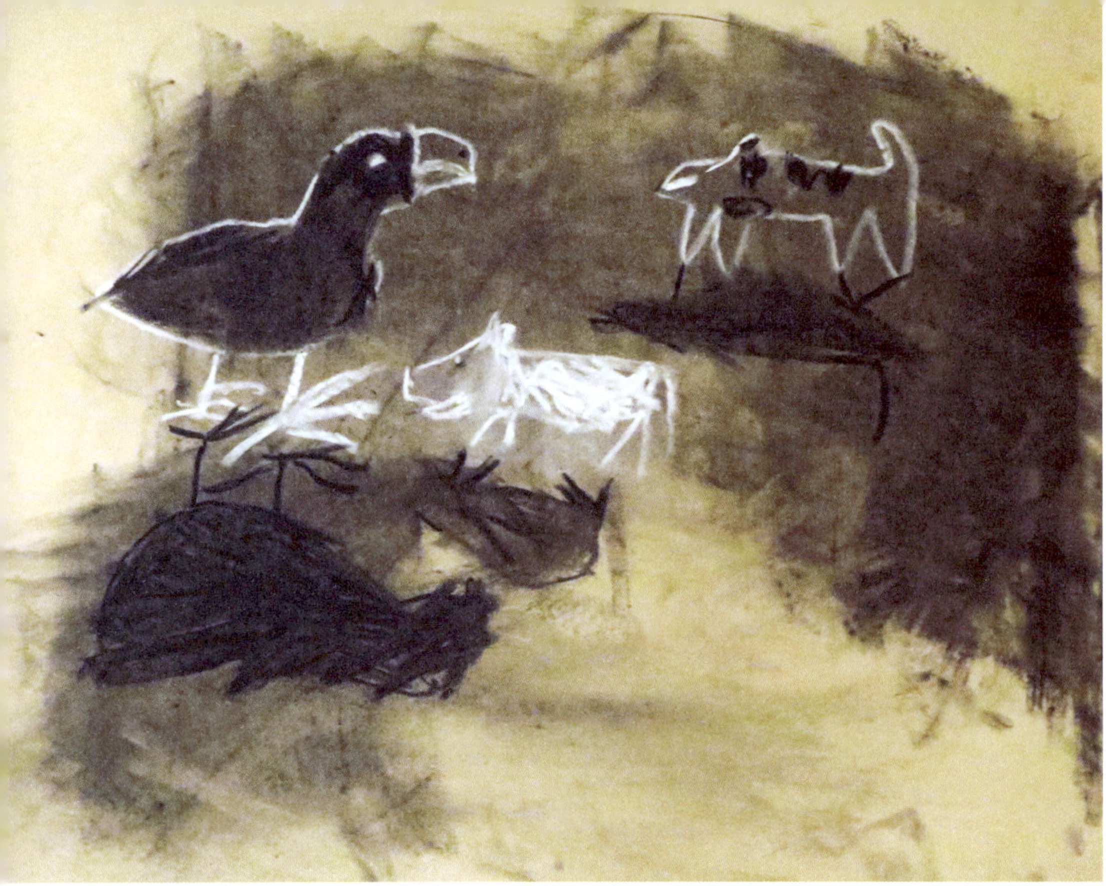

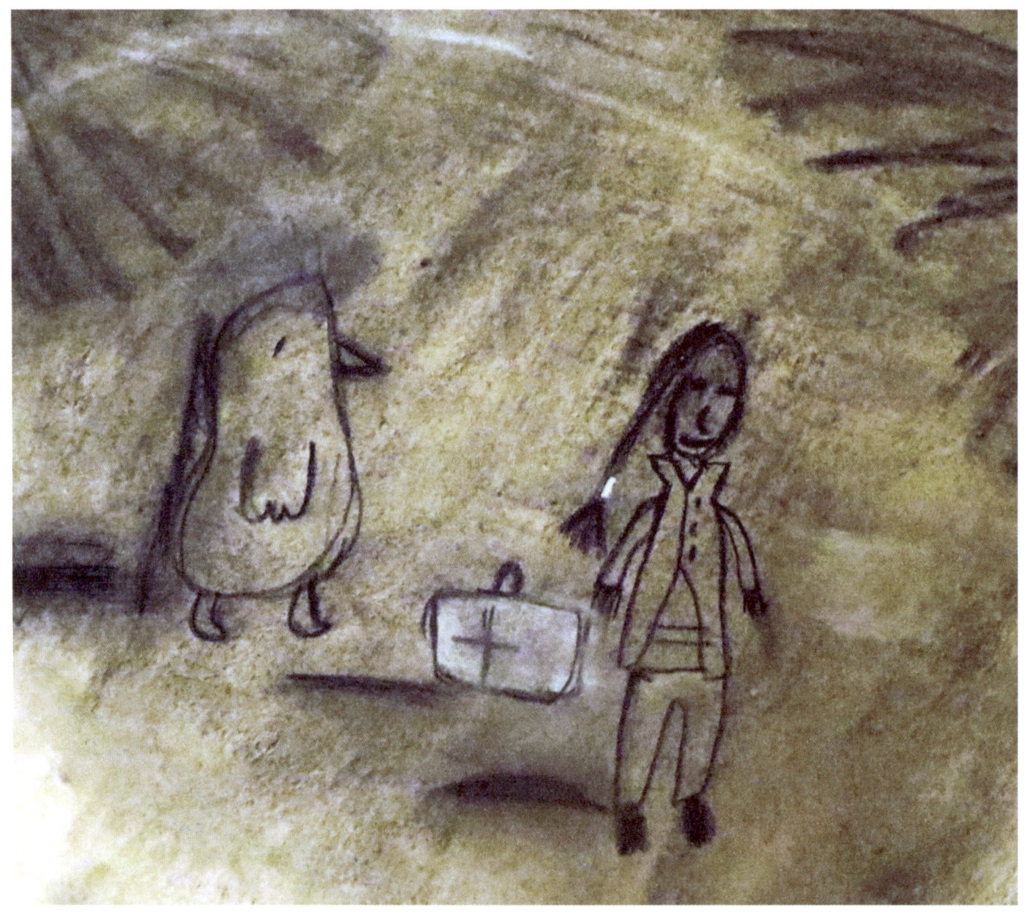

DRAWING BY TORCHLIGHT

This project requires you to use your imagination to create your own still life, then dramatically light it and make an equally dramatic charcoal drawing of it.

Materials

- Charcoal
- Compressed charcoal pencil
- White chalk or pastel
- Erasers
- Brushes
- Torches
- A2 or A3 sugar paper

Subject Matter

You will need a selection of toys set up in a still life. Use a torch, or more than one if you need to, to light the toy scene in a dramatic way. This works well in a darkened room. In daylight you could create the scene inside a box.

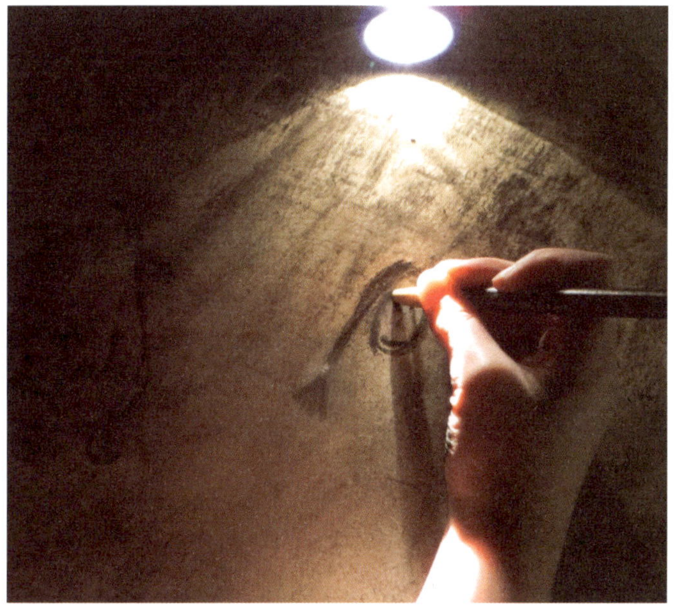

Activity

1 Make a charcoal drawing of the torch-lit still life scene. Charcoal can be tricky to handle if you try to use it like a pencil, and it is not really suited to detailed work unless you work on a large scale. Instead, aim for bold marks. While you are drawing your still life, think about what drama might be taking place. How do the shadows cast by torchlight change the story? Do they make it more dramatic?

2 When making your charcoal drawing, start by rubbing charcoal across the page and using your hand to rub the dust into the paper. This will create a background.

3 Then work back into the charcoal dust with an eraser to reveal 'light', or work back with more charcoal to portray 'dark'. It can be easy to overwork a charcoal drawing so try to use the blackest blacks and the lightest whites to show shadow and light, and create highlights or lowlights.

4 If you change the torch from pointing at your still life to your drawing each time you look at one of these, you will get used to the pattern of looking, then drawing, then looking, then drawing, etc.

5 Do not let your eyes get too tired! After about 30 minutes, raise the level of light in the room to finish off your drawing.

DRAWING INVENTIONS

Be curious about the world around you! This project recycles everyday objects to make collaged drawings of incredible inventions.

Materials

- Soft (B) and hard (H) pencils
- Pens
- Erasers
- Oil pastels
- Glue sticks
- Scissors
- Carbon paper
- Tracing paper
- Graph paper
- A4 and A3 drawing paper

Subject Matter

Gather together a collection of man-made objects: paper clips, magnets, bulldog clips, elastic bands, hinges, handles, pegs, brushes, and kitchenware items, such as whisks.

Try to choose a variety of objects made of different materials, and with interesting forms. These objects will provide the inspiration for your drawn inventions.

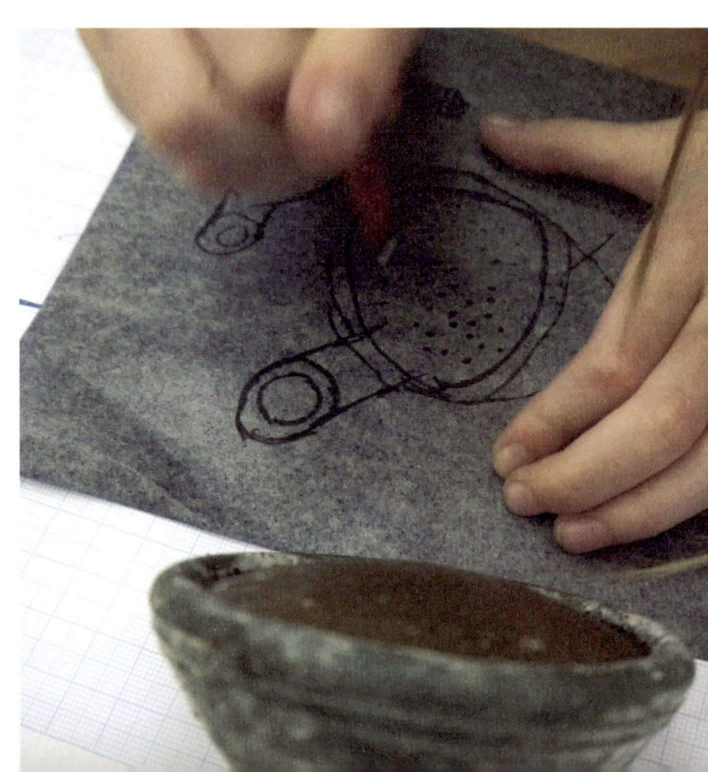

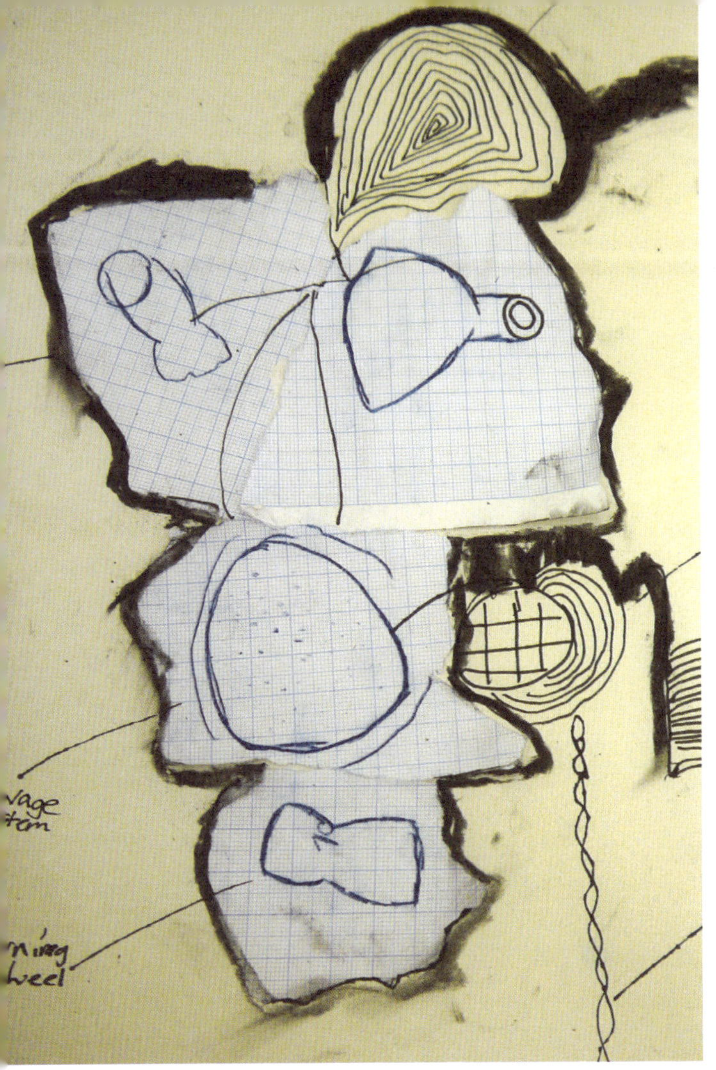

Activity

1 Start by choosing three objects. Draw each one on separate sheets of paper: one on tracing paper, one on graph paper, and one on carbon paper (a monoprint—see the Carbon Paper Monoprints project (p 194) for more details on this technique).

2 Think about shapes and materials that might inspire an invention. Which other objects might you might need to complete your invention?

3 Now the fun begins. Become an inventor. Cut, tear or copy your drawings and stick them together to create a collage. Draw new objects in between and over the original objects.

4 You might also like to make notes on your drawing.

5 Your finished collages will have a lovely tactile feel to them, with the use of different paper surfaces and drawn elements.

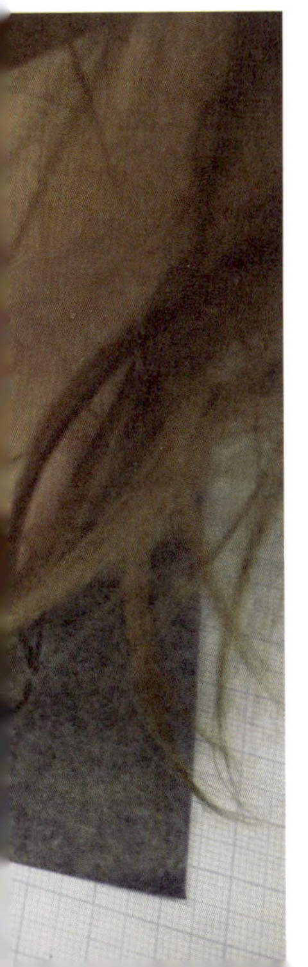

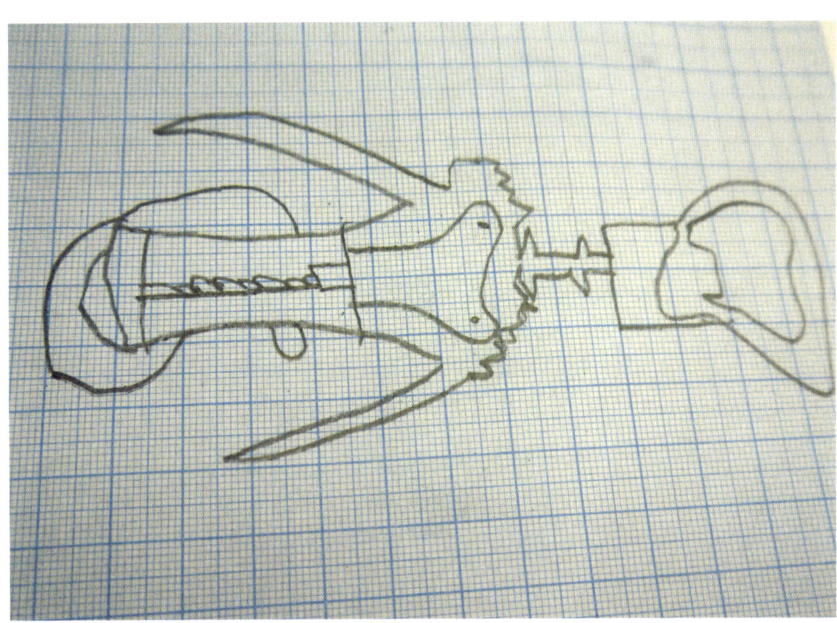

MAKING ILLUSTRATIONS

In this project, you will combine drawing with storytelling and play, to create drawings which bring stories to life!

Materials

- Charcoal
- Compressed charcoal
- White chalk or chalk pastels
- Erasers
- Cardboard and sticks
- A2 sugar paper

Subject Matter

A collection of small toys, such as farmyard animals and character toys.

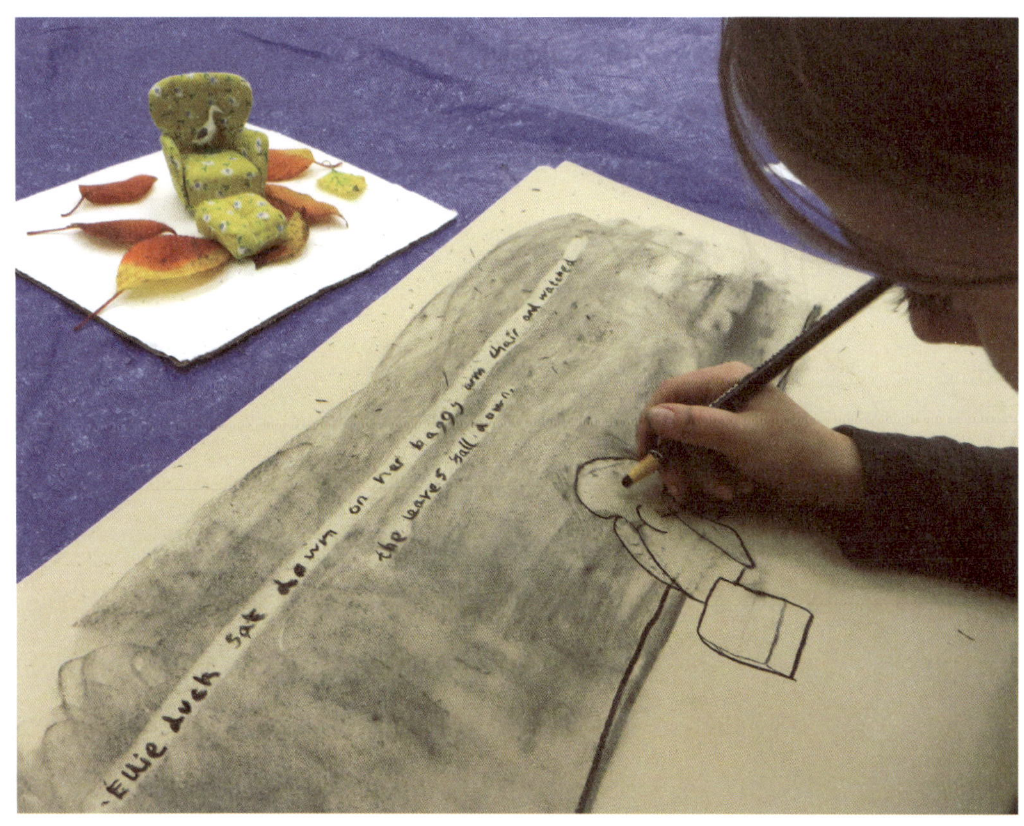

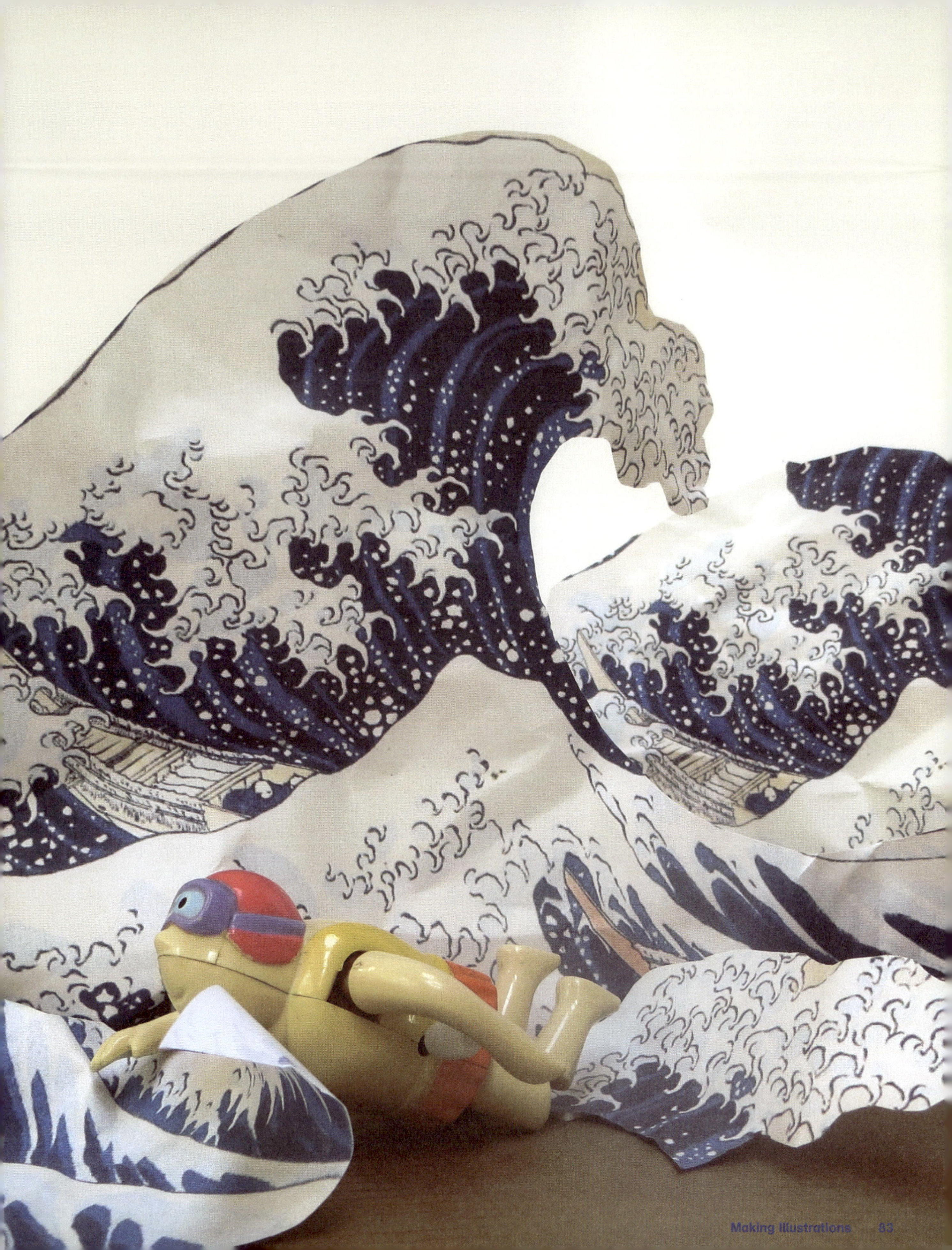

1 Using three of four toys, create a small scene that will become your subject matter. You can use cardboard and sticks to help prop up your scene, or as a background or foreground. Think carefully about how your chosen items work together or affect each other. Think of, and write down, a single sentence that is inspired by the scene.

2 Make a drawing of your scene using the charcoal and chalks. Remember that making a small, detailed drawing with large charcoal sticks can be very frustrating. Instead, try to work on a large scale and use the richness of the charcoal in your drawing. Allow both the words and the objects to inspire your sense of narrative.

3 Re-write your descriptive sentences on your drawing in a decorative way, so that the text and image work together on the page. How might the text sit in the white space of the drawing? How might the text relate to the image?

4 If you enjoyed this session, you may want to try illustrating the line of a poem or a line from a storybook. Then, with a collection of these, you can create your own illustrated storybook.

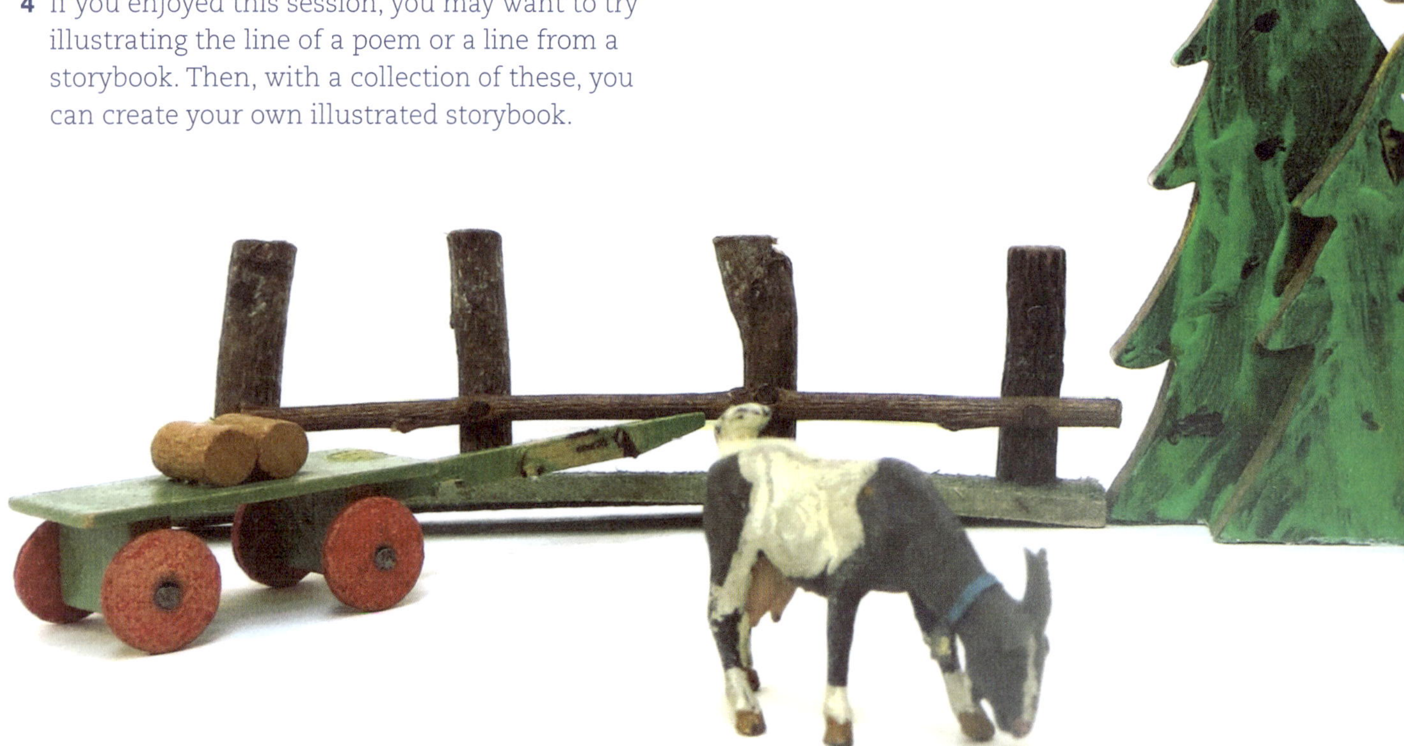

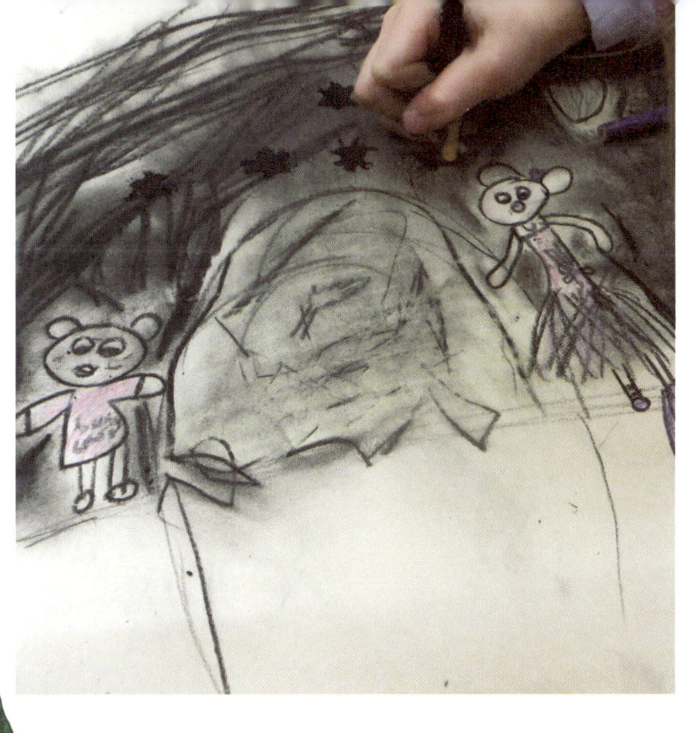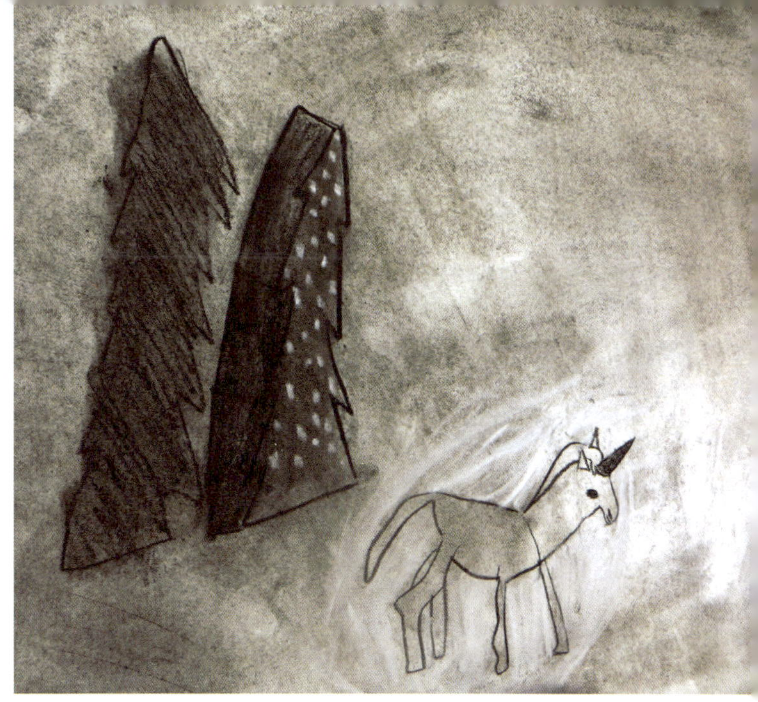

Facilitator's Note

If the child is focusing on a small scale, you may
be able to help them make the leap from small
drawing to larger charcoal mark making by having
them watch your hand as it 'air draws' on the paper,
alongside a commentary: "So the arm might be this
big and be here, the head here, the ears here…", etc.
As soon as children can start to visualise marks on
an empty sheet of paper, they usually feel confident
to make larger drawings on their own.

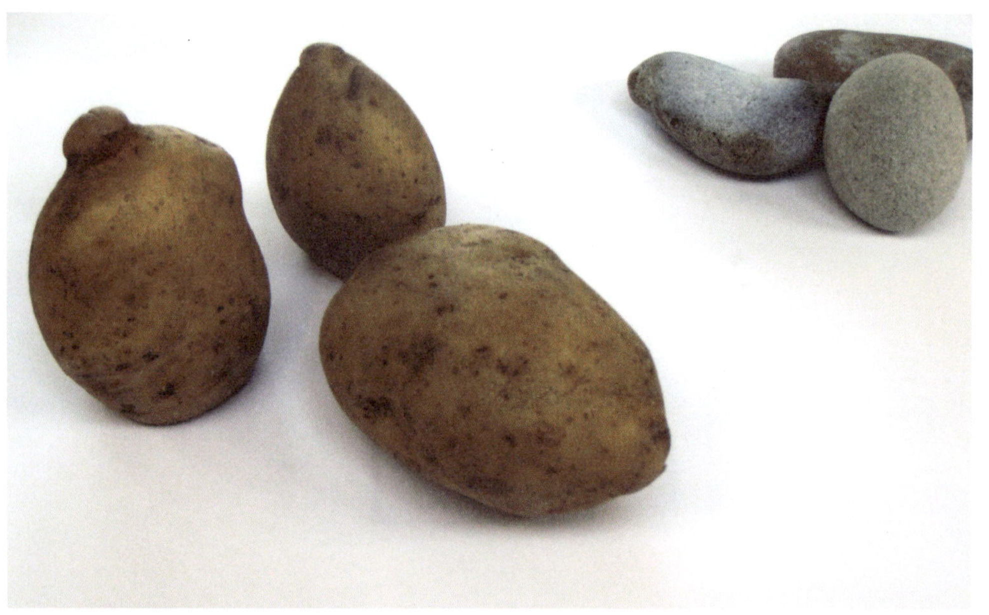

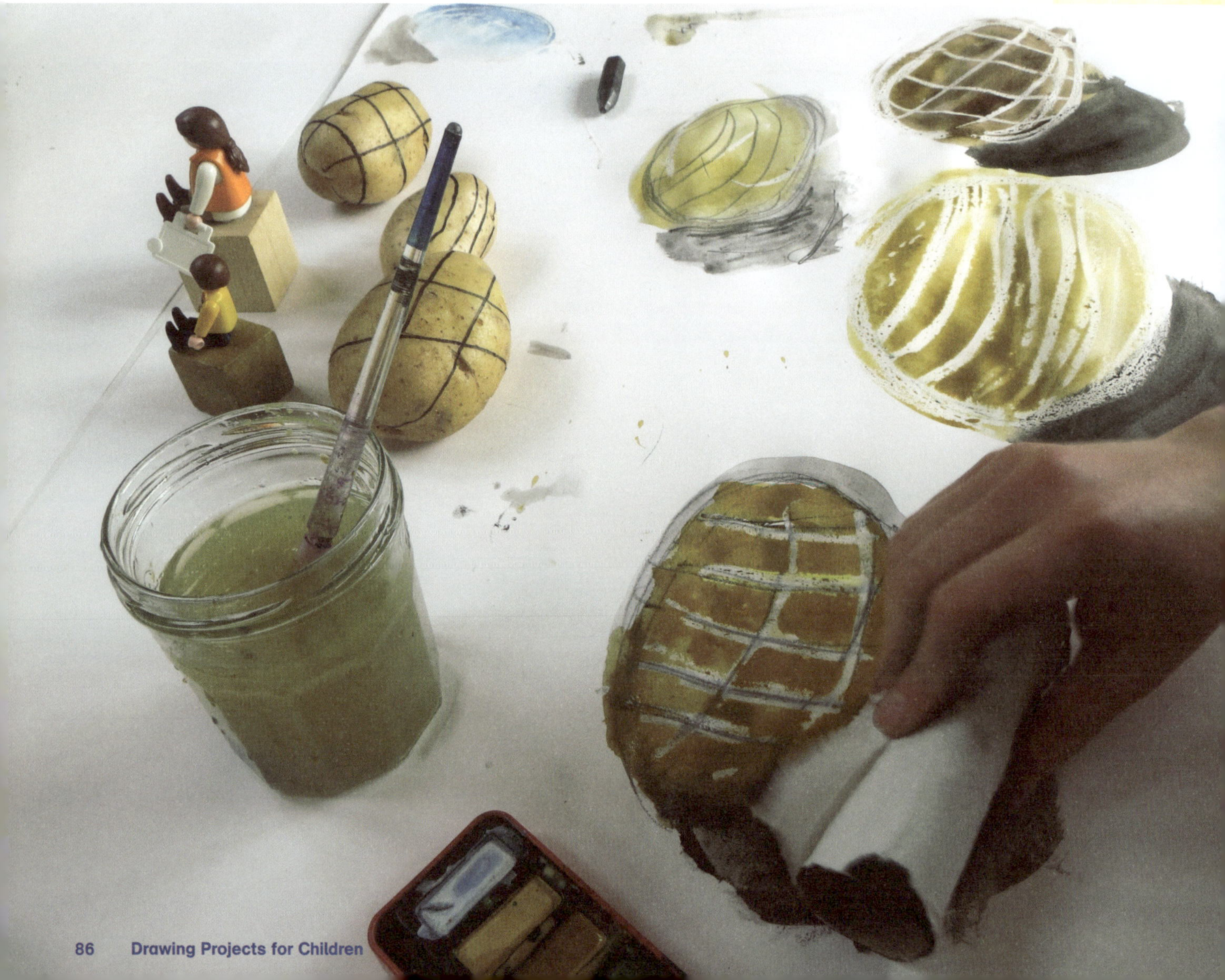

MAKING WEIGHTY DRAWINGS

In this project you will make drawings that have a sense of weight and volume, with contour lines to show form—just like the drawings of many sculptors.

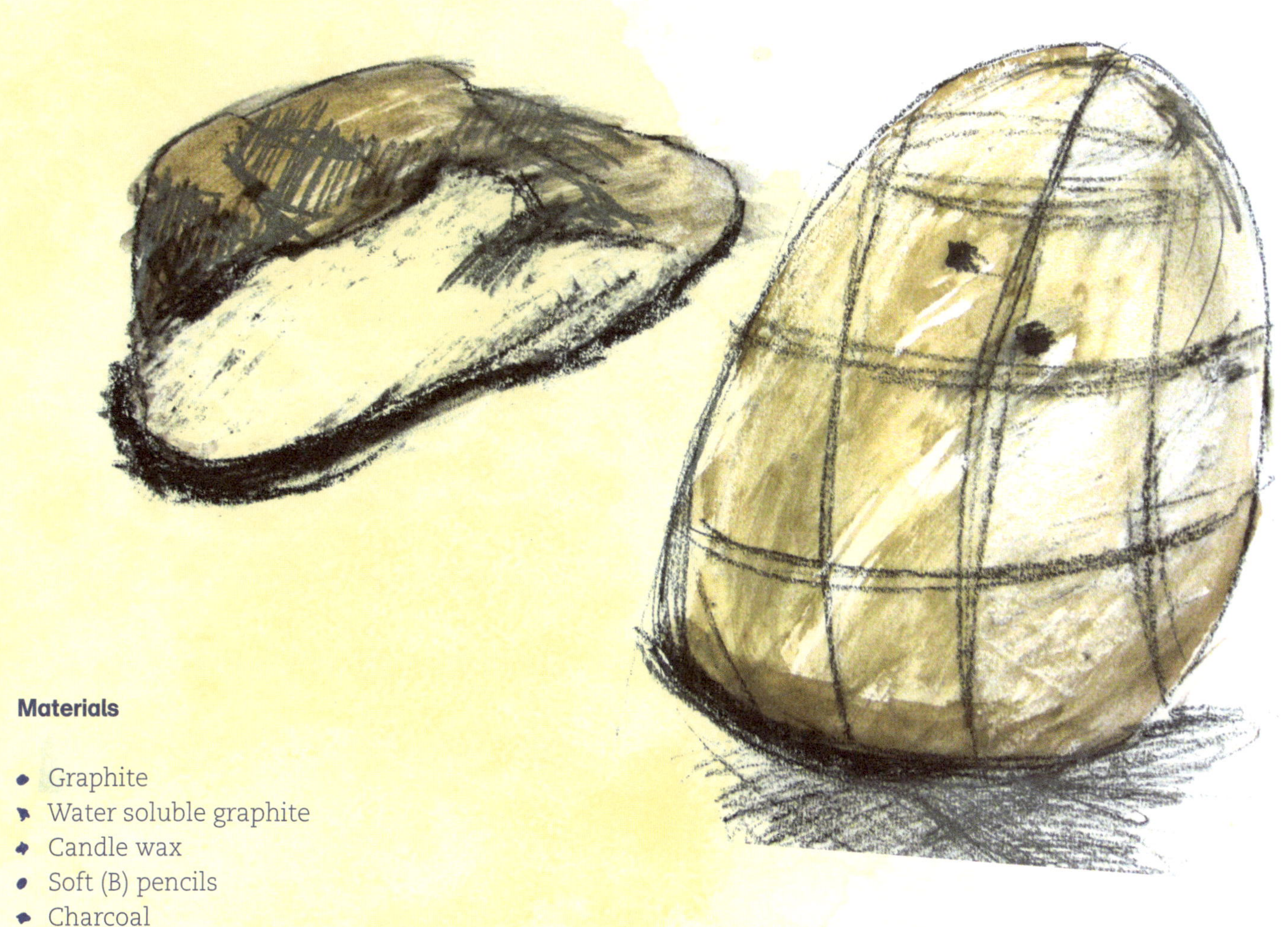

Materials

- Graphite
- Water soluble graphite
- Candle wax
- Soft (B) pencils
- Charcoal
- Watercolours
- Permanent marker pens
- A2 and A3 drawing paper

Subject Matter

Gather together a collection of pebbles and large potatoes.

1 Using a permanent marker pen, draw contour
  lines over the surface of the potatoes and pebbles
  to help show their form. Then place the pebbles
  and potatoes on a white background.

2 Looking at your pebbles and potatoes, think about
  how chunky they are. Hold them in your hand. How
  heavy are they? What do their textures feel like? Try
  arranging them in different positions and groups of
  twos and threes. What new things can you learn about
  each object when you pair them with another object?

3 Make some drawings that make the objects seem
  huge and weighty. Try using contour lines, wax
  resist, watercolour washes, graphite and an eraser
  to do this. Remember that these drawings are
  going to be chunky, solid and messy, so try working
  on a large scale, being careful not to make your
  drawing too delicate. You can use broad gestures,
  rather than thin lines to help with this. You may
  wish to start by drawing with a thick piece of
  candle wax, and then washing over this with a
  watercolour to reveal the drawing (a 'resist' effect).

4 Add some shadows to make the objects feel
  weighted to the ground.

5 Create several drawings in this way, each time
  exploring how your drawing materials can
  help create a sense of weight and volume in
  your drawings.

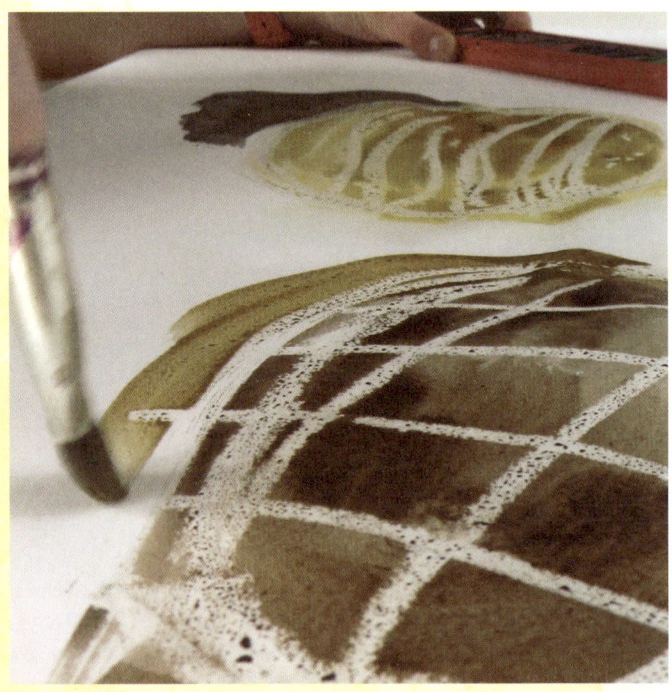

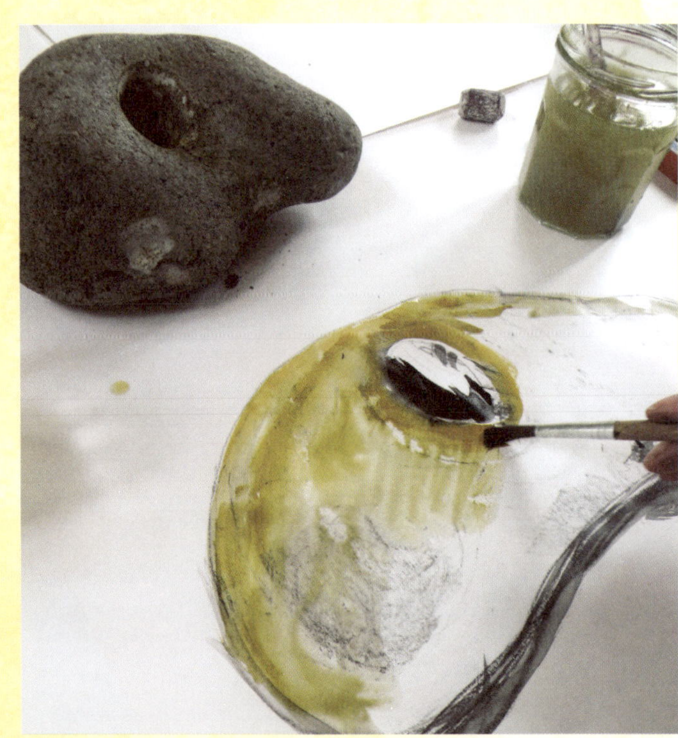

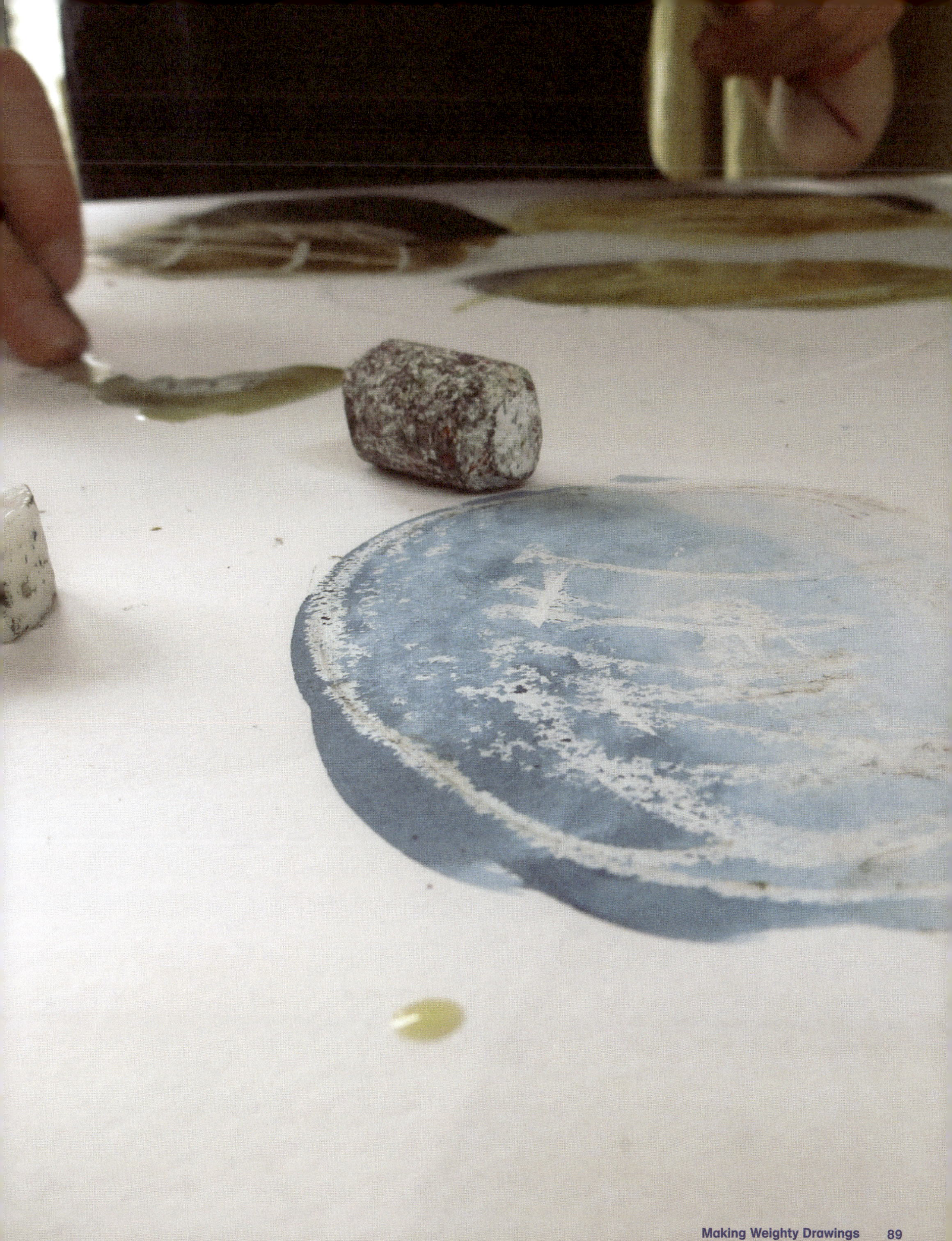

MAKING MARKS WHICH TELL A STORY

In this project, you will create two drawings: one of a storm cloud and one of a fair weather cloud. By thinking carefully about the marks you make as you go along, you will see how making different marks in different areas of your picture can help you build a story in your pictures.

Materials

- Soft (B) pencils
- Graphite
- Erasers
- A3 drawing paper

Subject Matter

Your subject matter in this project is your imagination!

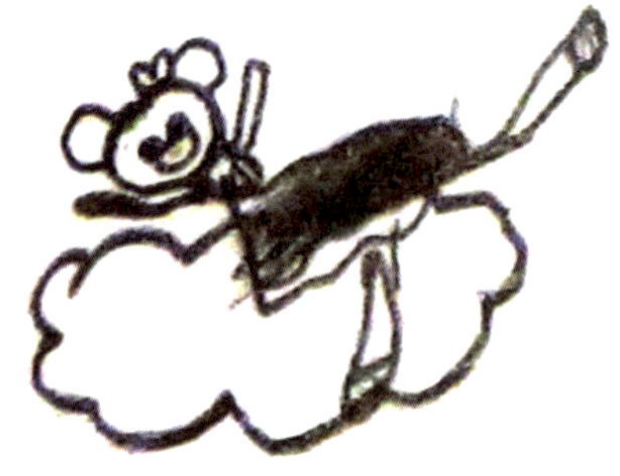

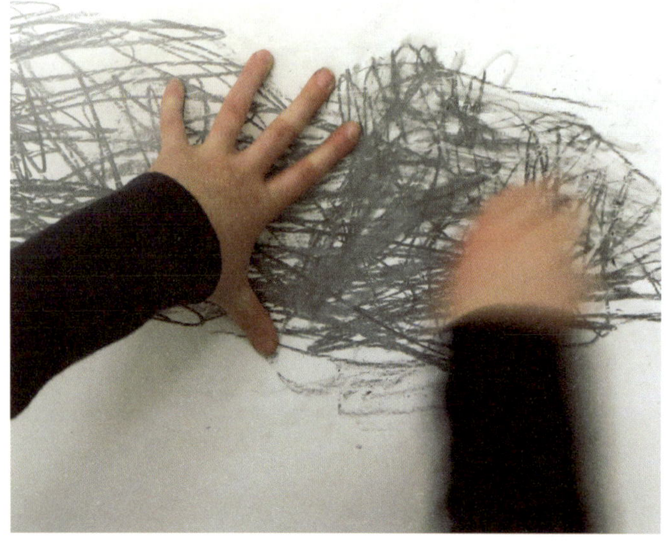

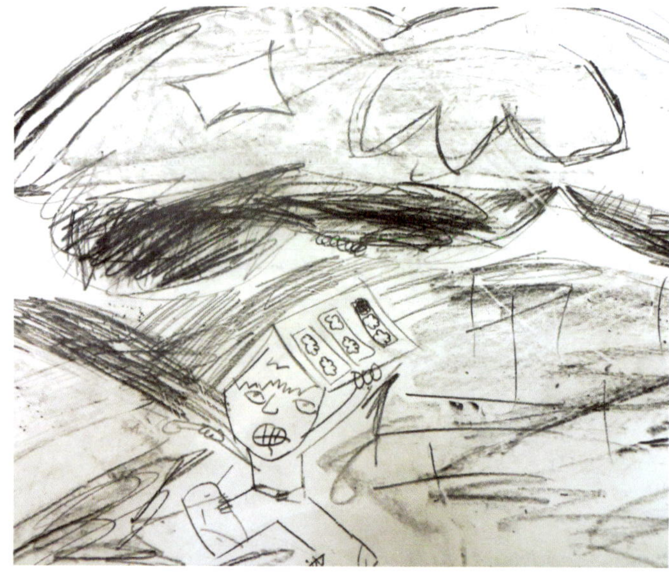

Activity

1 Imagine a light, fluffy cloud floating high on a
summer's day. Stare at your blank sheet of A3
paper, and imagine the cloud floating across the
sheet. What kinds of marks might you make to
show this type of cloud? What kind of pencil
would you use? How would you make sure the
cloud felt light and fluffy?

2 Start drawing the cloud. Stick to the following two
rules: only draw the cloud in the top two thirds of
the paper; and do not draw anything other than the
cloud (ie no fields below and no sun peeking out!).

3 Once you have finished your cloud, put it to one
side and take a second sheet of paper. This time
imagine a storm cloud. How might you portray
the anger of the storm in a single cloud? Would
your drawing actions have a different energy to
capture the anger? How dense might the marks be?
What shape will the cloud be? Will the cloud be
darker at the bottom where the rain gathers? This
time, use an eraser as well to help work the graphite.
Again, only draw in the top two thirds of the paper,
and do not draw anything other than the cloud. Try
to put physical energy into these drawings so that
you feel physically tired afterwards. This energy will
really show in the drawing.

4 Put your storm cloud drawing to one side and
return to your summer cloud drawing. Look again
at the summer cloud drawing and then make a
drawing in the white space underneath the cloud.
This drawing is completely up to you, but try to
explore the mark making as much as you did
when you were drawing the clouds. While you are
making this drawing, try to think about how the
bottom and top parts of your drawing tie together.

5 Finally, do the same with your storm cloud drawing.

Facilitator's Note

Reflection is a key drawing skill. This project aims
to challenge children to experiment with how far
they can push their drawing tools to help them
create drawings with a sense of drama, while
reflecting on the drawing at each stage. Consider
using photography as a way of helping the children
push their drawings as far as they can and to take
risks in their work; by taking photos of their work
at every stage, a child knows that a record of that
stage has been made should they push too far and
lose a quality in their drawing.

MAKING YOUR DRAWINGS YOUR OWN

This project is all about gaining confidence and learning more about choosing appropriate drawing materials, and deciding where and how to use them.

Materials

- A large selection of drawing materials
- A variety of drawing paper
- A newspaper
- Coloured sugar paper, cut into simple geometric shapes

Subject Matter

This project would work well with a variety of subjects, but in this project we used fresh fish. Arrange some fresh sardines or sprats on plates. Take a newspaper and place one of the coloured shapes on it. Then place the plate containing the fish on top of the shape, so you have a composition made up of newspaper, coloured shape, plate and fish.

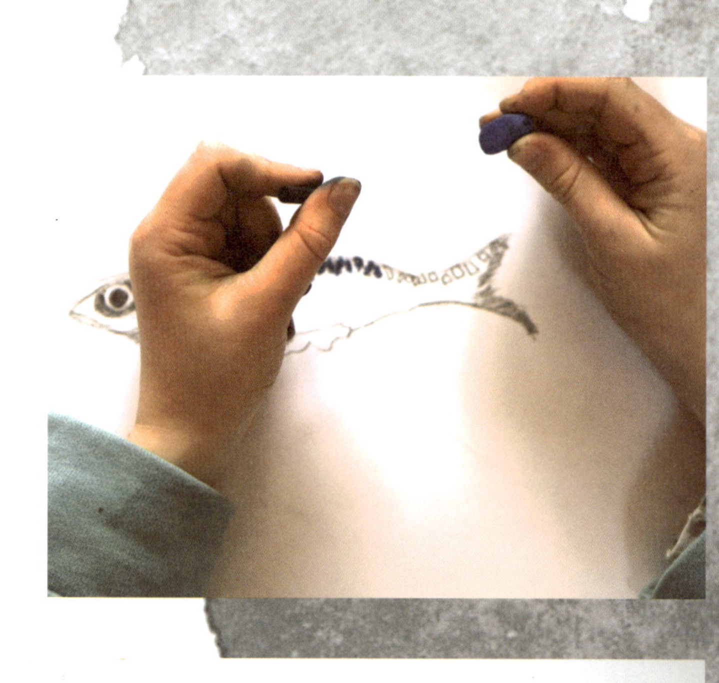

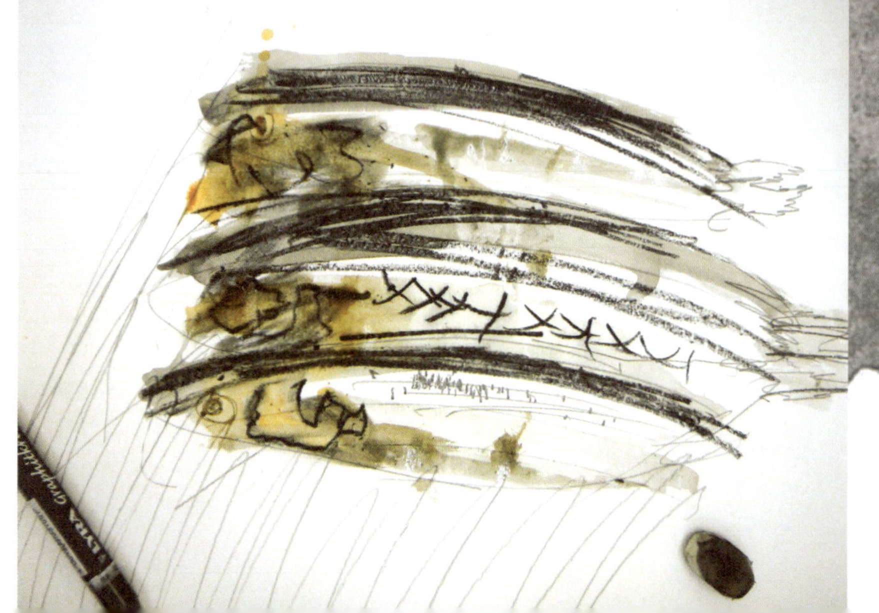

Activity

1 Before starting your drawing, you may wish to do a few warm up exercises. Try some Backwards Forwards Sketching (p 30) and Continuous Line Drawings (p 28), or Drawing to a Slow Rhythm (p 36).

2 Now make a new drawing of the fish on a separate sheet of paper. Use your instinct or intuition to choose a drawing material, and start making your drawing. Challenge yourself to add new lines with new drawing materials. Think of your drawing as a series of layers, each layer containing a new material or colour.

3 Be brave, and make brave drawing decisions! Remember to keep stepping back from your work to look at it from a distance. What does it need? Where and when will the drawing end?

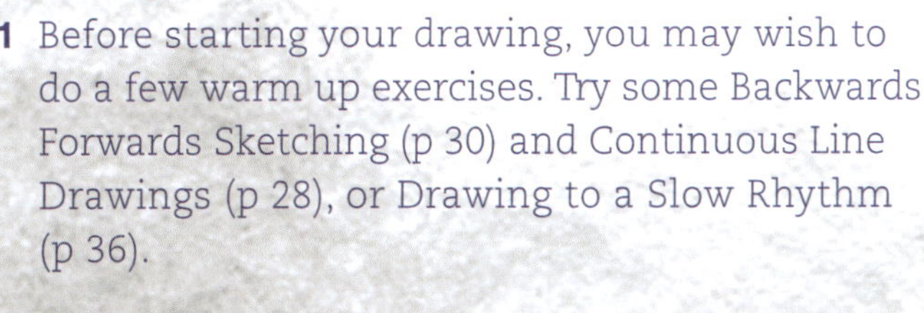

Facilitator's Note

This project is designed to promote the notion of the drawing journey. The drawing journey describes a process not from rough sketch to finished drawing as is so often promoted, but instead it describes an evolution of confidence during which children feel increasingly able to make intelligent and informed drawing decisions, to reflect and react, and to take complete ownership of their work.

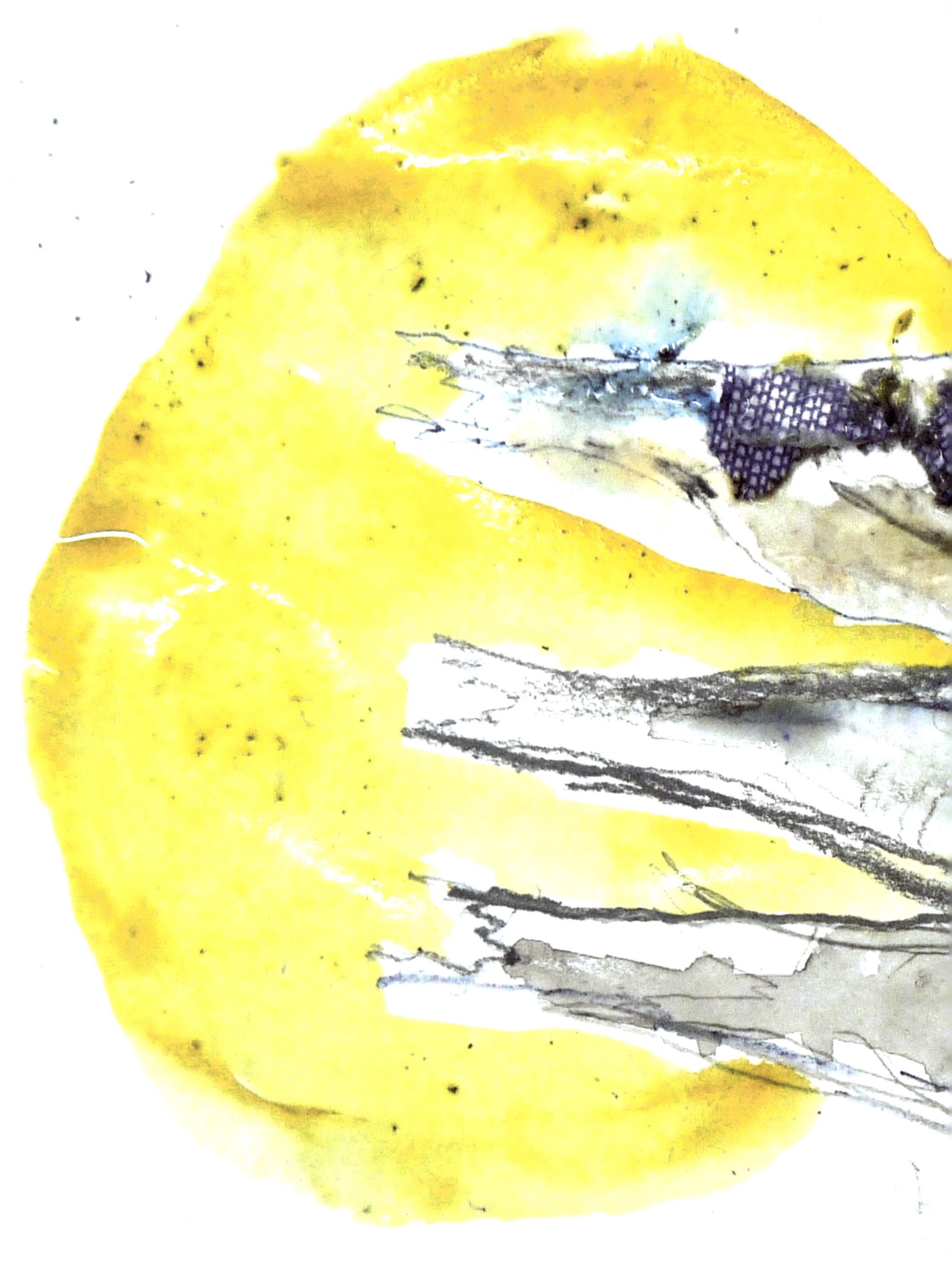

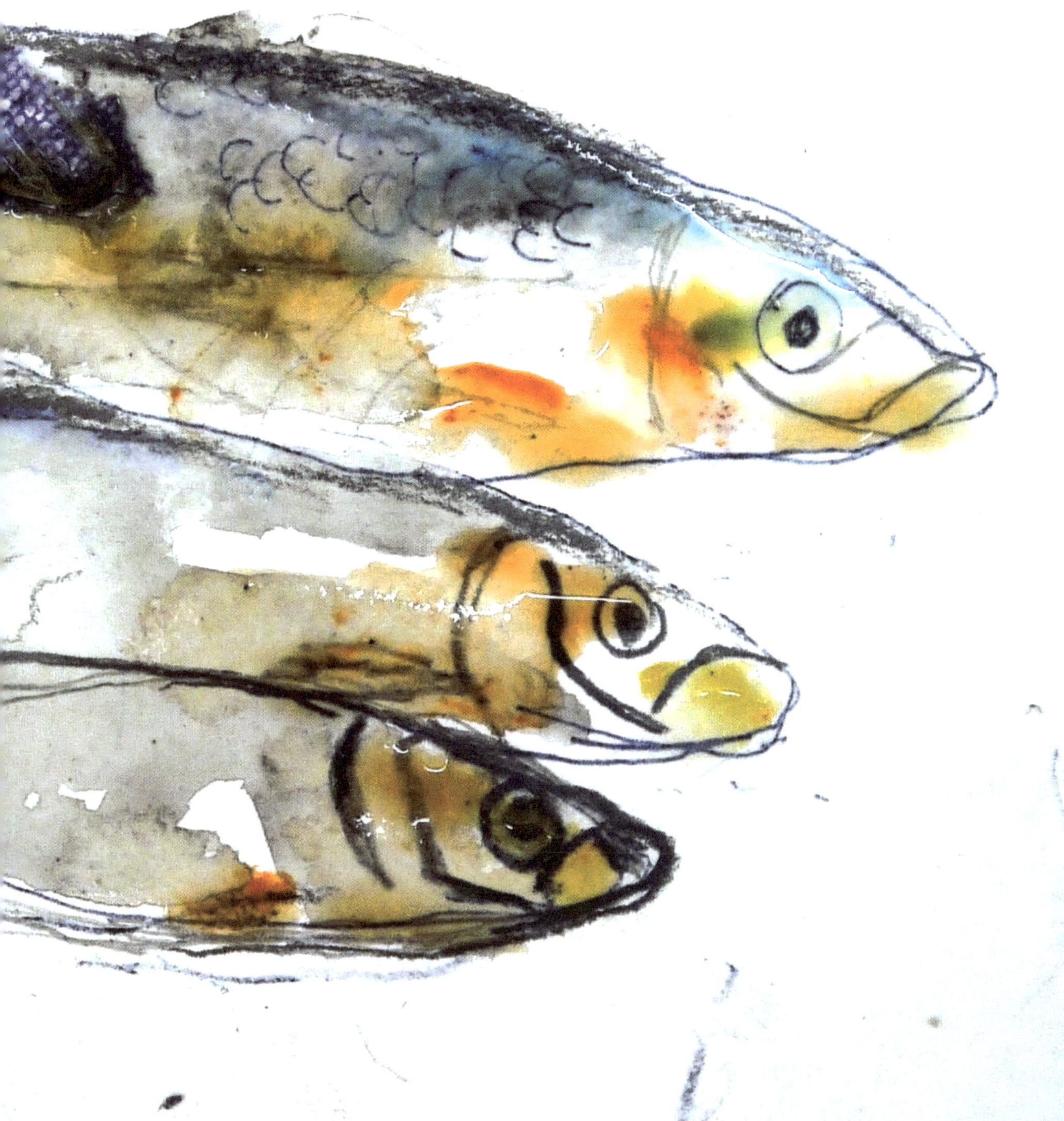

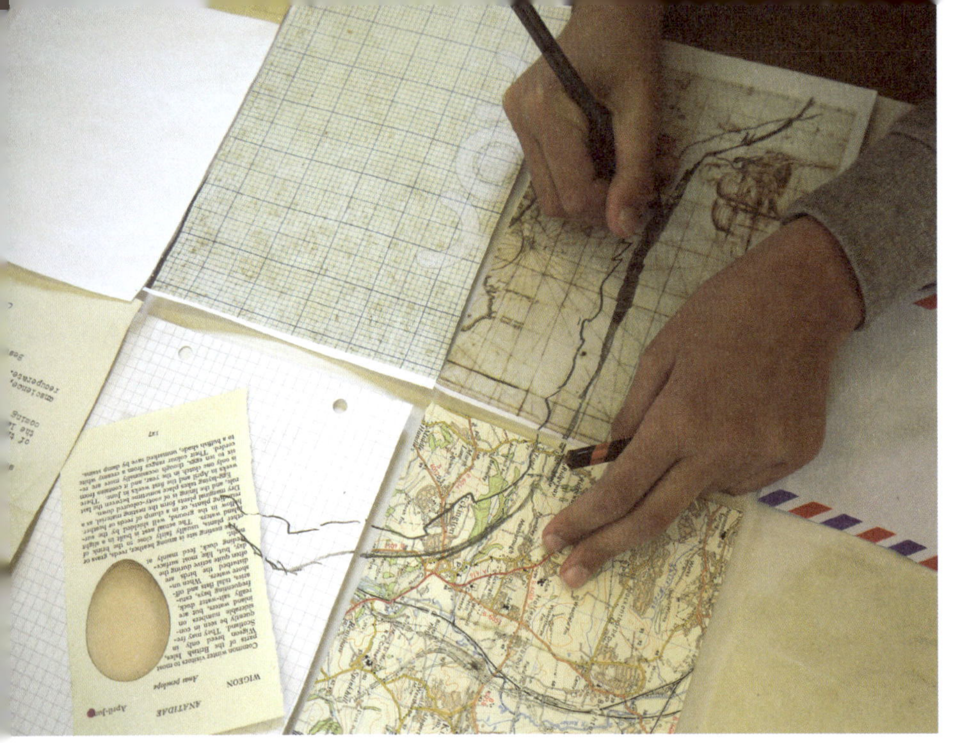

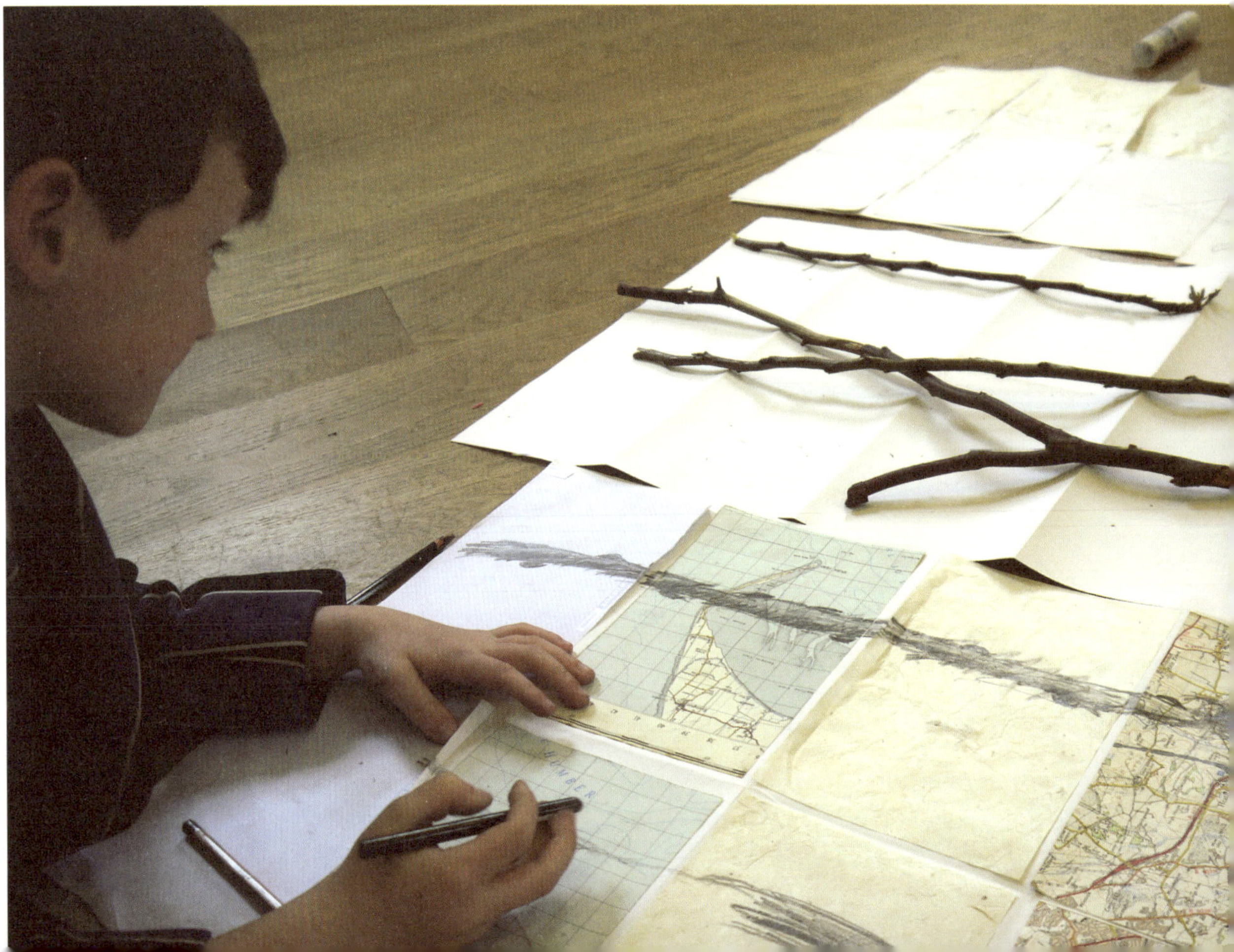

MAKING AN ARTIST'S BOOK

This project builds on two warm up exercises: Making Larger Drawings (p 42) and Making Stronger Drawings (p 44). You will make a drawing on an A2 sheet and then turn it into an artist's book. You will also have to think about which types of marks to make on paper that already has some marks on, and how those marks may also inspire you.

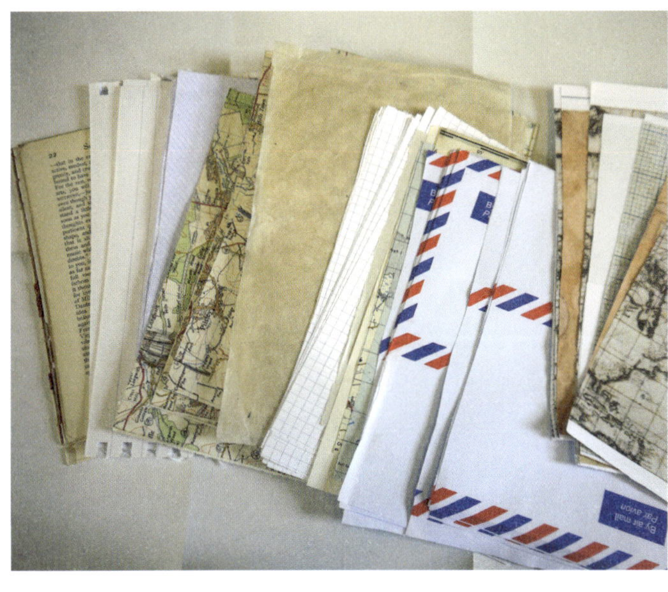

Materials

- Soft (B) pencils
- Graphite
- Erasers
- Glue
- Scissors
- Two sheets of A2 drawing paper
- Cardboard
- A selection of papers: graph, tracing, tissue, old maps, photocopies of fabric, pages from old books etc.

Subject Matter

Fold an A2 piece of paper four times. Unfold the paper so that you have a sheet with eight panels. Then arrange a collection of sticks and twigs on your unfolded sheet of paper, making sure that some of the sticks cross the individual panels.

1 Before starting your drawing, you will need to prepare a sheet to draw on. Fold a second sheet of A2 paper four times and then unravel it to reveal eight panels. Open it out and lay it flat. Then make a cardboard template the same shape and size as one of the panels. Next, tear up some old papers to the size of one of the individual panels using your cardboard template. You will need eight papers, preferably all different types. Finally, stick down your eight papers to the panels of the A2 sheet, creating a patchwork of papers on one sheet. This is your drawing sheet!

2 Now make a drawing of the sticks and twigs at exactly the same size as the real life sticks and twigs onto your drawing sheet. Try to use the creases in the subject matter paper to help you see where to draw your sticks and twigs.

3 You may need to change the type of marks you make for each panel. If you are drawing over a panel that has lots of writing on it, or a busy map, your marks might need to be stronger. If your line then moves onto a panel of delicate tracing paper, how will your mark making change?

4 Although you are working on eight different types of paper, try to remember you are making a drawing on one large sheet. Keep looking at the subject matter, then the drawing, then the subject matter, then the drawing again, etc.

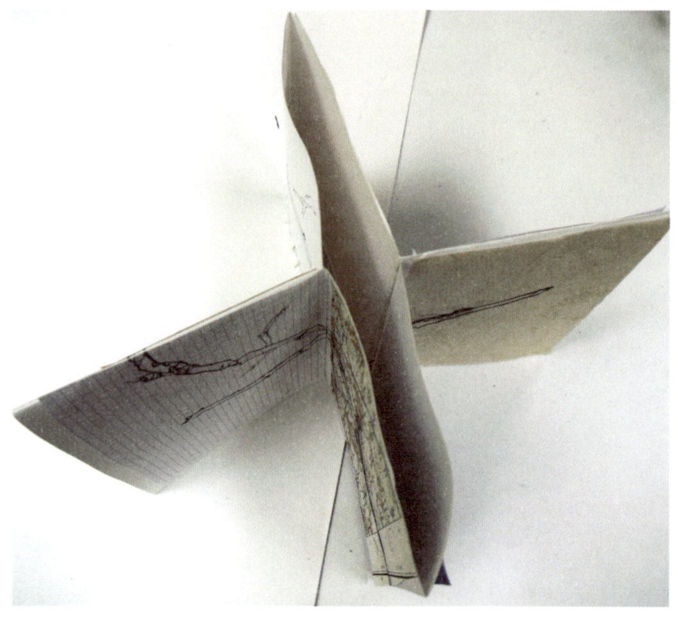

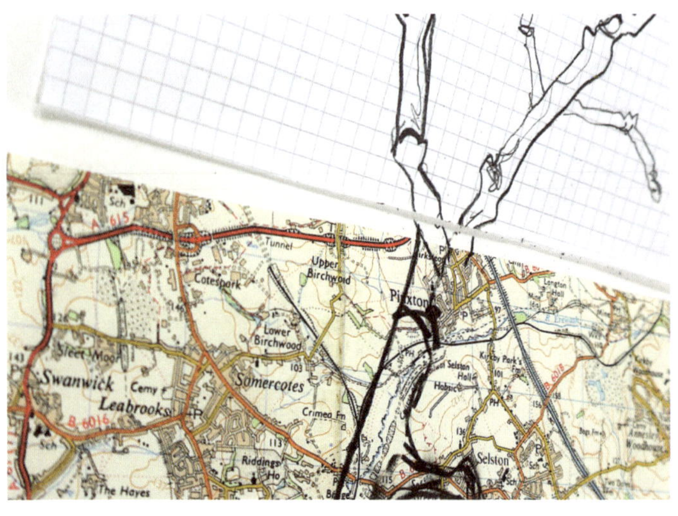

5 Once you have finished your drawing, cut a single slit across the two middle folds. Turn the sheet into a 'book' by pushing up through the slit and letting the pages fall and fold downwards. The book can start wherever you like! Take a look at your book; your whole drawing has turned into a series of pages. How have the line and composition changed?

6 Go back into your book and add some extra drawings on certain pages that fit with the marks, spaces and lines already there. You might want to pick a new, small subject matter to draw in the spaces between your first drawings.

7 Why not unfold your book again after adding new drawings, to see how they have once again changed the whole sheet.

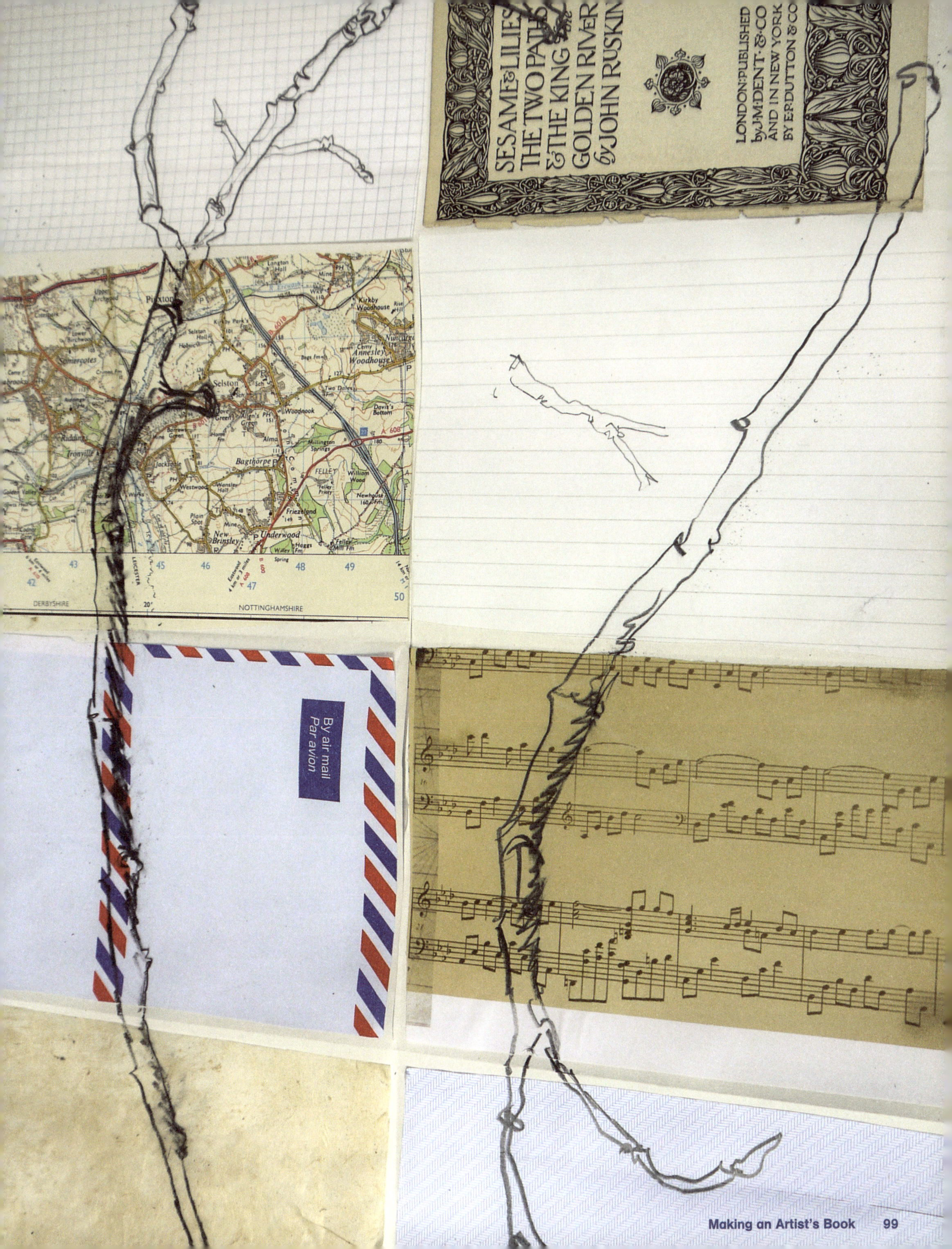

SESAME & LILIES
THE TWO PATHS
& THE KING OF THE
GOLDEN RIVER
by JOHN RUSKIN
LONDON: PUBLISHED
by J·M·DENT·&·CO
AND IN NEW YORK
BY E·P·DUTTON & CO

By air mail
Par avion

DRAWING ON PLASTER

In this project you will be able to try drawing on a new surface: plaster. This also means that instead of just creating a drawing, you will be making a 'drawing object'.

Materials

For the plaster canvas:
- Modelling foam
- Waterproof tape
- Fine casting plaster
- Scissors
- Buckets

For the drawing:
- Oil pastels
- Graphite or soft (B) pencils
- Linseed oil
- Cotton buds

Subject Matter

Set up a still life. For example, you could use a piece of card as a background, a patterned cloth as a foreground, and a jam jar with a flower as the subject.

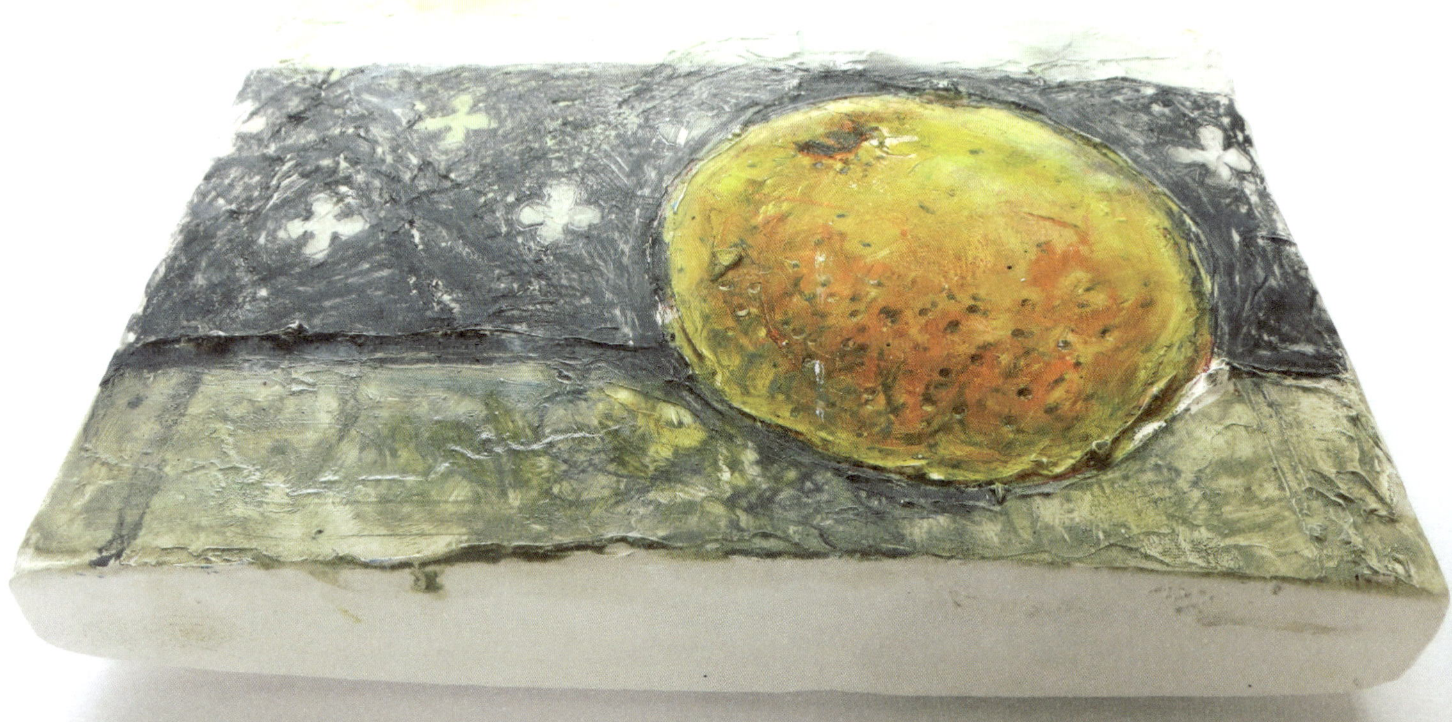

Activity

Before starting your drawing, you will need to create a plaster canvas. Make sure you get some help with this part, and remember that the plaster canvas will need about a week to dry before you can move on to making your drawing.

To make the plaster canvas, first create a temporary mould out of modelling foam. Use one sheet of foam for the base, and cut walls approximately 6 cm high. Tape the walls in place, and make sure there are no gaps through which the plaster might escape. Mix the fine casting plaster according to instructions and pour it into the mould to a depth of 3 cm or 4 cm. When the plaster has set, remove the mould to reveal the plaster canvas. Then allow the plaster to dry for about a week.

When you come to make your drawing, start with this simple warm up exercise. Make a viewfinder by cutting a rectangular shape out of a piece of card. The hole should be the same size as your plaster canvas. Then, looking through the viewfinder, find a part of the still life that you would like to draw. Working on paper that has also been cut to the same size as your plaster canvas, use a H pencil to quickly draw what you see through the viewfinder with very faint lines. This quick placement drawing will help you fix the position of key elements on the page.

Then, using a softer B pencil, make a Continuous Line Drawing (p 28) over the top of your placement drawing. The final drawing will help you when you turn to your plaster canvas.

1 Now you are ready to start work on your plaster canvas. While doing so, remember that the aim of using these materials is not to use the thick oil pastels to 'colour in' the canvas, but to turn them into a type of paint with linseed oil, and for the graphite to create detail.

2 Begin with a faint line drawing in graphite. This does not need to be detailed yet.

3 Then, start working on the background of your picture with oil pastel. You only need to apply a little bit of pressure—do not be too forceful with your delicate plaster canvas! You might want to try using more than one shade of the same colour, layering the pastels.

4 Use a cotton bud dipped in linseed oil to blend the oil pastel, like a paint.

5 Use graphite to redraw the initial lines, add detail and shading. Enjoy the way the oil pastel and linseed oil make the graphite look heavier. Then repeat this process, adding a little more oil pastel, then a little more pencil.

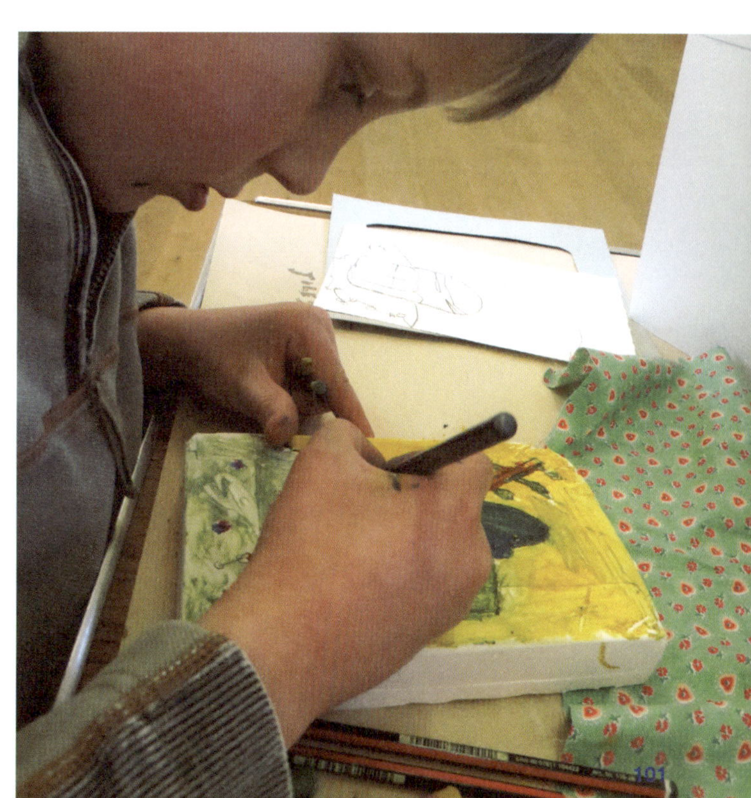

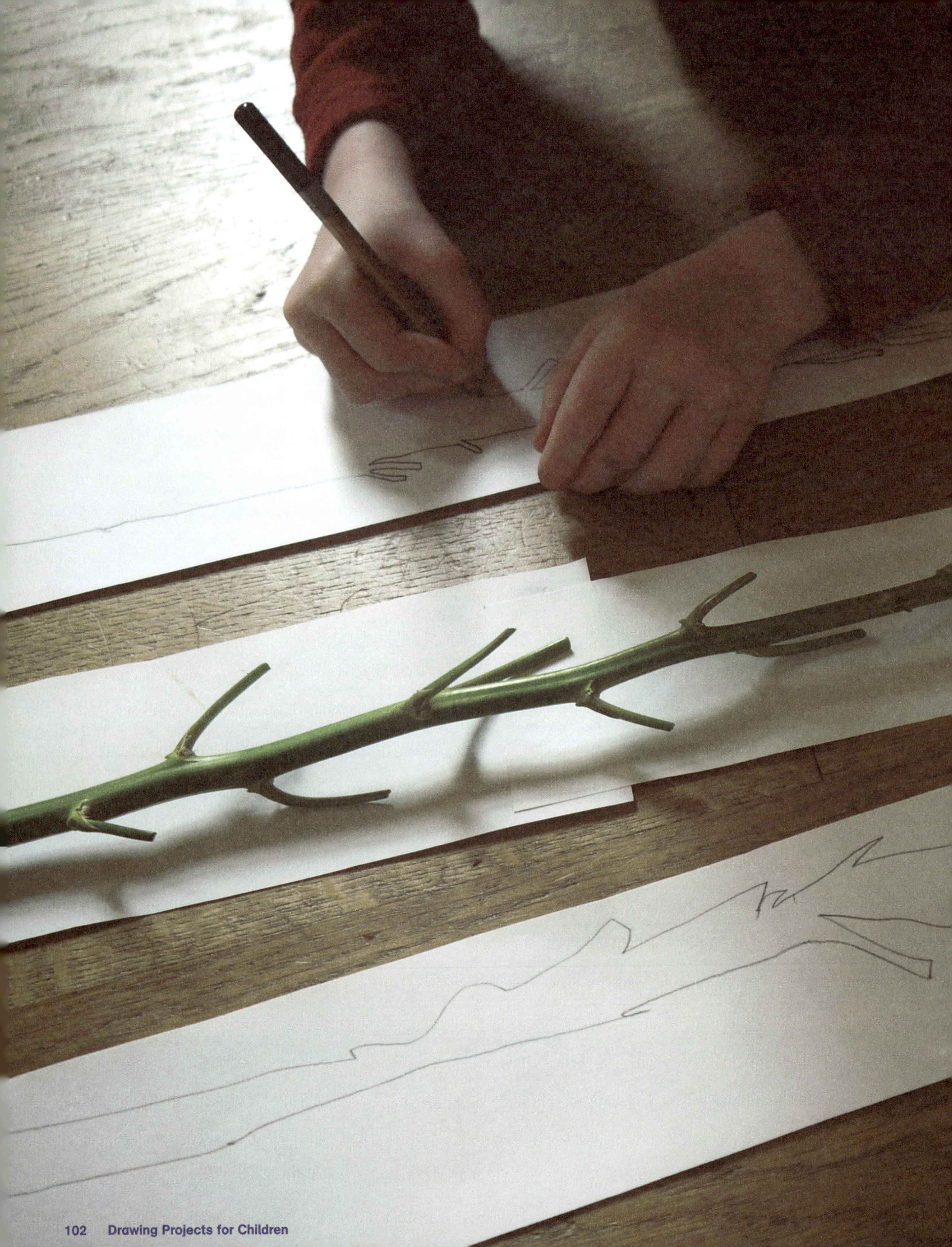

LARGE AS LIFE SCROLL DRAWINGS

In this project you will make a long thin life-sized drawing, and then turn it into a scroll book. Working on a large scale means you will need to be physically involved in your drawing, moving your whole body up and down the long sheet of paper to make the drawing.

Materials

- Soft (B) pencils
- Graphite
- Compressed charcoal
- Erasers
- Long, thin sheets of drawing paper (approximately 10 cm x 3 m).
- Pieces of corrugated cardboard (approximately 10 cm x 20 cm)
- Glue or tape
- An elastic band

Subject Matter

The subject matter should be a mixture of long and thin items such as a 3 m length of rope, 3 m branches with side buds, tall shoots of asparagus or grasses, or a long line of cutlery displayed end to end.

Lay each item on a long thin sheet of paper, the exact same dimensions as the paper on which you are going to make your drawing. You might need to cut and stick paper to create the right length.

Lay the sheets with the subject matter on the floor.

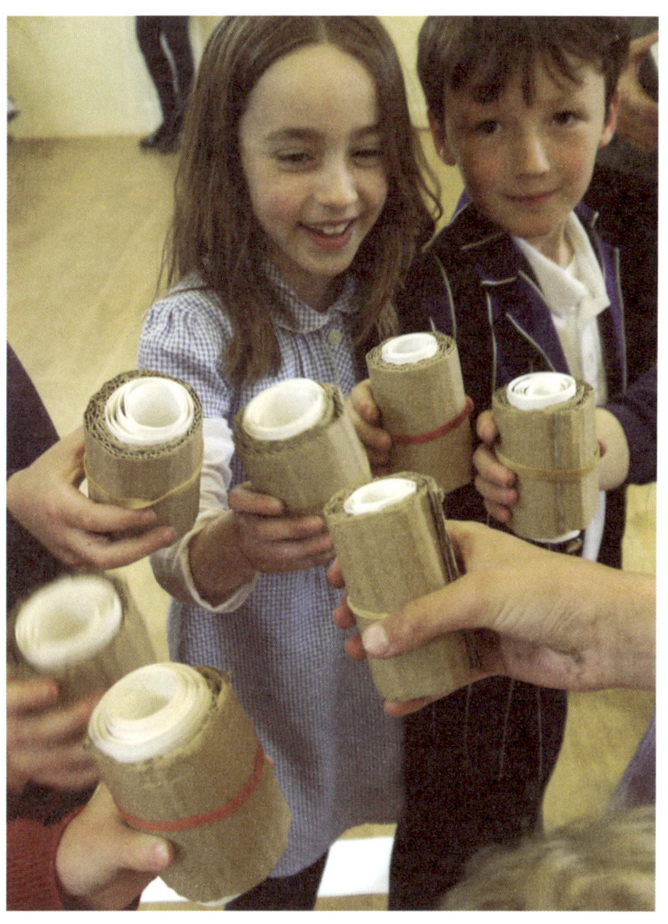

1 This project works best on the floor so you have plenty of room. Lay out your drawing paper alongside the subject matter, leaving enough room between each sheet of paper to move along the length of it as you make your drawing.

2 Make a drawing the exact same size as the subject matter (a one to one ratio). For every centimetre your eye travels over the subject matter, your hand should travel the same distance over your drawing.

3 If you need to slow down your looking and drawing you could try some techniques such as Backwards and Forwards Sketching (p 30) and Continuous Line Drawing (p 28).

4 Remember that when you are making this drawing you should be moving your whole body back and forth along the length of the paper. Why not try changing your drawing material as you go up and down the sheet of paper?

5 Once the drawing is finished you can make it into a scroll book. Take a piece of corrugated cardboard and curl it to make a coil. Unwind it, and taking some glue or tape, attach one end of the long drawing to one end of the cardboard.

Starting from the other end of the drawing, roll it up until you reach the end of the cardboard and allow the card to become the 'cover' for the scroll book. Roll it all up and secure with an elastic band.

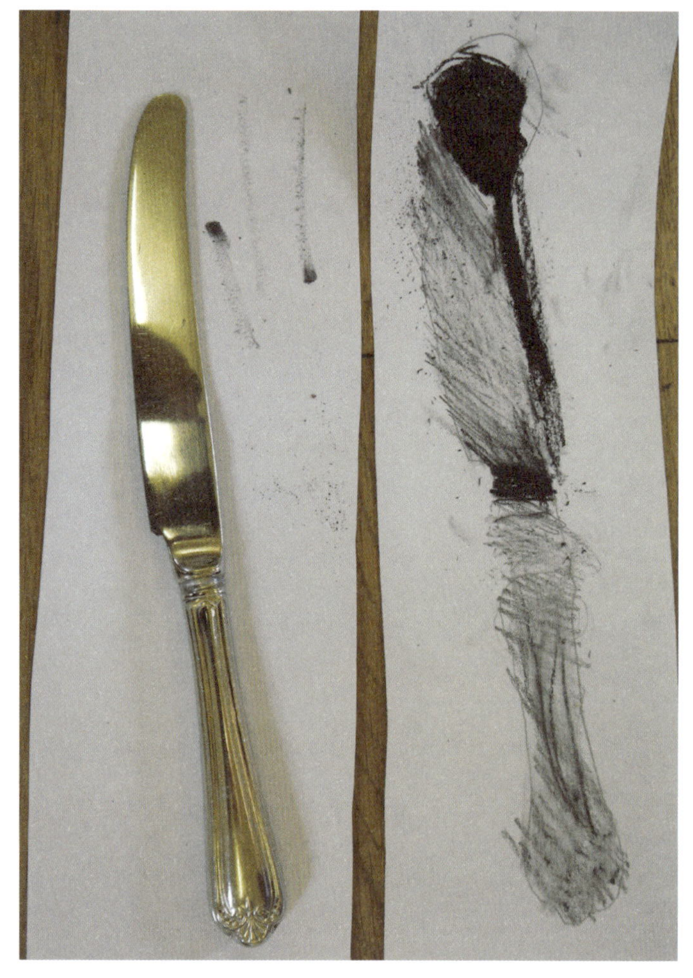

Facilitator's Note

When the subject matter is close at hand, making life size drawings helps children coordinate speed of looking with speed of drawing as their eyes and hands move the same distance at the same speed. In addition, it can help children who by nature make tiny drawings to work at a larger scale.

This project provides an opportunity for children to make exciting drawings at a scale that they might not normally work. It also encourages them to move their bodies to make a drawing, enabling them to become actively involved with drawing as a physical process.

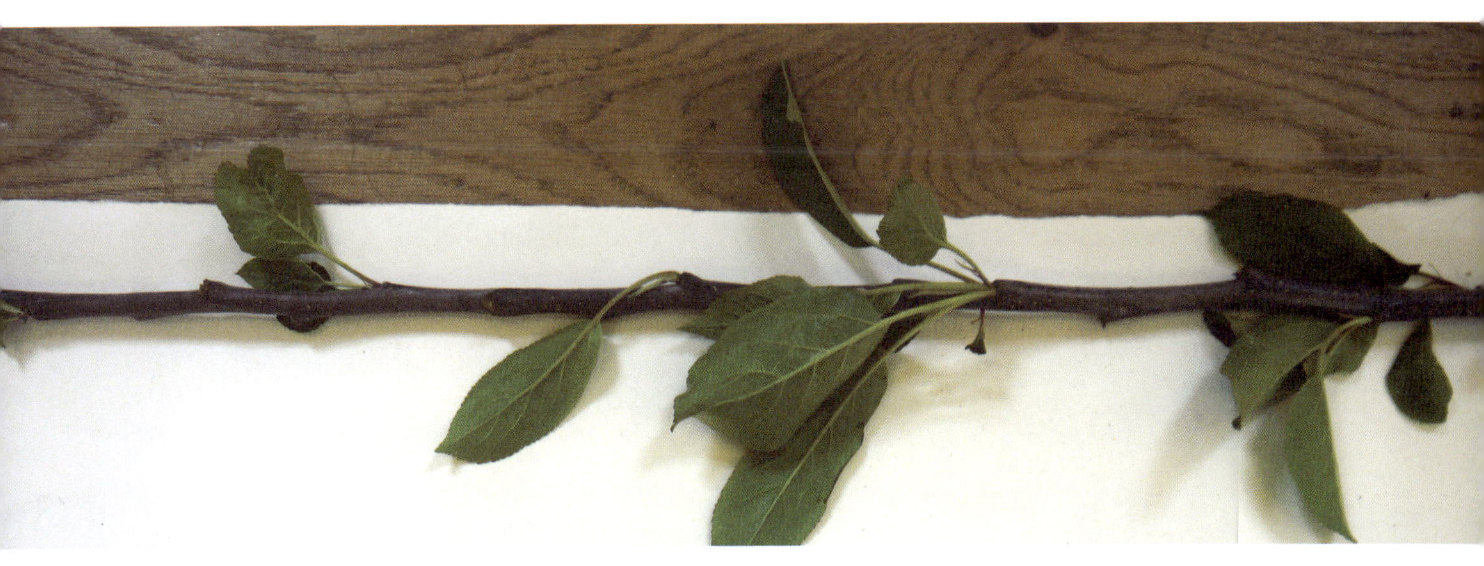

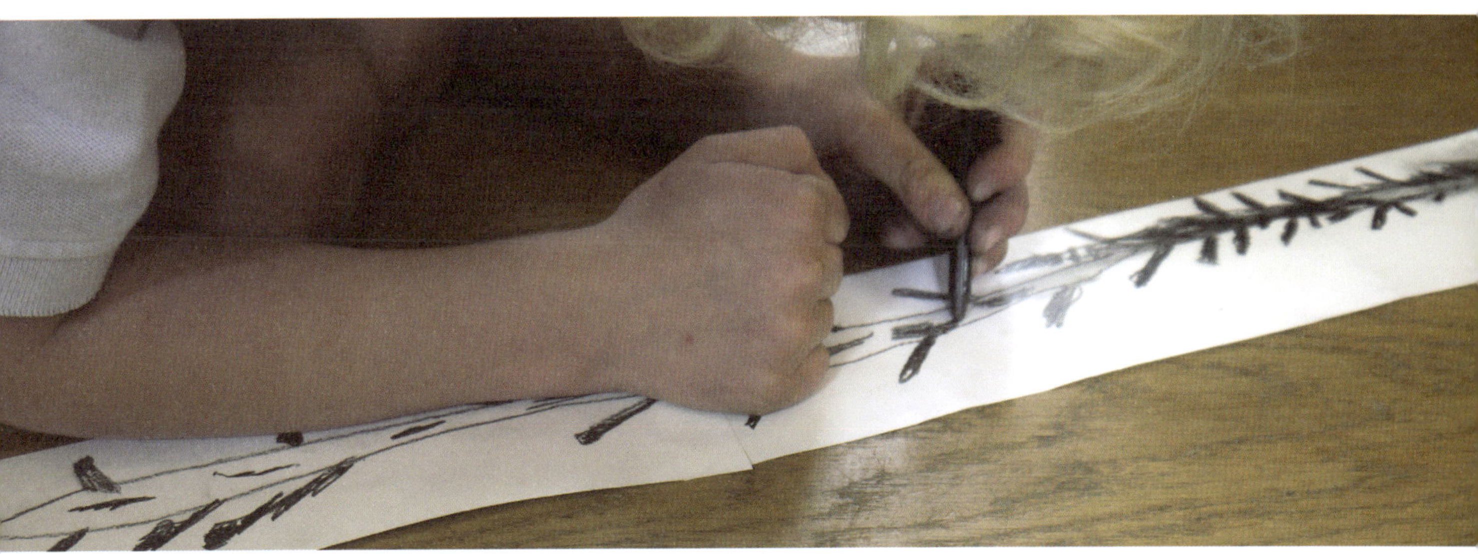

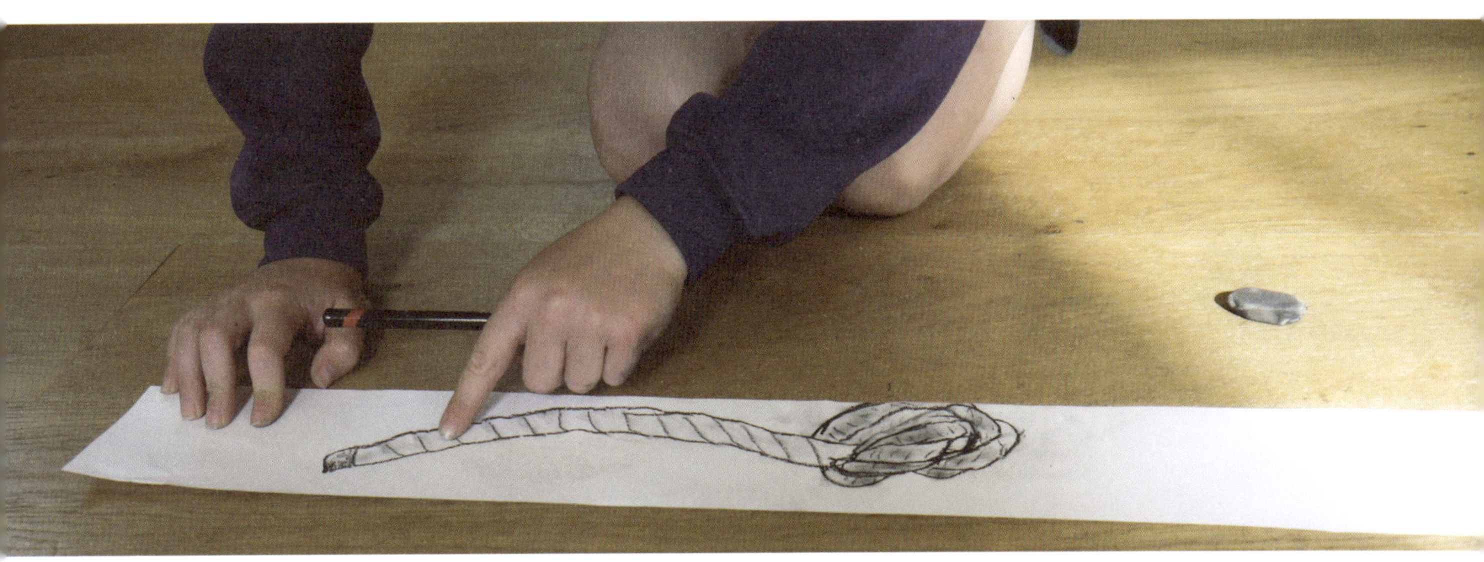

SEASONAL DRAWINGS

This activity has three main stages: carefully drawing from observation, cutting out and collaging, and then adding some colour.

Materials

- Hard (H) pencils
- Handwriting pens
- Permanent marker pens
- Erasers
- Watercolours
- Glue
- Scissors
- A4 drawing paper

Subject Matter

Gather some seasonal food such as mince pies or panettone and seasonal plants such as Ivy, Holly and Christmas tree branches.

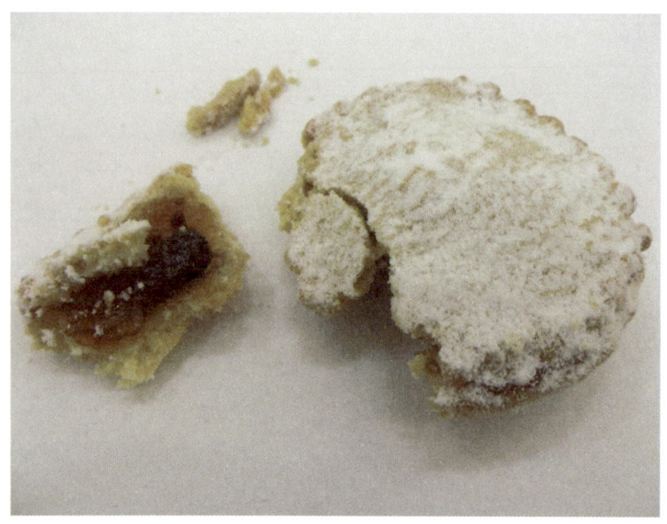

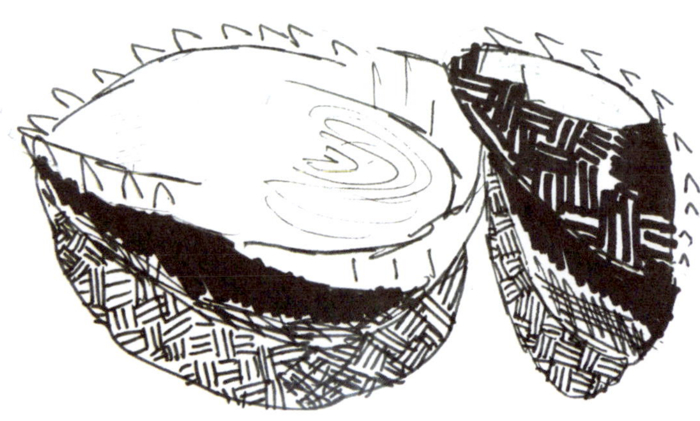

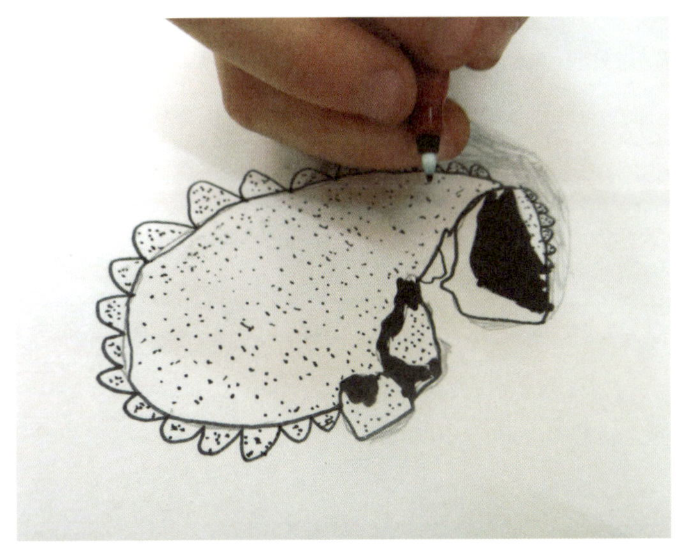

Activity

1 Begin by using a hard pencil to make some line drawings of the mince pies and panettone using a Backwards Forwards Sketching (p 30). Draw the food on its own, without a background.

2 Then, on top of the first drawing, make another drawing with a black handwriting pen and a black permanent marker. Think carefully about when to use the thick black marker and when to use the thin pen. Thick lines may work well for the outer edge of the food, with thin lines for the detail, for example.

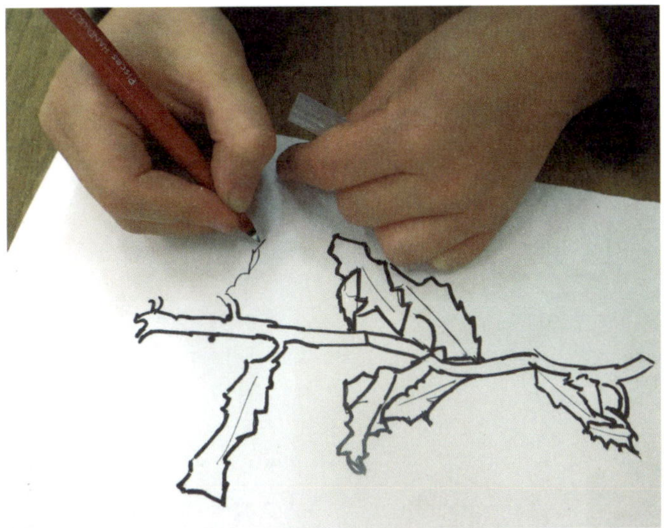

3 Carefully cut out your drawings, making sure you only cut outside of your pen lines. Remember, if you cut slowly, you will cut more carefully, just like in drawing. Save your cut out drawings until later.

4 Repeat stages one to three, this time drawing seasonal sprigs of Holly, Ivy and Christmas tree branches.

5 Create a collage with your cut out drawings by sticking them onto a new piece of A4 drawing paper. You could even draw a background for them or add some text on this new sheet.

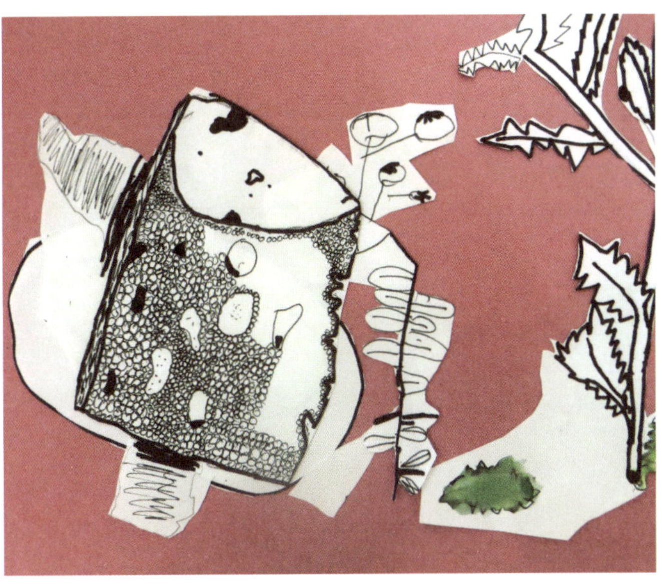

6 Use watercolours to add some colour to your drawing or the background.

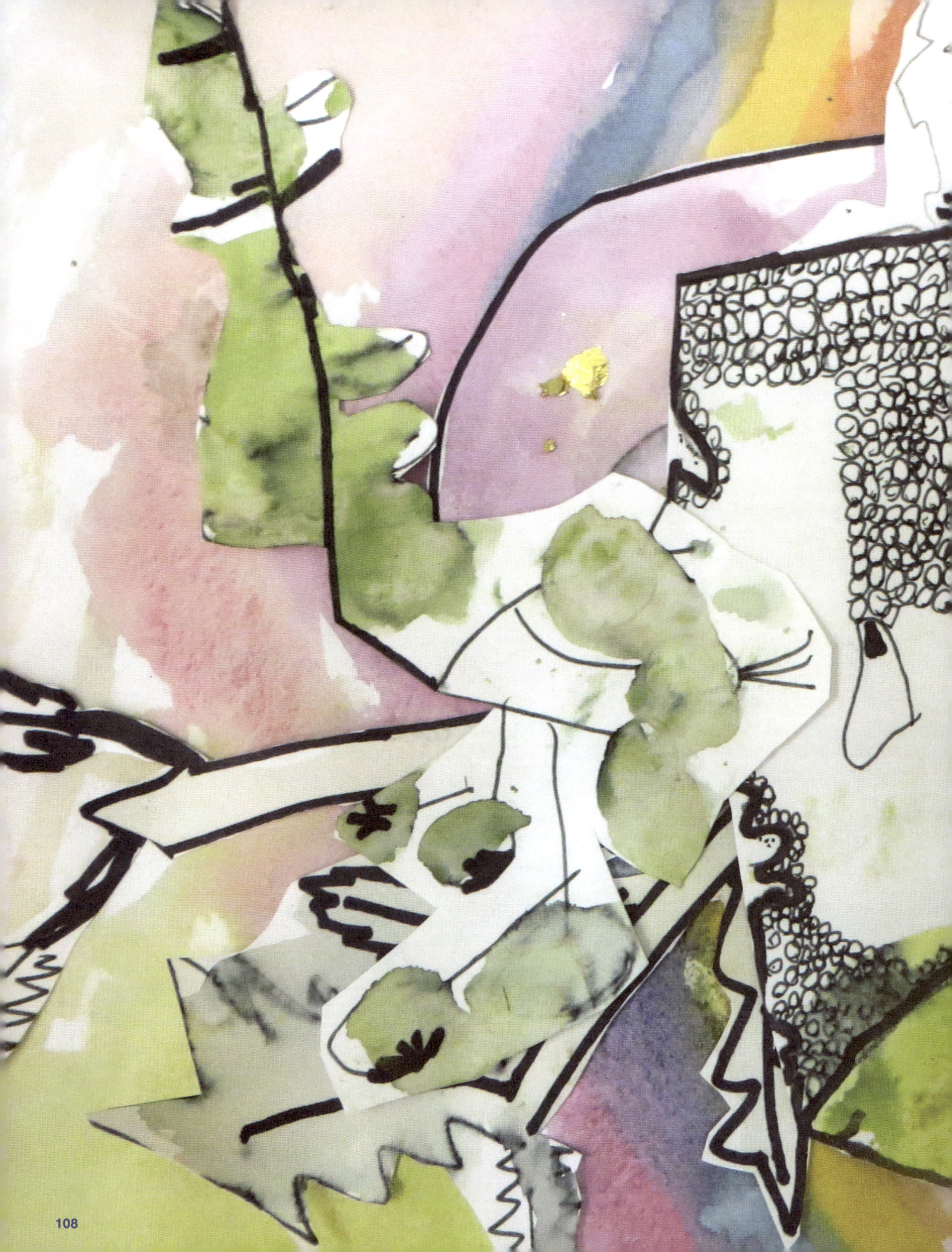

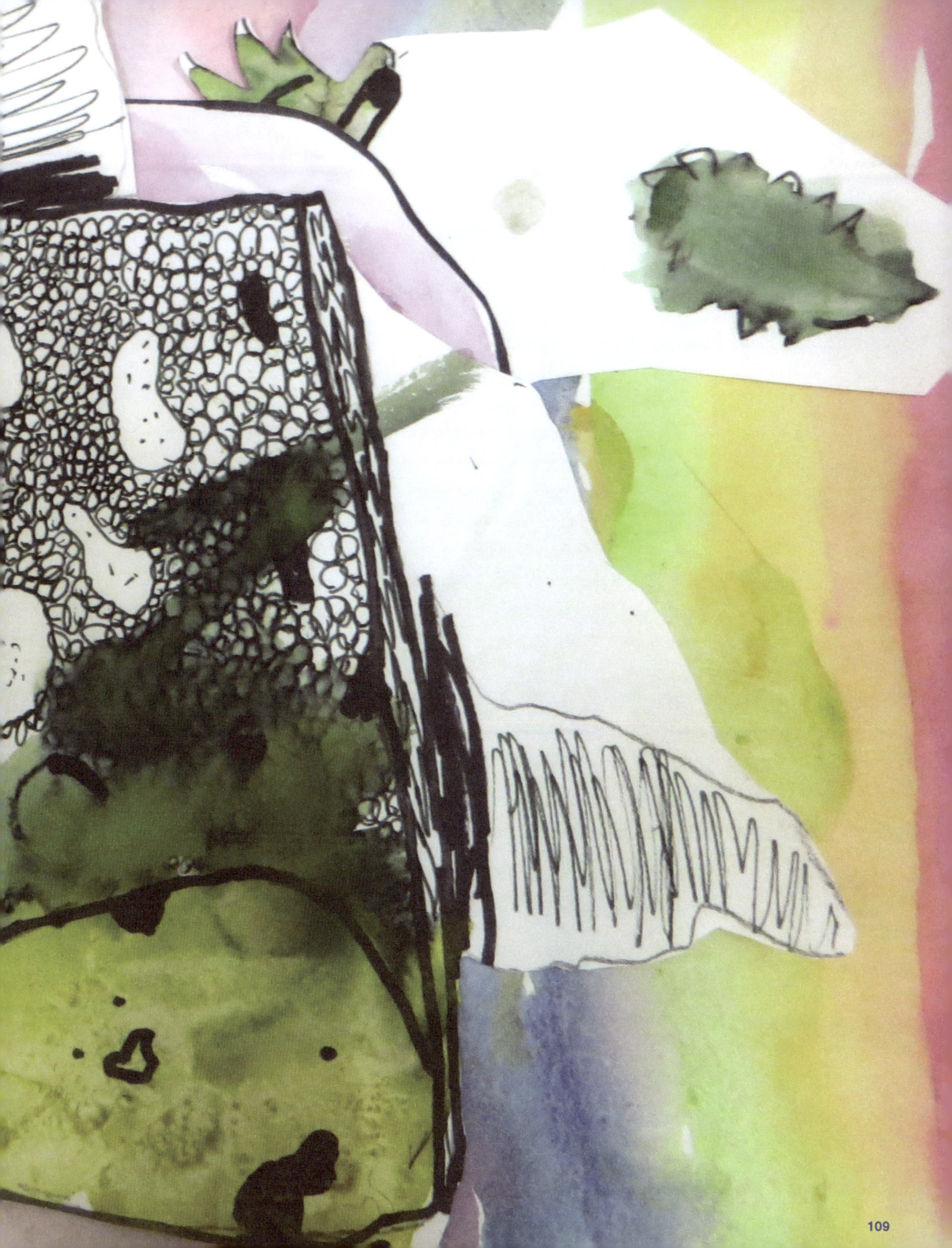

MATERIAL MARK CARDS

This is a great project for exploring lots of different drawing materials. In this project you will explore each drawing material, and think carefully about what marks they make by creating a set of sample cards. These cards will be good reference tools and inspiration for your future drawings!

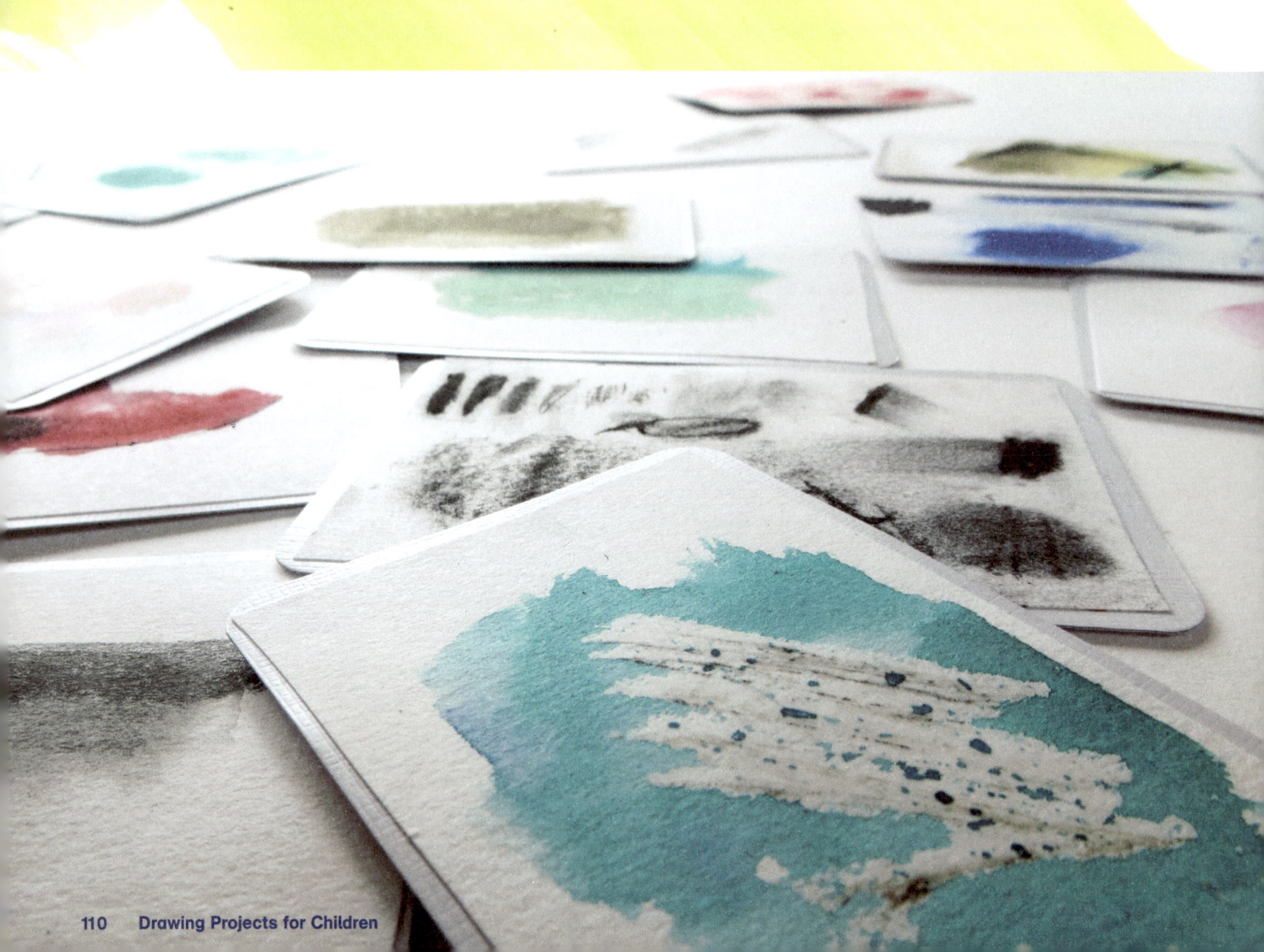

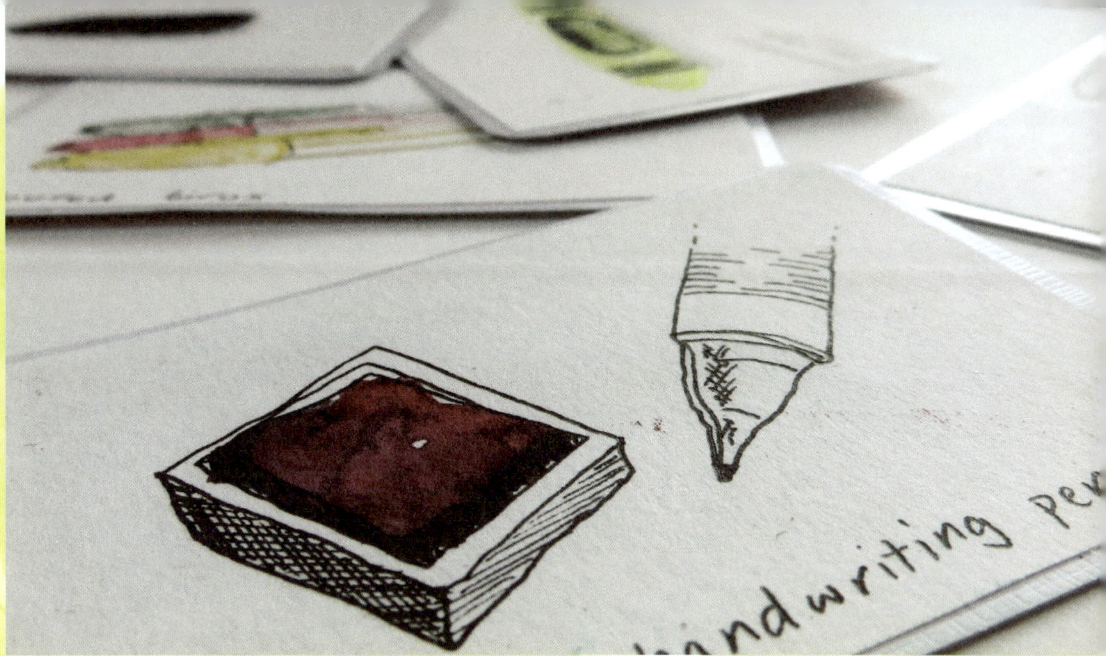

Materials

- A large selection of drawing materials
- A pack of playing cards
- Drawing paper
- Glue

Subject Matter

The subject matter for this exercise is the drawing materials themselves. You should have a large selection of drawing materials to choose from.

Activity

1 Prepare your drawing paper by tearing it into rectangular pieces that are slightly smaller than the playing cards.

2 Then make two drawings. First, an 'illustration' image. For this, you should choose a drawing material to draw, making your image on one of the small pieces of paper using either the same drawing medium you are illustrating, or a pencil or handwriting pen.

3 On a separate piece of paper, make a 'demonstration' image. For this, experiment with what types of marks your chosen drawing medium can make.

4 Use fixative in a ventilated area to fix any images made with graphite, soft pastel, chalk or charcoal.

5 Then, take a playing card, stick one of your drawings to the front and the other one to the back—creating a material sample card.

6 Carry on doing this until you have an entire set of sample material cards. You may even want to make some cards that feature two drawing materials, showing what happens when you combine watercolour and handwriting pen, or watercolour and wax resist, for example.

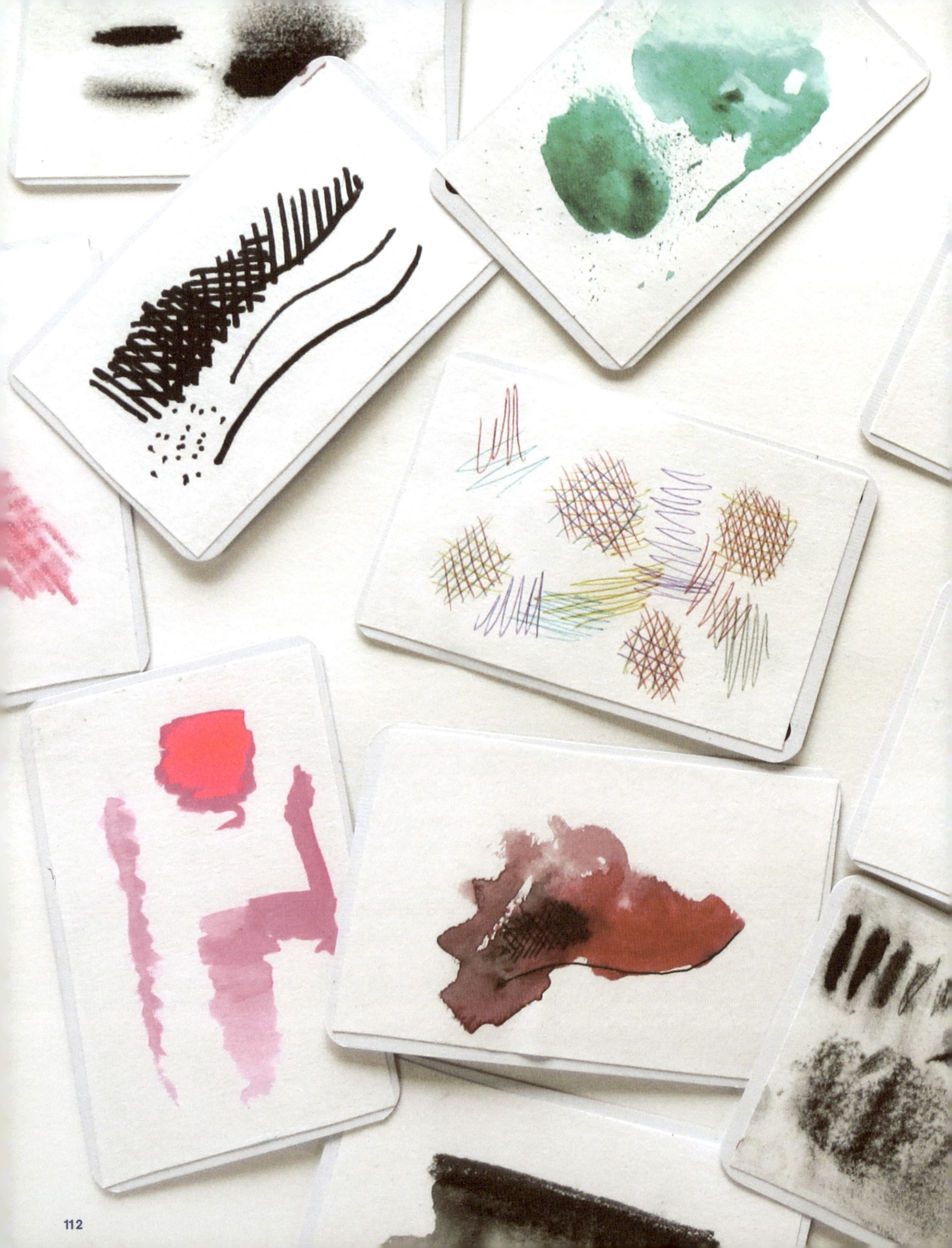

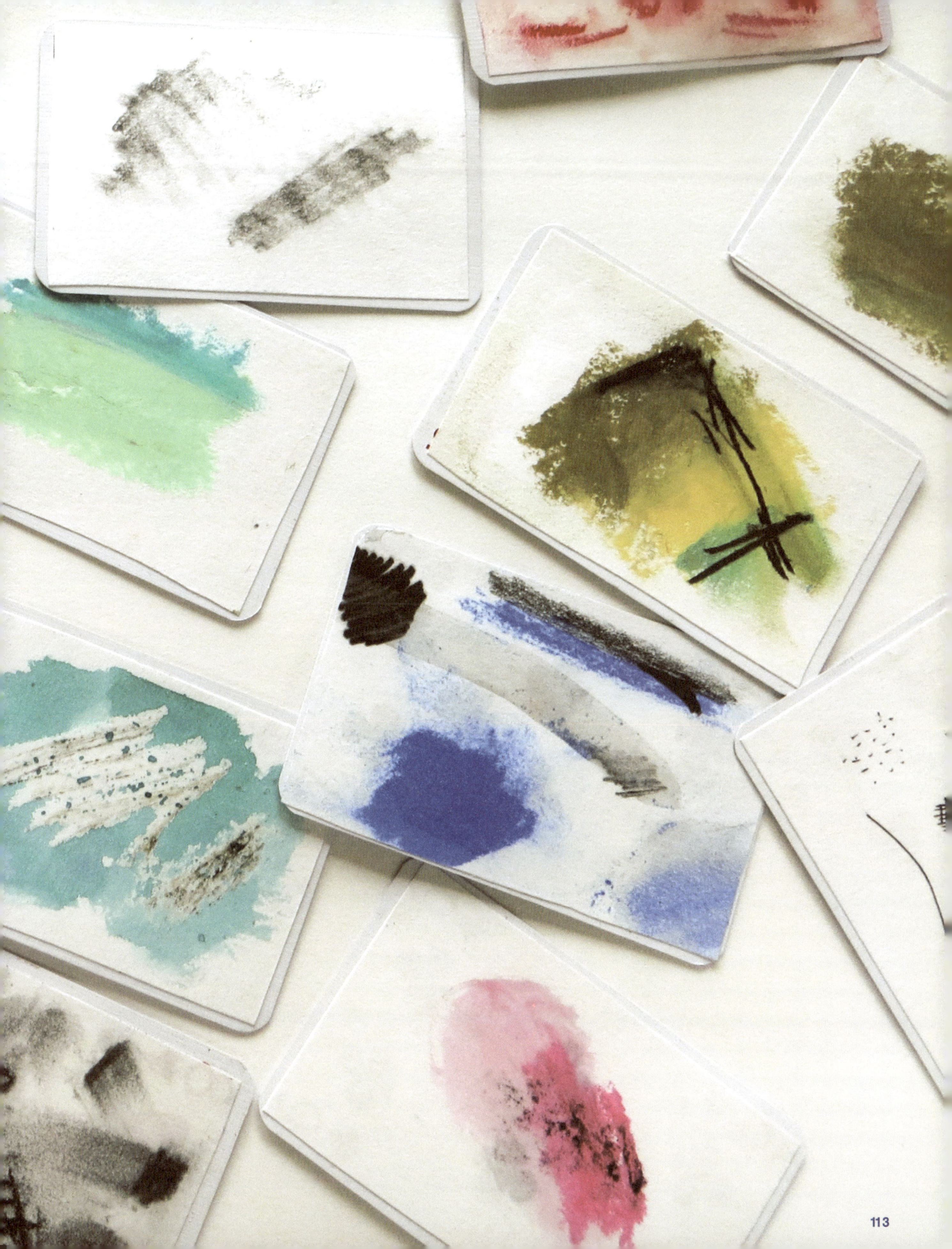

CARBON PAPER MONOPRINTS

Making monoprints is a great way to generate lots of drawings and to be spontaneous. Using carbon copy paper is a fun and easy way to work. In making monoprints, you draw on a top layer of paper and, when you are finished, peel away the layer to reveal the final print.

Materials

- Pencils
- Oil pastels
- Tracing paper
- Carbon paper
- A4 drawing paper

Subject Matter

This activity is suitable for any subject matter, from objects you can observe in front of you, to your own experimental mark making.

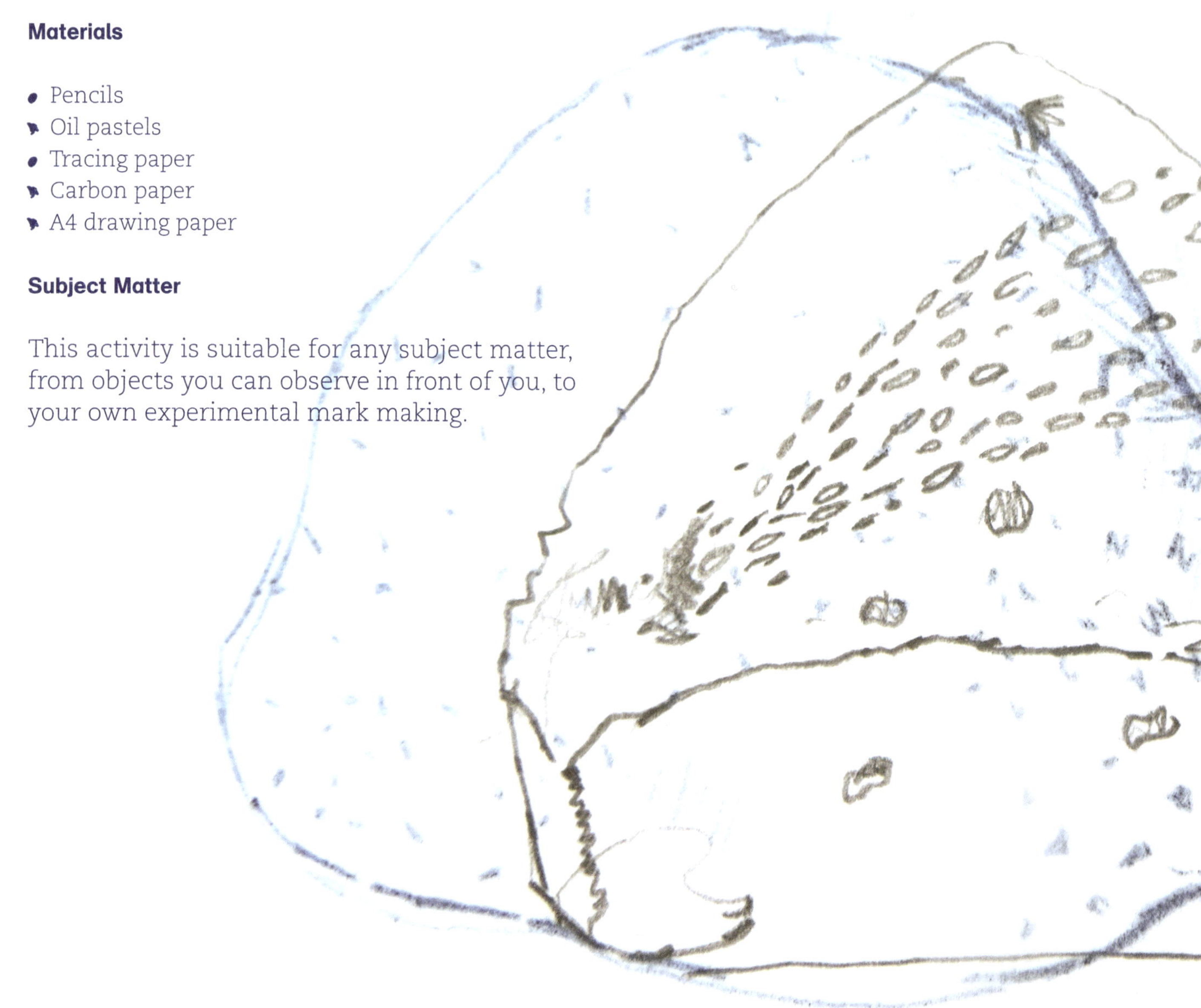

Activity

1 First, prepare your paper for the printmaking. Lay the drawing paper on the table with the drawing side facing up. Lay the carbon copy paper on top of the drawing paper with the inked side facing down. Then, lay a sheet of tracing paper over the carbon copy paper. Make sure that all the layers of paper in this paper 'sandwich' are lined up and secure them with a paper clip.

2 Draw on the top layer of tracing paper to create your print. You can make lots of different types of marks to create various effects. How do marks made with a sharp pencil compare to those made with your fingertips or the heel of your hand?

Why not try out all sorts of mark making? Sometimes monoprints work well when they are created quickly.

3 If you want your print to be colourful, you can add colour using some oil pastels. Peel back the carbon paper, making sure not to move the paper clip that is holding the paper together, and apply some oil pastel to the carbon paper's shiny side. Then carry on with your drawing.

4 Once the drawing is finished, remove the paper clip and peel off the carbon paper to reveal the print on the drawing paper. You can re-use the carbon paper by putting new oil pastel on the shiny side. You can even keep your original drawing on the top layer of tracing paper!

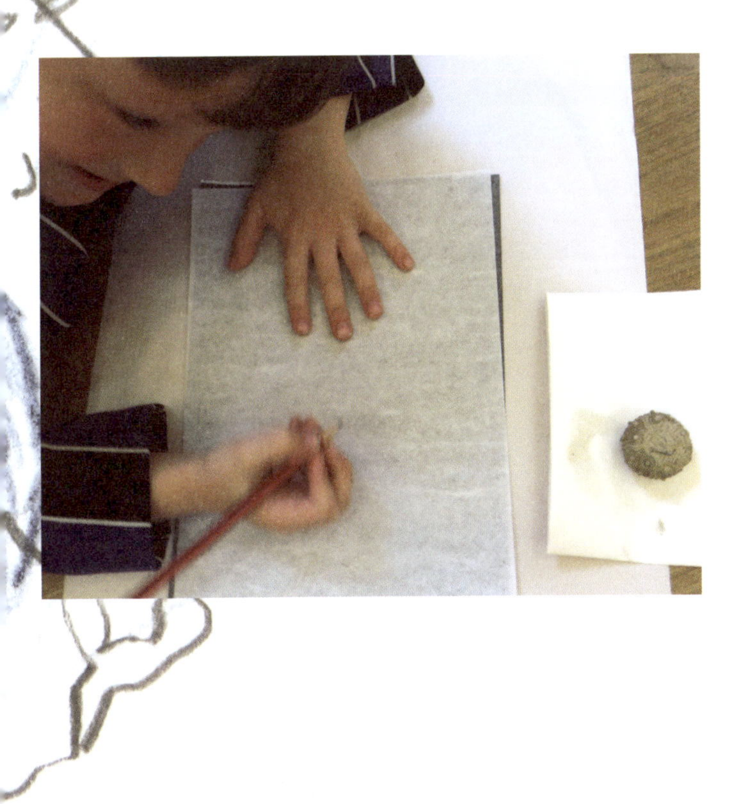

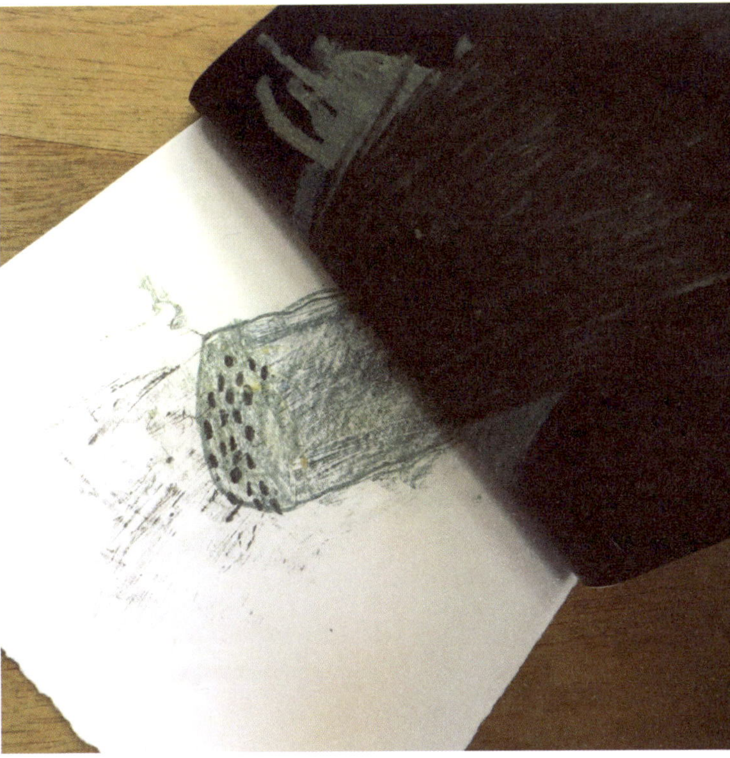

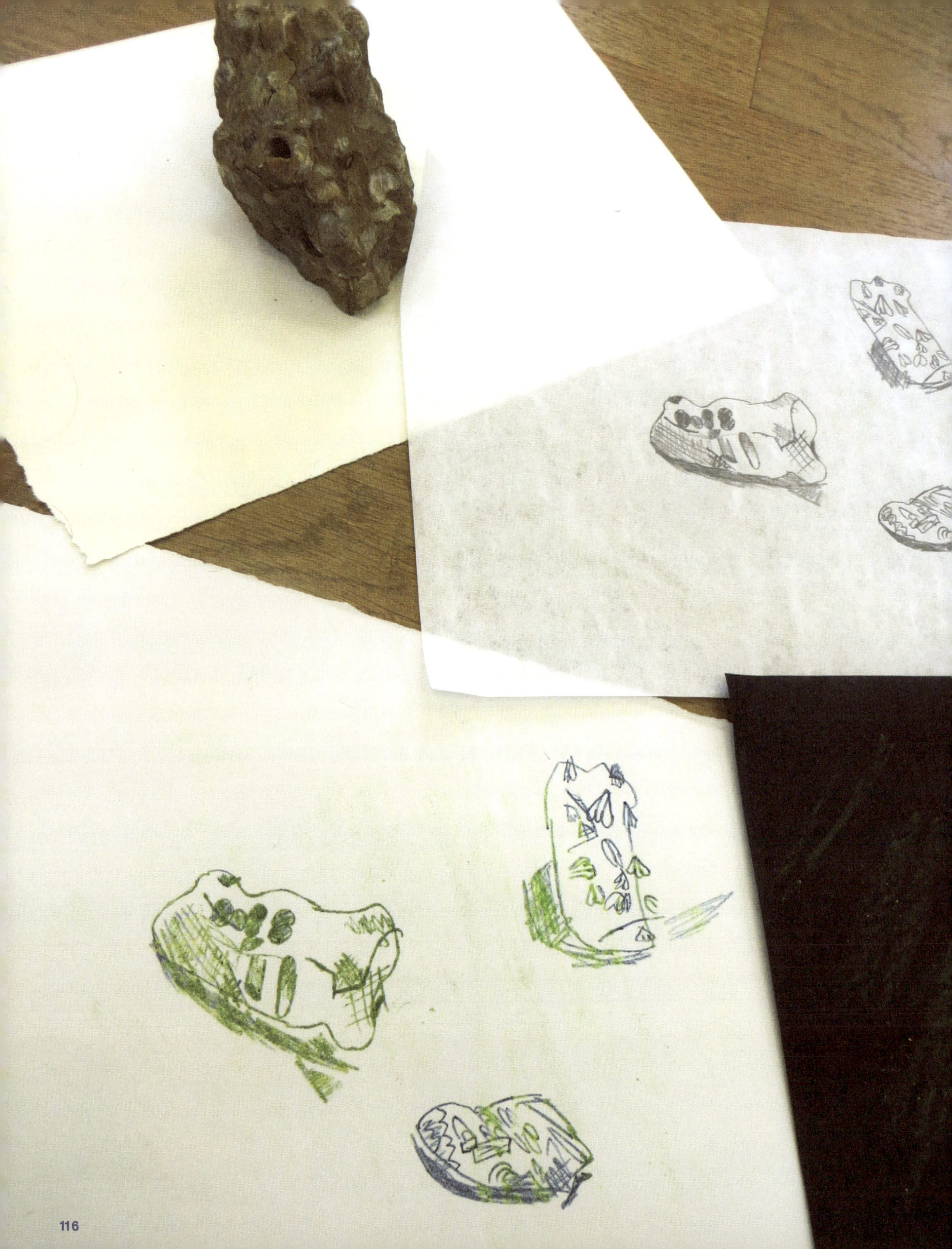

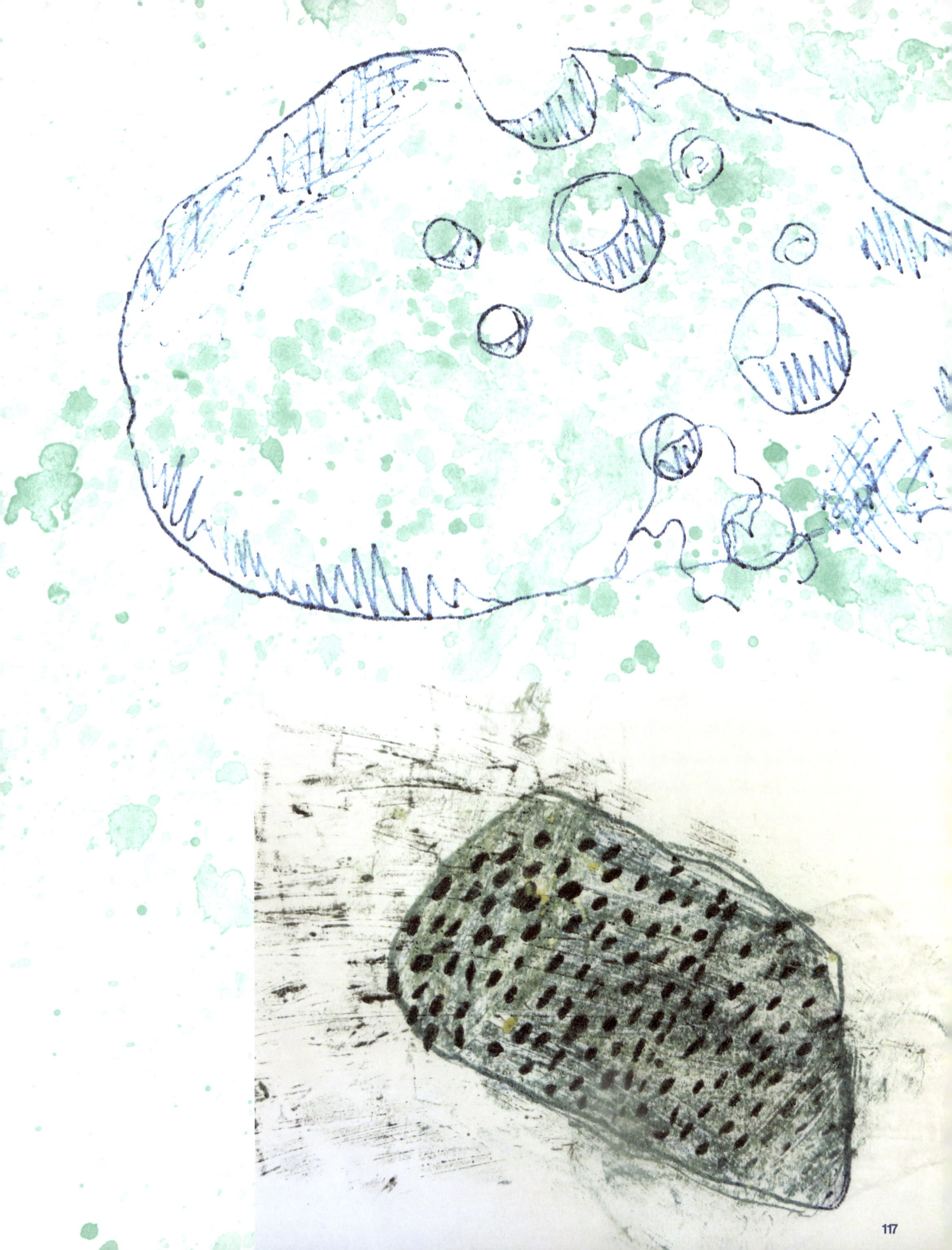

SCRAPERBOARD DRAWINGS

In this project you will make some scraperboards with oil pastels and black paint. When you make your drawing on the board, rather than make dark marks on a light surface, you are going to take away the black paint to reveal lighter areas beneath.

Materials

- Corrugated cardboard
- Oil pastels
- Black acrylic paint
- Washing up liquid
- Nails, flat screwdrivers, and other 'scraper' items

Subject Matter

Choose a simple still life, such as a piece of fruit.

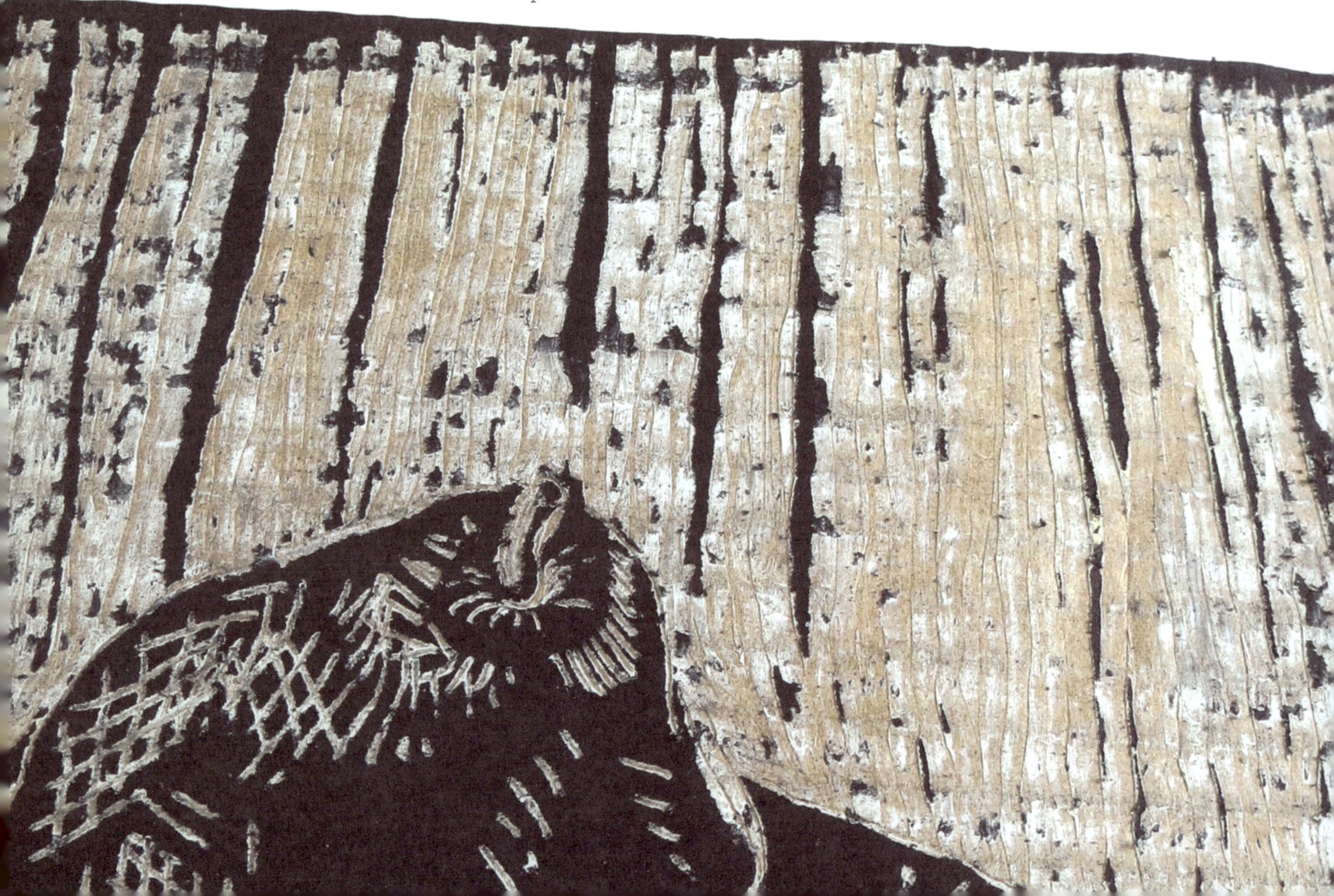

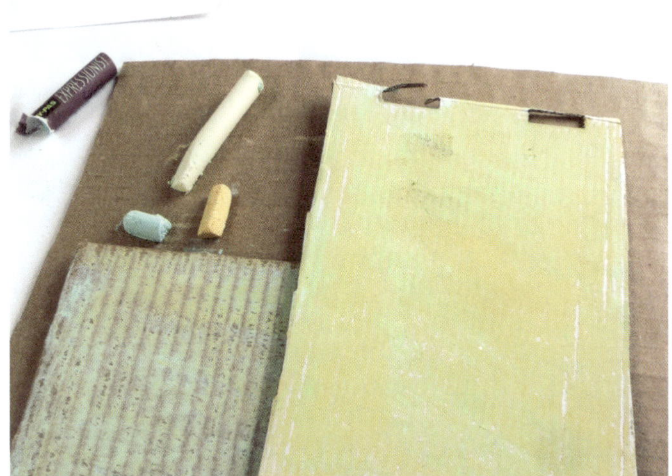

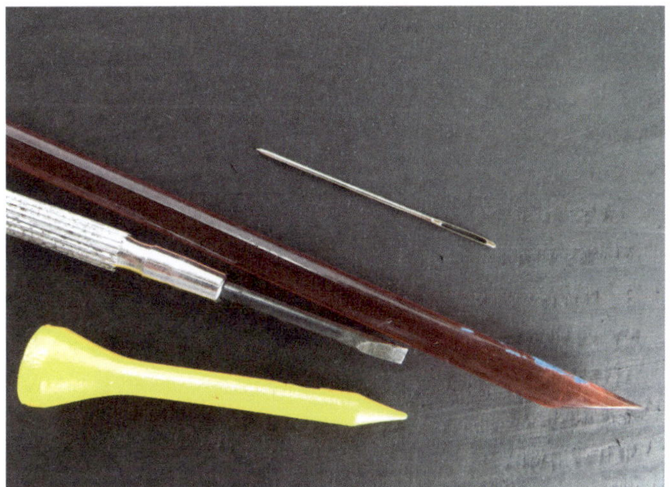

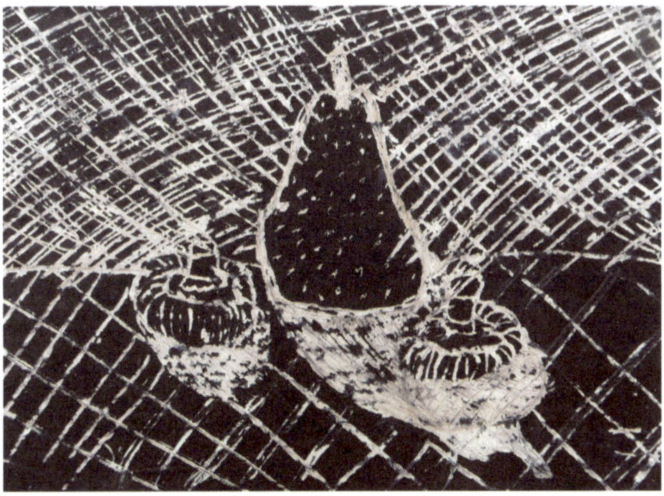

Activity

Before starting your piece, you might want to try out a warm up, such as Thoughtful Mark Making (p 50).

1 Prepare your cardboard by cutting it to an A5 size and covering one side with two pale colours of oil pastel. Make sure you press hard to create a good, even layer of oil pastel. Then mix the black acrylic paint with a small amount of washing up liquid (this will make it easier to remove the acrylic paint later on) and paint a layer of this over the top of the oil pastel layer. Finally, leave your cardboard to dry before starting your drawing.

2 To create an image on the card, scratch away part of the black surface to reveal the light oil pastels beneath. Try exploring how each of your mark making tools can be used to produce different types of lines. Try changing the angle you hold them at, or using a different edge against the painted surface of your cardboard.

3 When you start to draw your subject matter, try to do so on a large scale so that you can use lots of different marks within the object. Remember that you are working in a totally different way to how you would usually draw: normally you would add dark lines and shadows to a light background, but here you are showing lighter lines and areas of light on a dark background. How does this affect which areas you decide to scrape away?

4 After you have finished drawing your subject matter, why not add a patterned or lined foreground and a background to your picture.

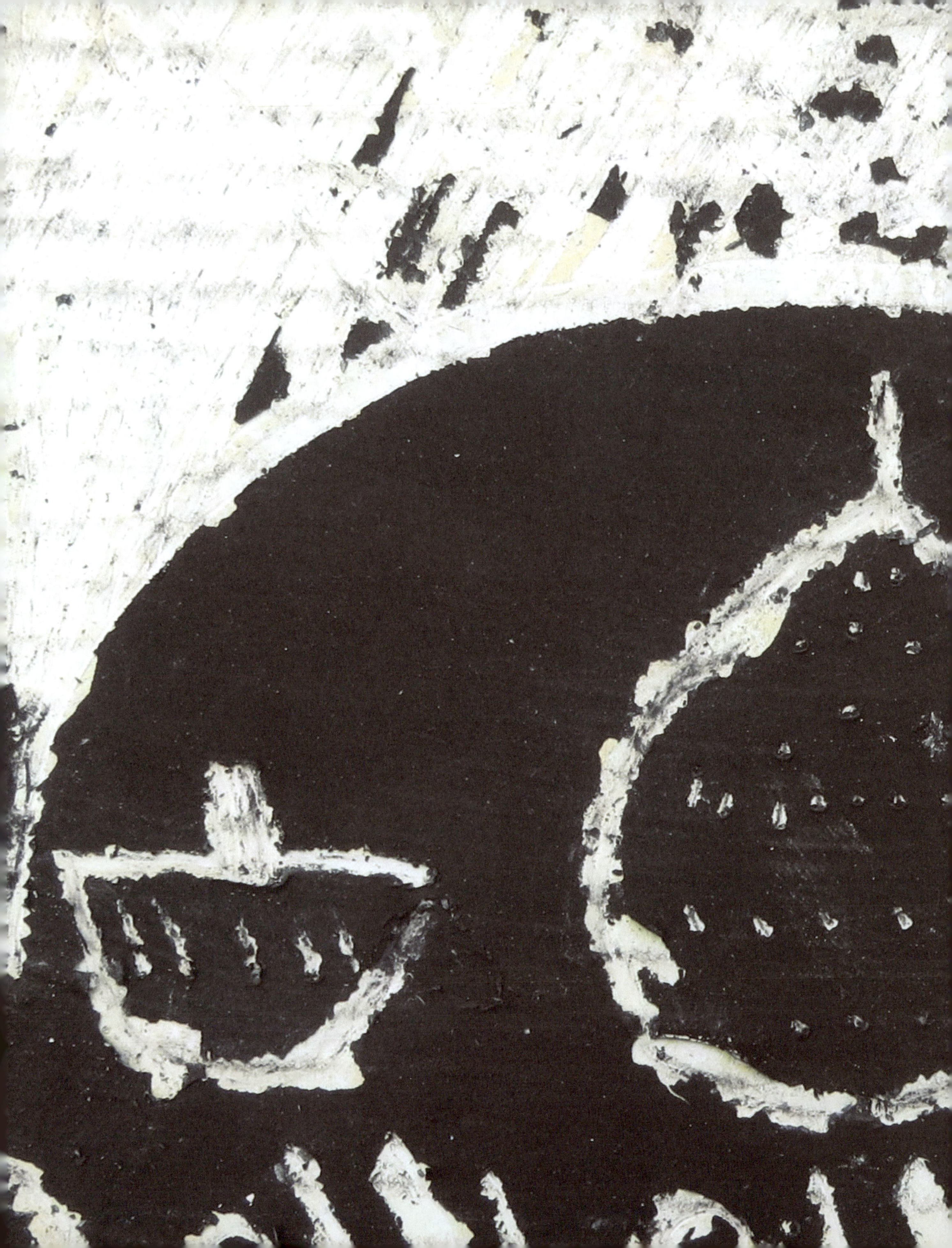

DRAWN AND COLLAGED BIRDS

These striking birds are easy to make and combine drawing and making skills. Make one as a pet, or make a whole flock as a piece of sculpture or art installation. You could even make the birds a house to live in, or a tree to perch in!

Materials

- Corrugated cardboard or foam board
- Drawing paper or sugar paper
- Drawing materials (pencils, charcoal, oil pastels, chalk pastels, watercolours, pencil crayons, wax crayons, felt pens, inks)
- Wire
- Tape
- Glue
- Scissors
- Pliers

Subject Matter

You will need a selection of feathers, and some pictures of birds to see the shape of their bodies and feathers.

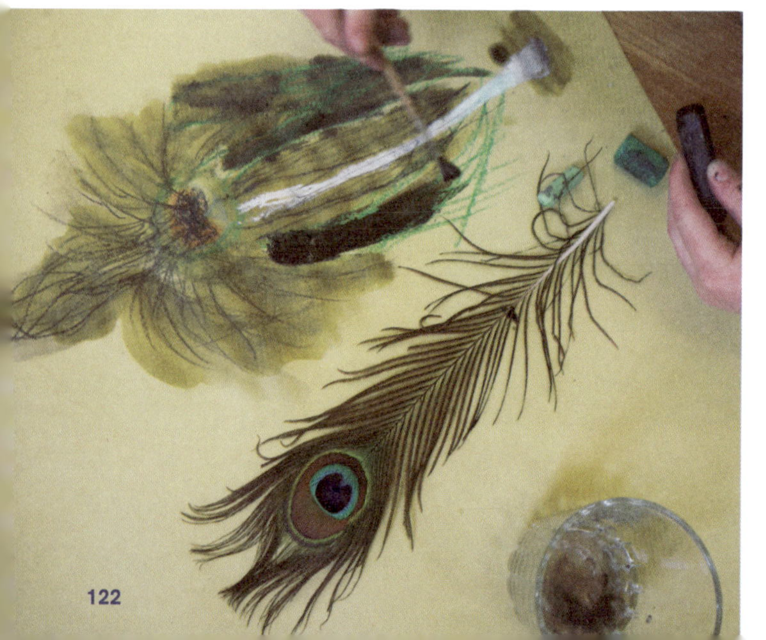

Activity

Making the Body and Legs:

1 Take a piece of cardboard or foam board and cut out an egg shape about the size of your hand. This single shape will become the body and head of the bird. The egg shape does not have to be perfect: cut a few and see which one you like best.

2 Next make the legs. Twist some wire into a rough foot shape, leaving a long bit for the leg. An uncurled and twisted paperclip may work well too. You will need two of these for your bird.

3 Finally, you need to attach the legs to the egg shaped body. This stage is all about balance! The legs are easy to attach to the bird, but it is slightly harder to make it balance. Push the long bit of wire into the edge of the egg-shaped body. The bird should stand on two legs, but if it does not stand at first, try the legs in a slightly different place, or try spreading the claws of the feet further apart. Once the bird balances, wrap a bit of tape around the part where the wire and the body meet, just to help keep it in place.

4 Take a moment to look at the standing bird. Get to know it! What kind of personality or character should it have? Will it be sweet and cute, or fierce and scary? Will it be cheeky or beautiful?

Mark Making:

1 For now, put the bird to one side. Instead, work on some drawings that you can use as collage material. These will be inspired by the textures and shapes of feathers, and will soon be torn up to form pieces with which you can decorate your bird.

2 Do not feel too worried about the end result of your drawing. You should experiment with lots of mark making, trying to cover a sheet of paper with 'featheriness'. Look at the selection of feathers for inspiration, and draw several feathers on the same sheet of paper. Try using a variety of drawing materials in combination. For example, what happens when you use wax as a resist and apply watercolour over the top?

3 You may want to take a photograph of your final drawing before you tear it up for your collage material.

Collage:

1 Cut or tear your feather drawing to create collage pieces. Think carefully about how you can use these pieces to add not just colour to the bird, but also texture and form. For example, you might crush or fold a piece of paper to make it into a three-dimensional shape. The collage does not have to be glued flat to the bird: it can also be glued at right angles to form wings or tail feathers.

You might like to try the Drawing Feathers project before you make these birds (p 60).

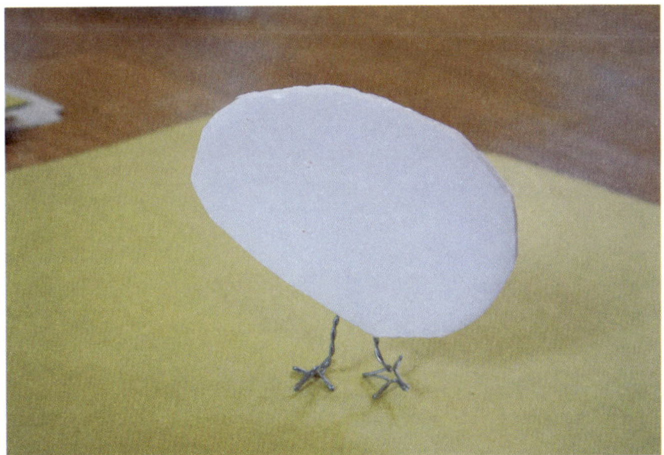

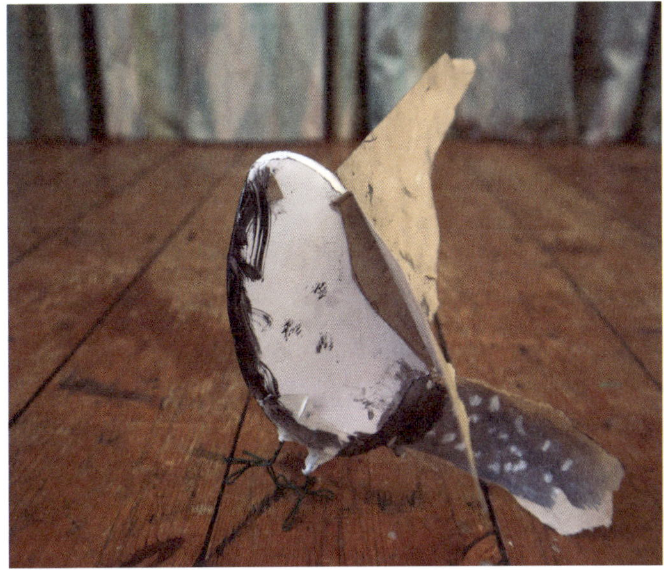

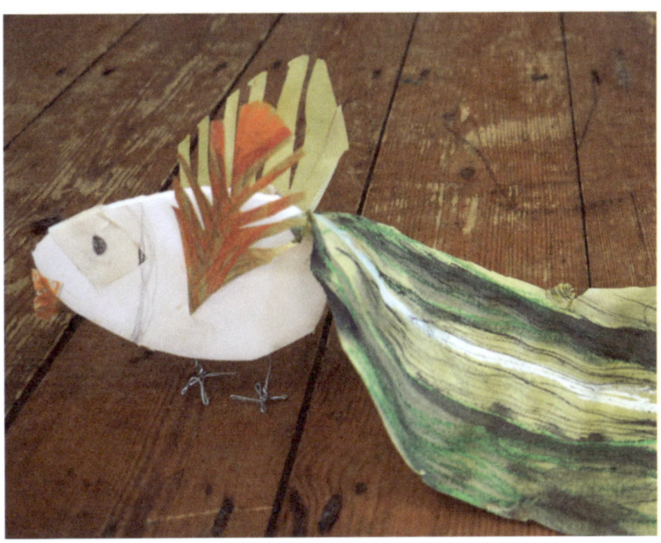

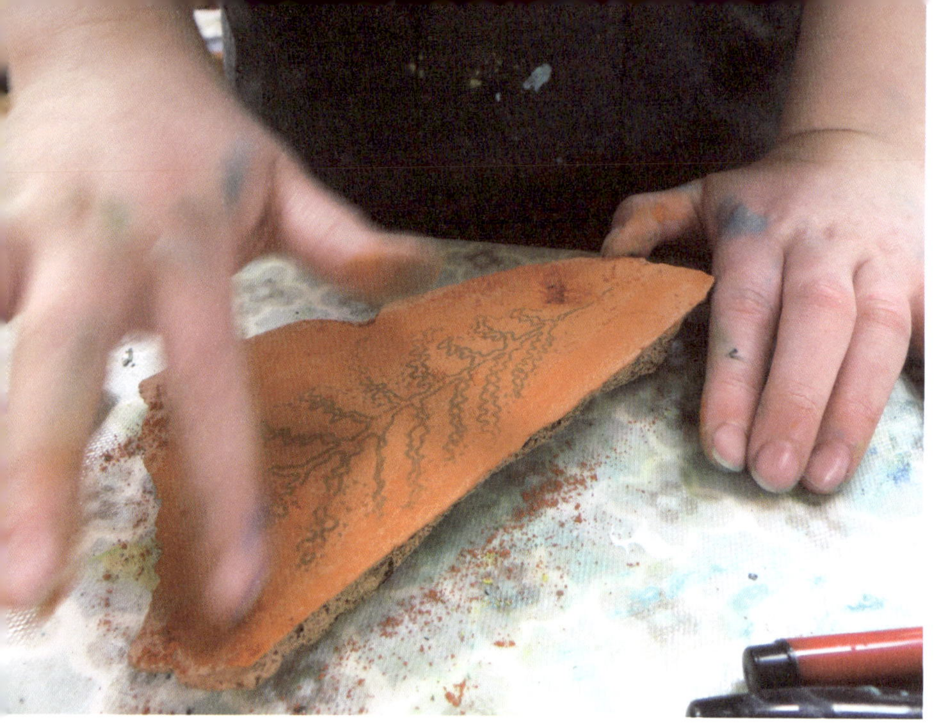

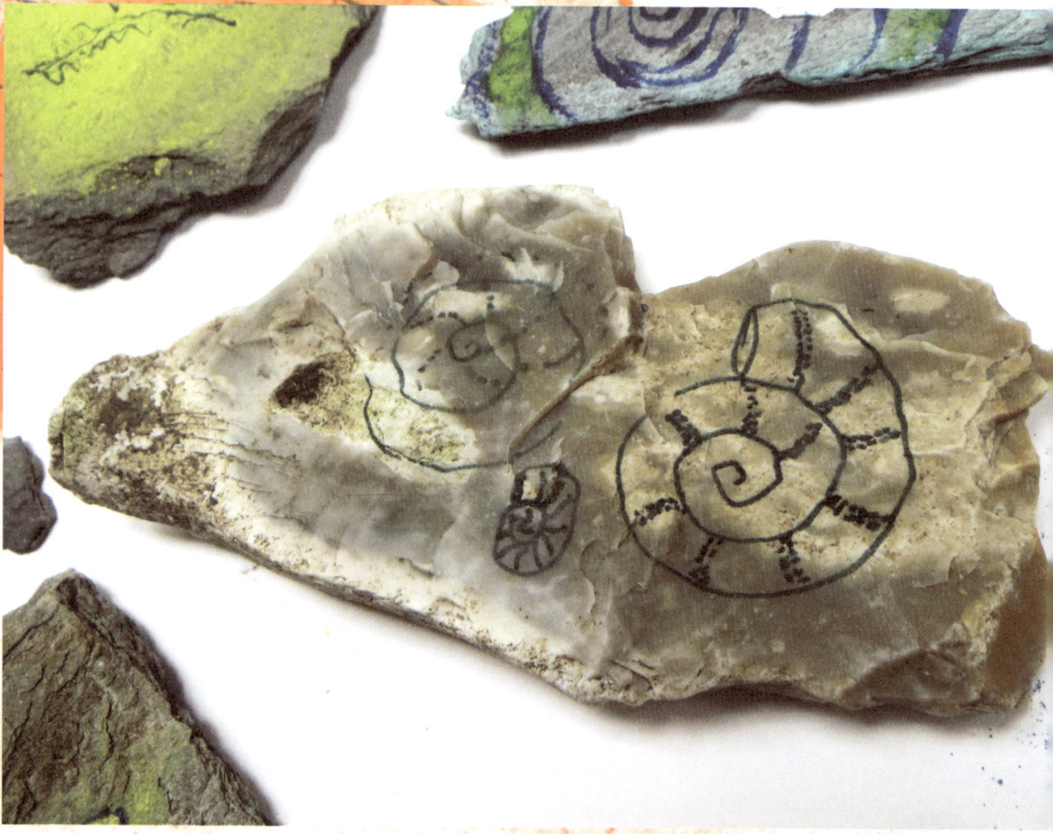

TREASURED FOSSILS

In this project you will use colour, texture and form to transform a stone into a fossil. This new challenge means trying out your drawing skills on new surfaces, which will change the way familiar drawing tools make their marks.

Materials

- A collection of small flat pieces of stone, such as slate, brick or flint
- Oil pastels
- Chalk pastels
- Handwriting pens
- Correction pens
- Watercolours and a fine brush
- Large nails to be used as mark making tools.

Subject Matter

You will need a selection of either real fossils or pictures of fossils.

Activity

1 Prepare your pieces of stone by scrubbing them clean. Once they have dried you can start your drawings.

2 Study your pieces of stone and brick. Which are your favourite colours and shapes?

3 Choose a piece of stone to transform into a fossil. Using your selection of drawing materials draw a fossil on to your piece of stone. Use colour and texture to create a background for your fossil. Make sure to take a look at your subject matter to see how fossils sit within rocks, their shape and their colours.

4 When you have finished your fossil, why not take another stone and make another one? Soon you will have a collection of your own treasured fossils.

Facilitator's Note

When selecting the drawing materials, you may decide to limit the colours of pastels and paint to one particular colour band, such as green/blue. If you are working with a group of children, encourage them to add their drawn fossils to a shared collection as they go along, so that they will see and be inspired by each other's work as they go. Celebrate new ideas and discoveries by sharing and reflecting at the end of the session, once the artwork is complete.

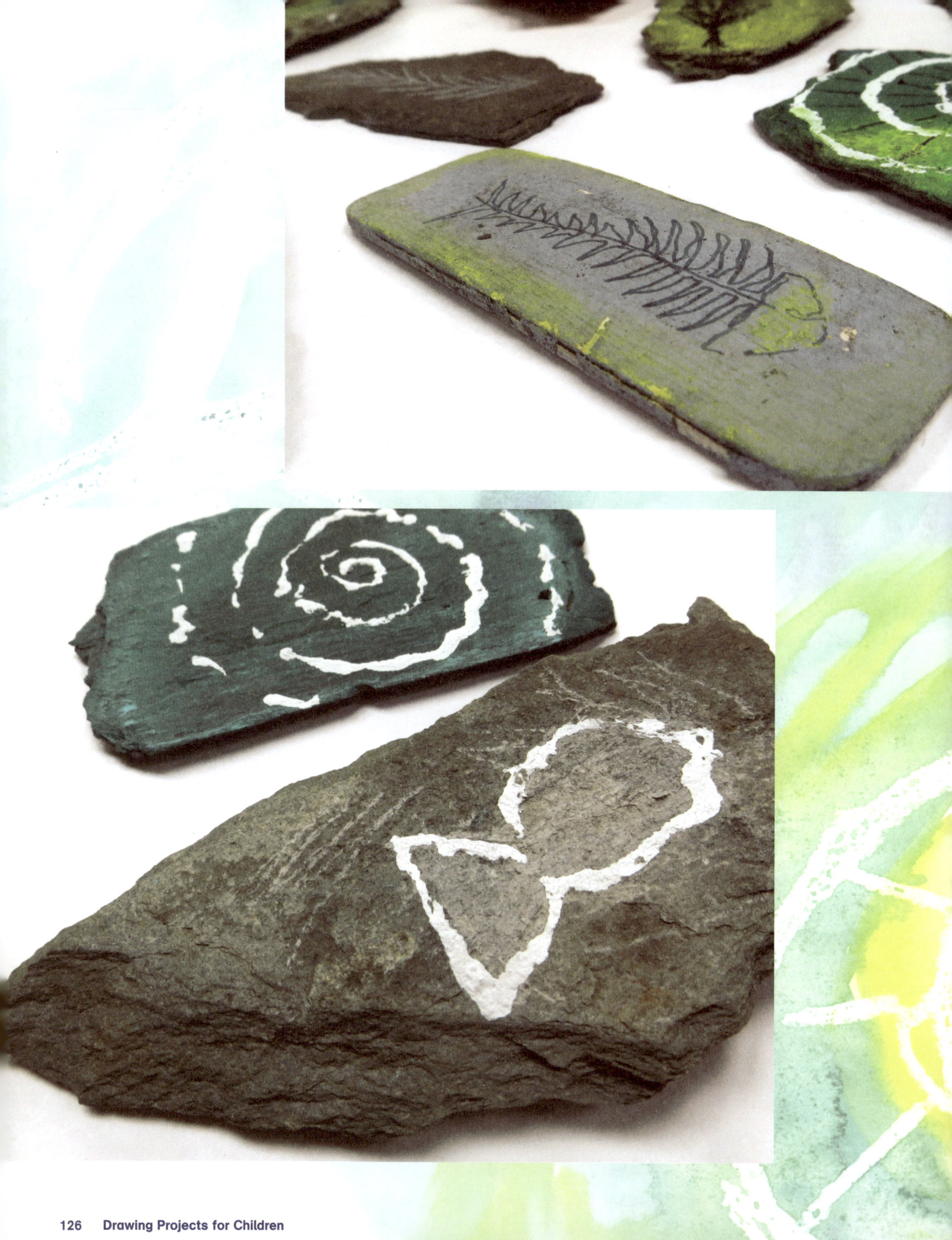

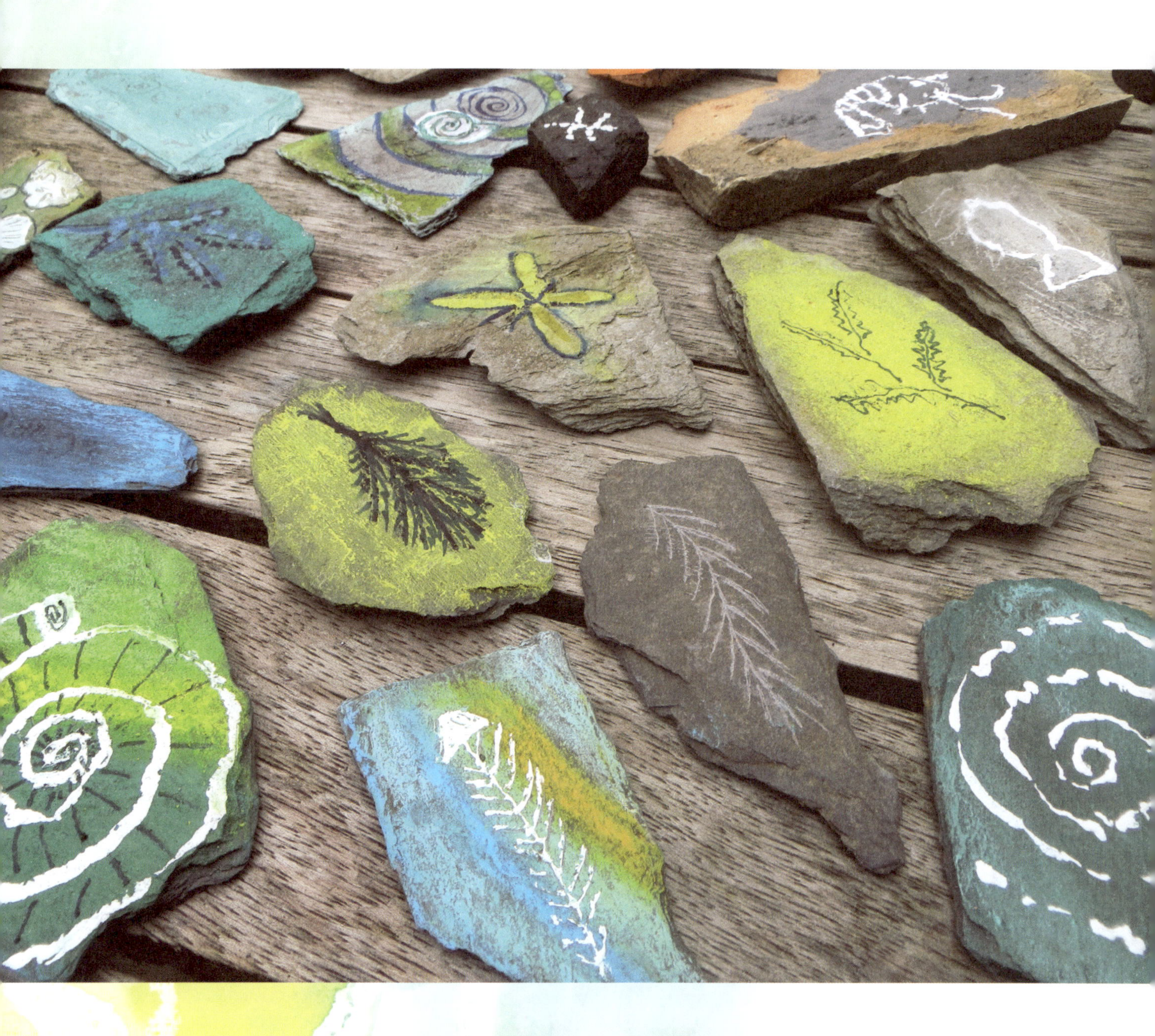

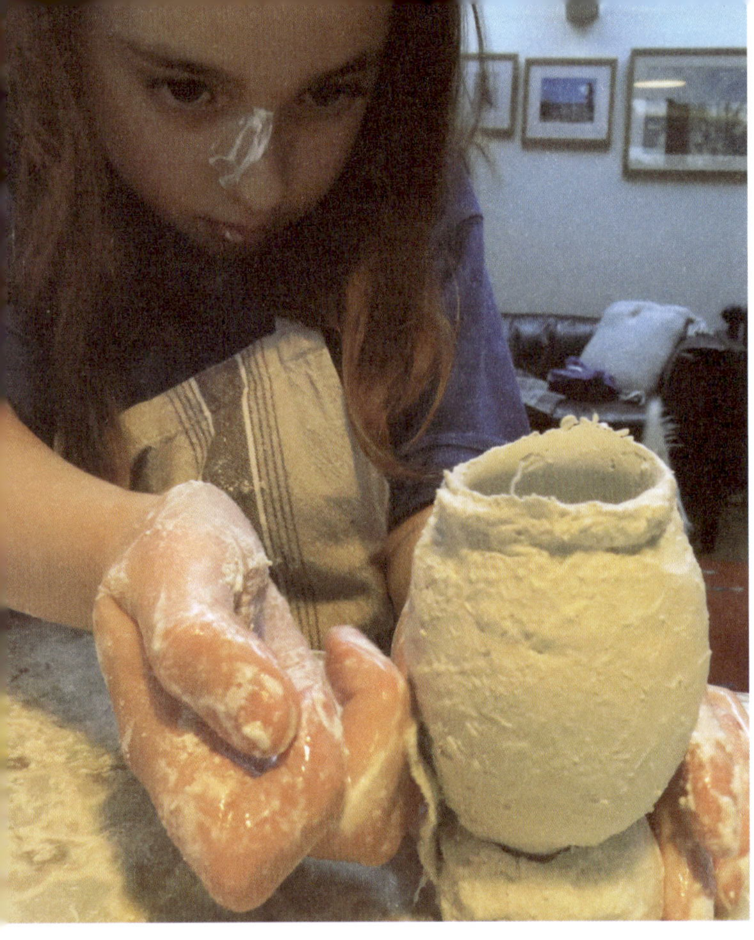

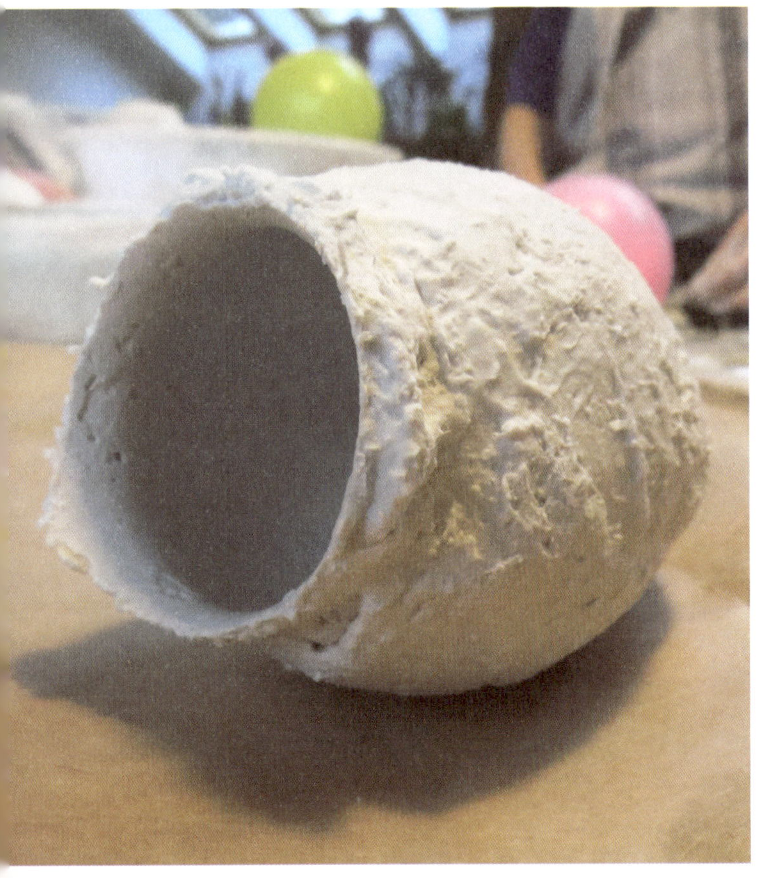

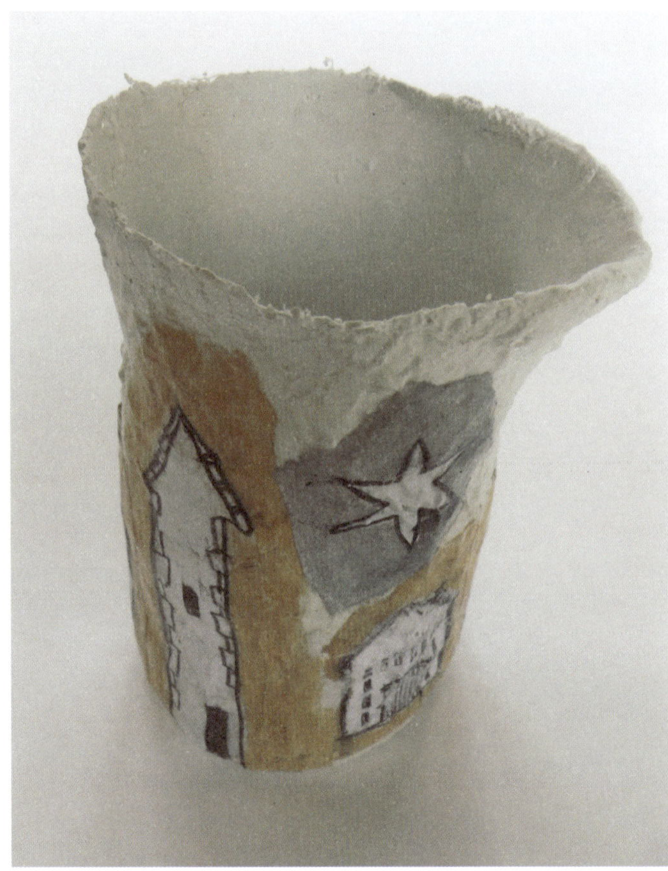

MAKING PATTERNED VESSELS

In this exercise you will create your own decorated 3D cup, vase or bowl.

Materials

To make the vessels:
- Modroc
- Balloons
- Scissors
- Cups

To make the decorative sheets:
- Tissue paper
- Drawing paper
- Oil pastels
- Graphite
- PVA glue

Subject Matter

Various objects might inspire the decoration of your vessel, including feathers, flowers, fruits or geometric shapes. It may also be helpful to take a look at pictures of some different types of vessels, such as jugs, cups, vases or bowls, and all of their different spouts, handles and lids.

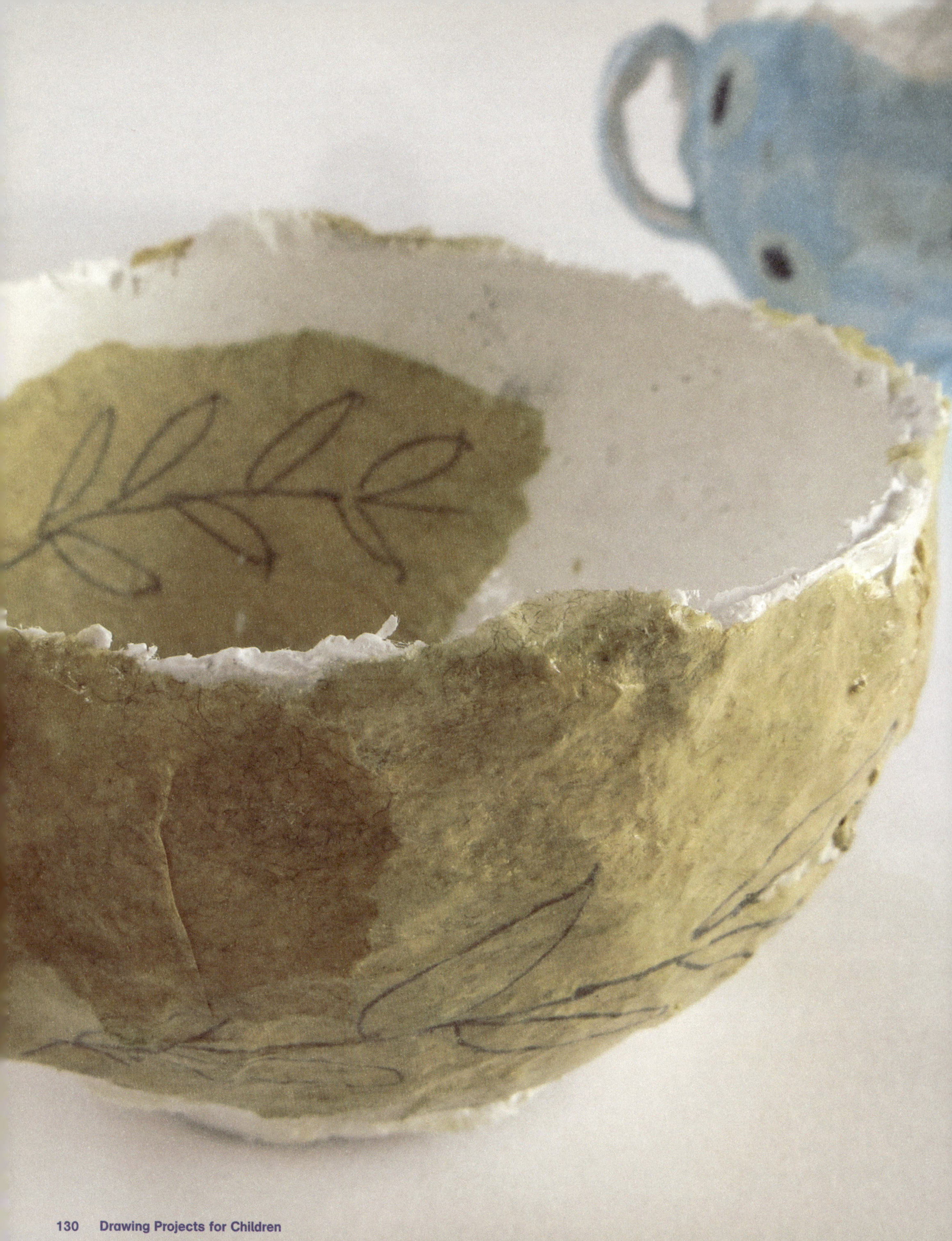

Making the Vessels:

1 Cut the modroc into strips, and blow up a balloon no larger than 10 cms in diametre.

2 Using a cup to hold the balloon in place, start to apply modroc over the top of the blown-up balloon, so that the modroc reaches about half way down its surface, creating an upside down bowl shape. You will only need one or two layers of modroc, but make sure you have blended it well with your fingers, as this will make your finished vessel strong.

3 Add any details, such as handles, whilst the modroc is still wet, using smaller, folded pieces of modroc. Whilst the vessel is upside down, you could add a band of modroc around the bottom of your vessel to help it stand.

4 Once the modroc has set and become hard, remove the vessel from the balloon.

5 To add a spout, make a single cut into the modroc, open out the new folds, and add a piece of modroc to cover the gap.

6 Leave your vessel to dry out for a few days.

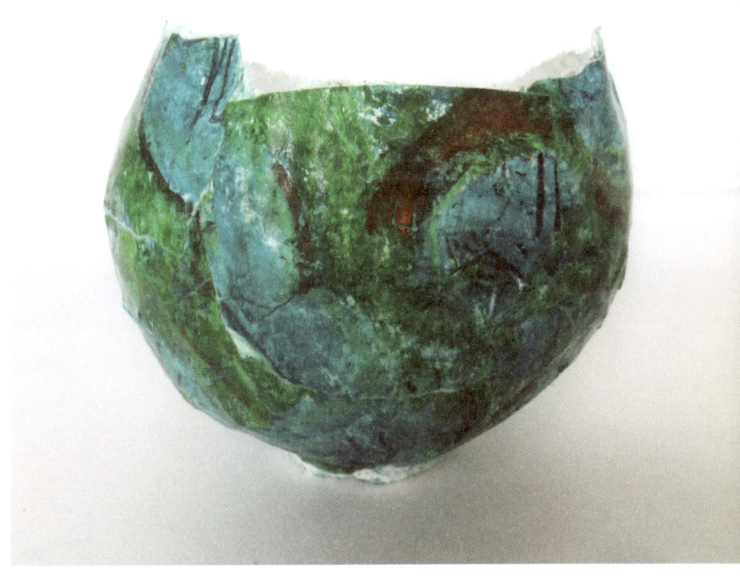

Decorating the Vessels:

1 For your decorative sheets, you will need to create a flat, repeated pattern. Using a small selection of colours, explore the ways in which a pattern or a shape can be repeated across the page. What about your background? Is your pattern abstract or figurative? You can do this on either tissue paper or drawing paper, adding more layers of tissue paper to add to the colour or patterns.

2 Now it is time to cover your vessel with your decorative sheet. If you have used tissue paper, cut or tear the sheet into smaller sections and use PVA glue and a brush to paste it onto the vessel. If you have used drawing paper for your sheet, begin by softening the paper. To do this scrunch the paper up and unfurl it again. You can also try to dampen the paper very briefly once it has been crumpled. The paper will then be soft enough to tear into smaller pieces and paste onto the vessel with PVA glue.

3 When you are pasting your decorative paper onto the vessel, consider how you will use your pattern. Are you going to match up the pattern so it flows across the vessel? Or are you going to use it more randomly? Are you going to decorate the inside of your vessel, or just the outside?

4 Let the PVA dry completely until it is translucent.

DRESSING UP AS FOSSILS

Sometimes, after working on a small scale, everyone needs to stretch their limbs (and creative horizons) and work on something bigger. In this project you will work on metre squares of fabric to create textured drawings. At the end, turn yourself into a piece of installation art by wearing your drawings!

Materials

- Watercolours
- Graphite
- Water soluble graphite
- Wax crayons
- Oil pastels
- Brushes
- A1 metre squares of cotton fabric (cheap or second hand bedsheets are ideal)
- A3 drawing paper or sugar paper

Subject Matter

You will need a selection of printed images of fossils. Try to choose images that fill the whole page.

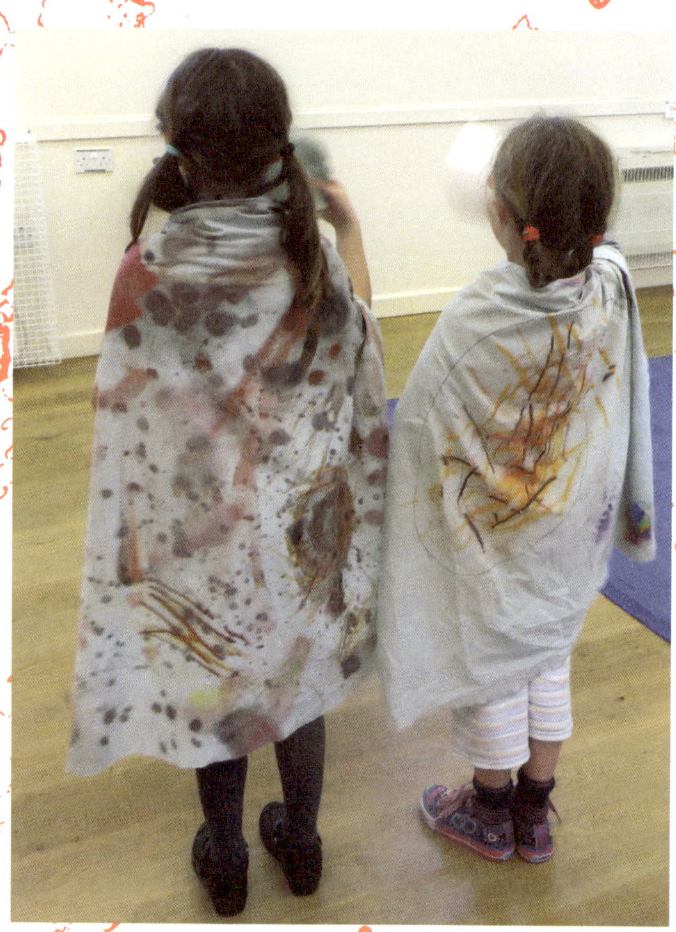

Activity

Before you start this project, you might want to try
a warm up exercise. Tear some sugar paper into
hand-sized pebble shapes. Taking one piece of pebble
paper, create a fossil or stone-like texture over the
whole surface. Only spend about two minutes doing
this. Once you have completed this, take another
pebble and create another fossil, but try using a new
material or a different way of mark making. How
does crumpling the paper, before or after making
your drawing, change the texture?

1 After finishing the warm up, turn to your metre
   square of fabric. Trying to cover the whole surface
   of the fabric, create a fossil in the same way you did
   on your practice pebbles. How might the marks you
   make balance out across the entire canvas? How
   might the colour or the thickness of your marks
   help your composition?

2 Try to remember to step back now and again to
   take a look at your fabric. This will help to see
   how the drawing is progressing. It is also helpful
   to remember that although when we make a
   drawing we usually move from the wrist, when
   you work on a larger scale you can try to move
   from the elbow, the shoulder or the waist. Try to
   involve your whole body in making the drawing!

3 Once your canvas is complete, allow it to dry.
   Then curl up and cover yourself with your
   drawing. You have turned into a fossil!

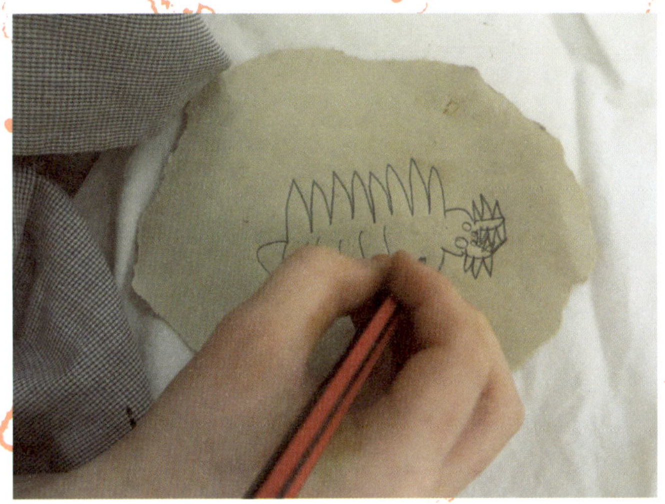

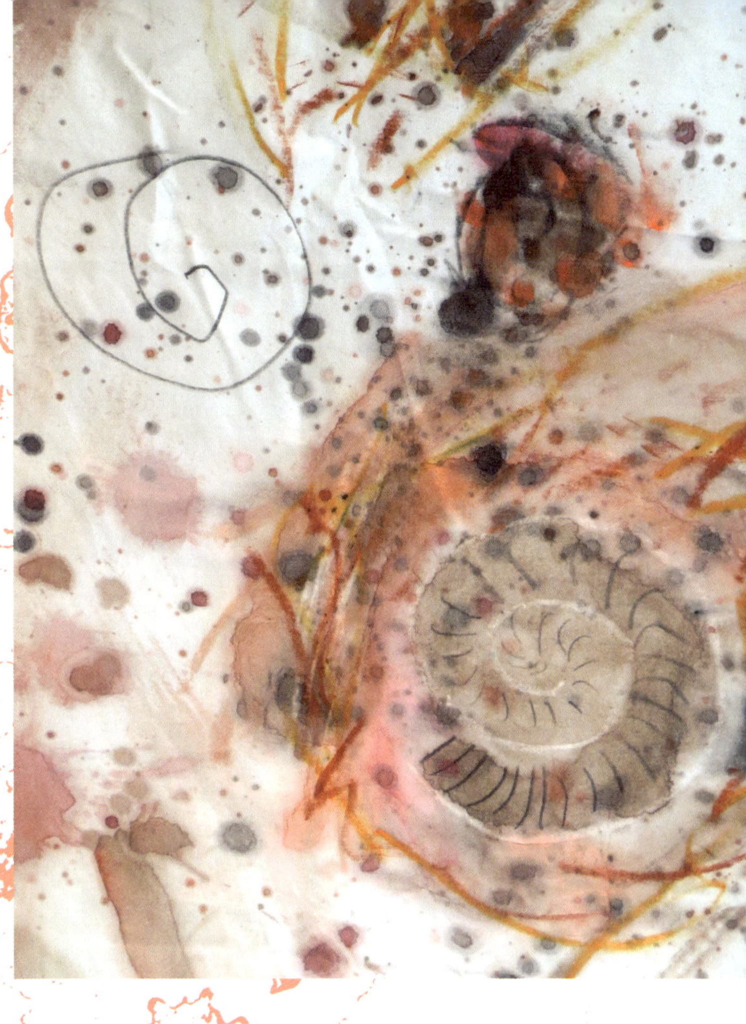

Facilitator's Note

It is a good idea to remind the child of the importance
of stepping back from their work to enable them to
make decisions about how the drawing is progressing.
For this reason, if possible, set the room up with the
child working at one end, and the materials on a
table at the other end, and ask them to choose only
one or two materials at a time before returning the
materials and choosing more. In this way, they will be
encouraged to see their work from a distance every
time they return to fetch more materials.

The metre square dimension of the fabric relates very
well to the size of a child's body. Without prompting
the child will likely begin to 'wear' the canvas as a
shawl, but as one last surprise have them curl up into
a ball on the floor and throw the canvas over them,
tucking it in. Enjoy the sudden quiet as the energy in
the room changes and the child becomes a rock!

MAKING SPELLS FROM STILL LIFES

Have you ever seen a drawing with lots of movement in it? Or seen a drawing which appears to be very still? In this project, you will get the opportunity to work on a series of drawings which are very still, and then transform them into a dynamic, swirling spell pot!

This project is split into two sessions.

Session One: Making Still Life Drawings

Materials

- Soft (B) and hard (H) pencils
- Graphite
- Handwriting pens
- Erasers
- A5 drawing paper

Subject Matter

Collect and arrange a variety of spell 'ingredients' on single sheets of paper. Try to make the ingredients as varied and interesting-looking as you can, including things like: rocks, shells, feathers, seed heads, seeds, grasses, twigs, scrunched paper (foil, tracing paper, bank note), treasure items (keys, beads, coins), wool, string, cotton, mushrooms, onions, teabags, etc.

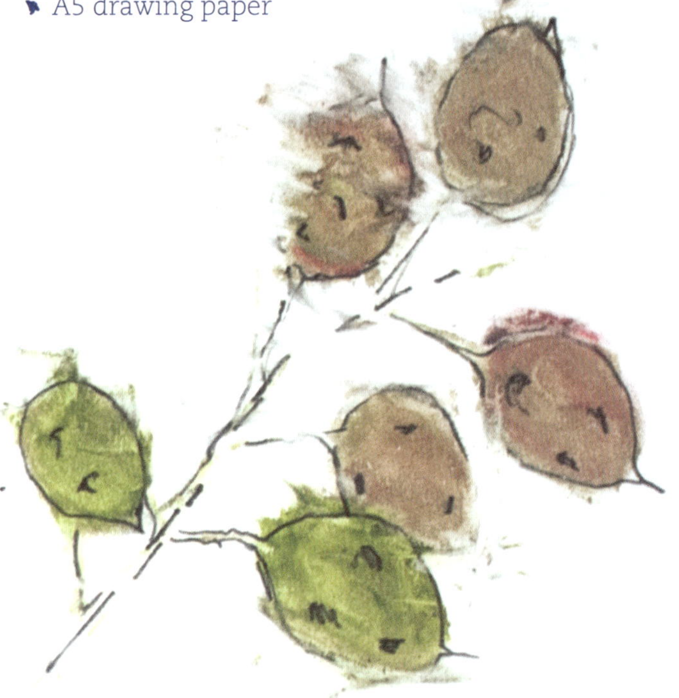

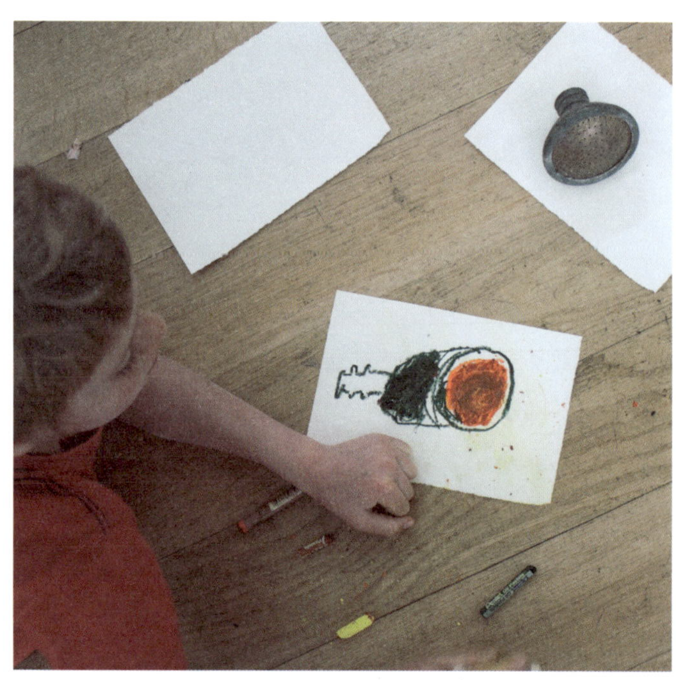

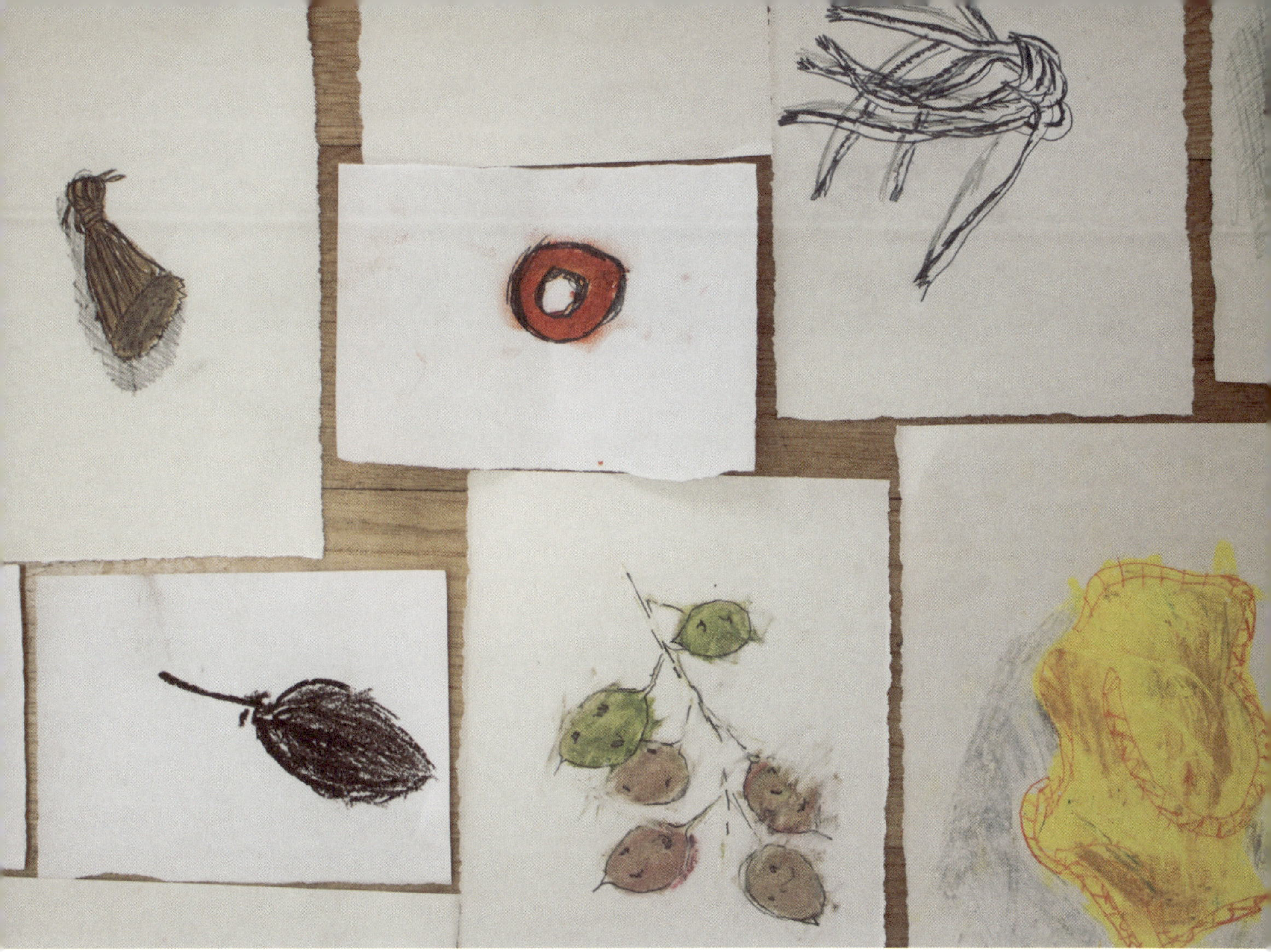

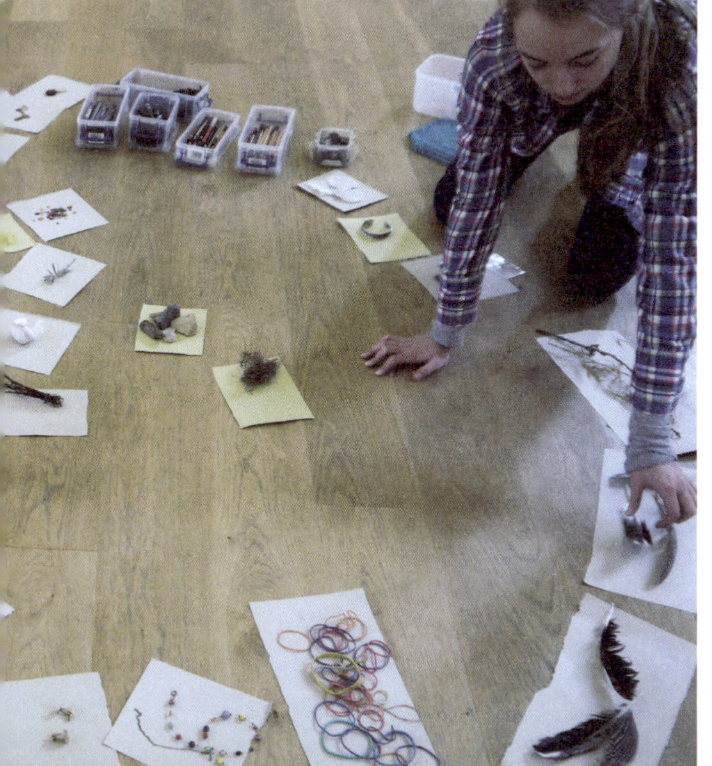

Activity

1 Arrange the subject matter in a circle on the floor, with space for you to sit on the outside of the circle, to draw your objects.

2 Choose a spell ingredient that you would like to draw, making a single drawing on a sheet of A5 paper, before moving on to the next ingredient on a new sheet. Feel free to choose whichever drawing material you would like to use for each object.

3 Keep going until you have a selection of spell ingredient drawings.

Session Two: Making Dynamic Drawings

In complete contrast to the calmness of session one, this session will be full of energy and colour! Your aim is to transform the still drawings from session one into a drawing full of movement and action.

Materials

- Soft (B) and hard (H) pencils
- Graphite
- Handwriting pens
- Erasers
- Chalk pastels
- Oil pastels
- Eight or more A2 sheets of drawing paper taped together to make one large canvas

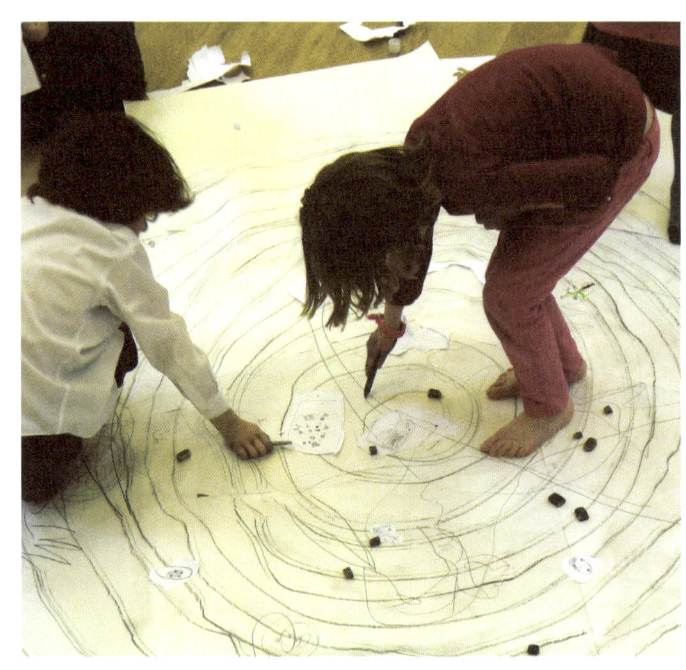

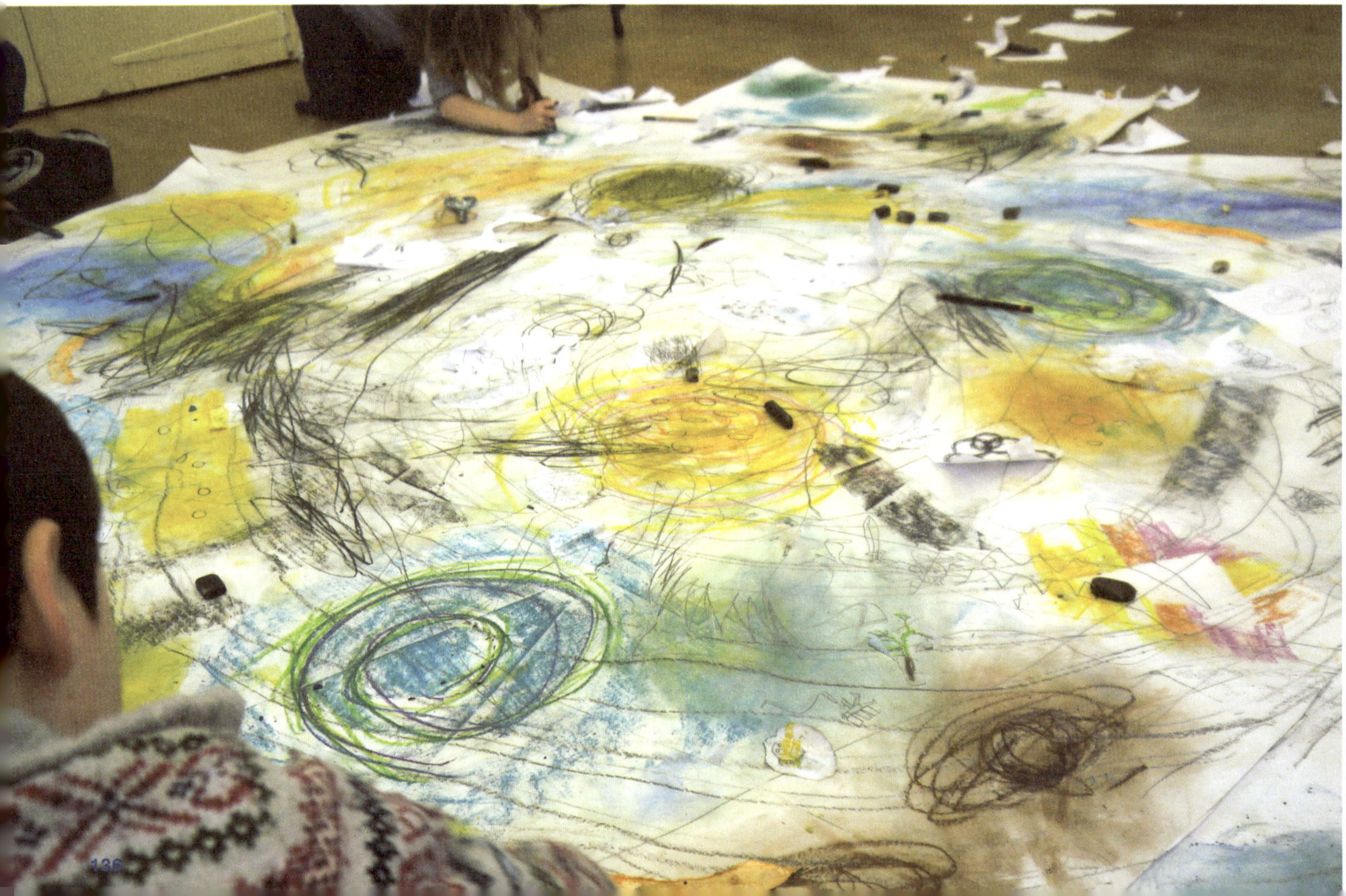

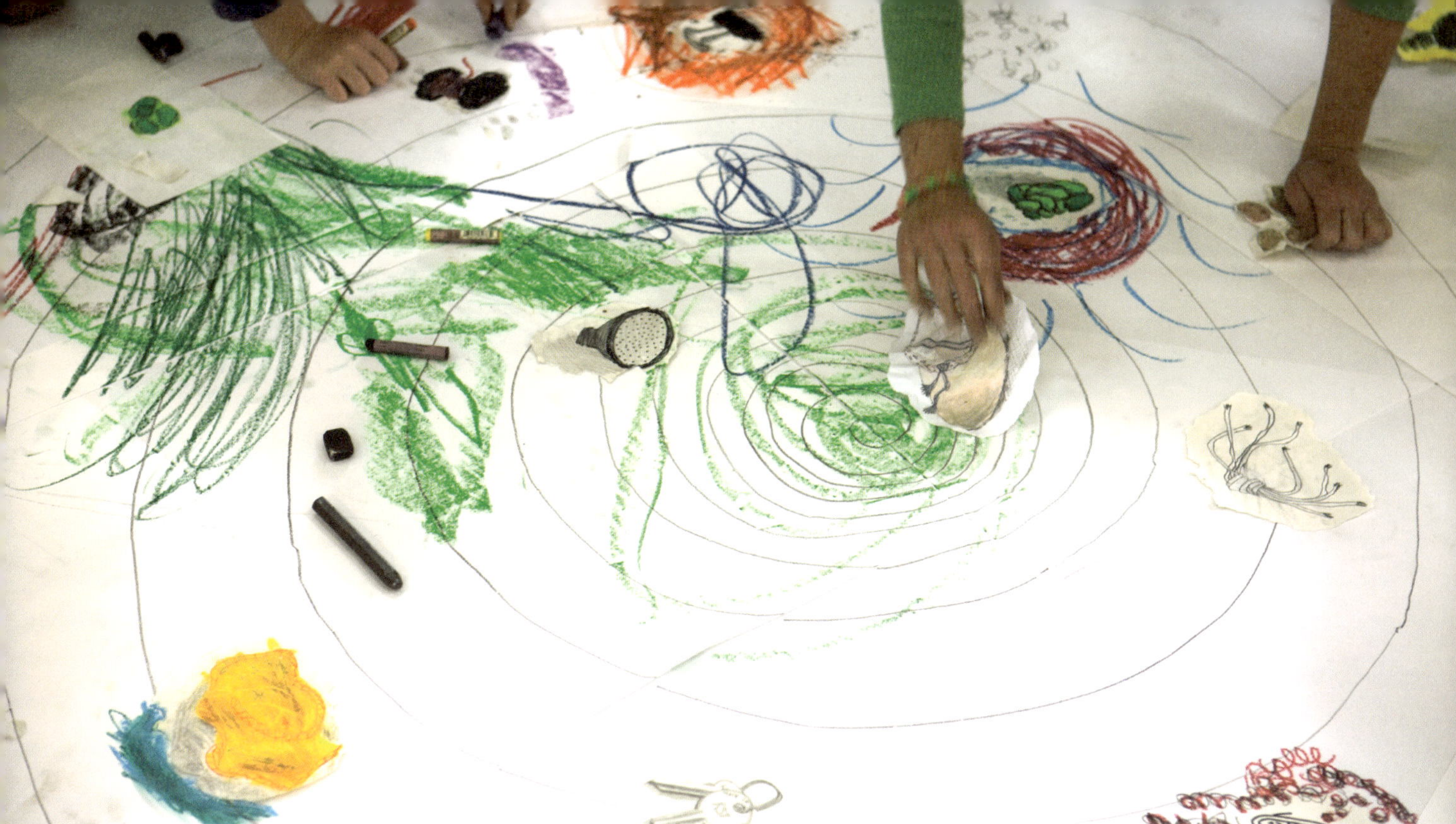

Activity

Before you begin the shared drawing, start with an expressive mark making warm up exercise to get you into the right frame of mind. Work on a large sheet of paper, with a water soluble graphite stick, water and paint brush. The challenge is simple: to make a drawing that is about turbulent, swirling water! Work for about ten minutes on this warm up drawing. Knowing when to stop is always difficult—you need time to push the drawings, and also to get seduced by the materials, but you need to stop before the drawing crosses a line and loses its focus.

1 The plan is to make a shared drawing of a swirling spell pot, full of the ingredients drawn in the previous session.

2 Stick several large sheets of paper together to make an area large enough to accommodate all the still life images. Think carefully about which drawing materials to allow onto the shared drawing. You will be climbing all over the drawing, so you might not want to choose materials that will smudge or cause too much mess, like chalk

or water soluble graphite. Graphite sticks, erasers and pastels will work well.

3 You might want to start with a spiral or vortex to act as the backbone of the drawing.

4 Once the background of your swirling spell pot is finished, begin to collage the drawn ingredients, sticking them down on the large canvas. Challenge yourself with questions like "How do I make these images feel like they are somehow embedded into the drawing?" Use colour to help this process, and also make marks with graphite and then use erasers to blur boundaries

5 Let the layers of the dynamic drawing really start to build up and enjoy watching your swirling spell pot take shape!

If you are working with a group of children, the second part of this project could be a shared drawing, a great way to demonstrate to students that drawings can be still or dynamic, personal or shared.

If the children find the idea of other children reworking their drawings troublesome, scan or photocopy the original drawings and use the copies in the shared drawing, leaving the original intact. Working on a shared drawing is a sophisticated process—one has to be able to let go to allow the drawing to proceed. From the outset agree as a group what is and is not permitted. You might agree that children can draw over or around someone else's drawings in the same way that you might develop your own work—but not just for the sake of it.

Session one should be calm and focused, but session two will be energetic and spontaneous. Sessions like this test the resourcefulness of the facilitator. It is vital to have a number of activities taking place at one time, and to direct the children to their own activity: in effect to manage the drawing (in terms of both process and outcome). Section out the activities; get one child to draw the spiral vortex, whilst the others start tearing the copies of the 'still' drawings ready to place them as ingredients in the spell pot.

Your job as facilitator is to oversee the drawing and help children see the image develop as a whole, as well as a series of parts. Keep the drawing balanced and stop halfway through to consider how the drawing is coming along, asking "What does it need?".

Give individual children 'challenges' to help direct the drawing, and stretch their skills. For example you may recruit a 'spy' whose job it is to draw small bubbles in the spell pot, unnoticed, whilst another could be asked to cut the still drawings out neatly (as opposed to tear), to place over existing drawings. Other children could be challenged to work only with rubbers, or to create areas of negative colour by using a pastel over cut-out paper shapes, which are then removed.

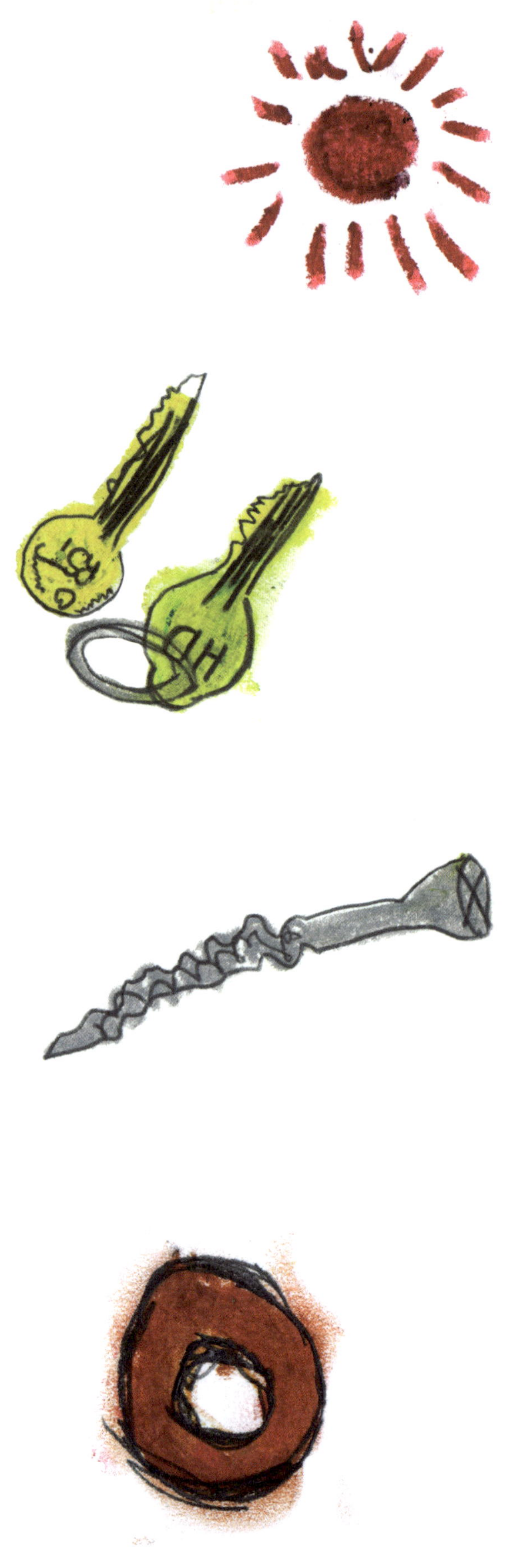

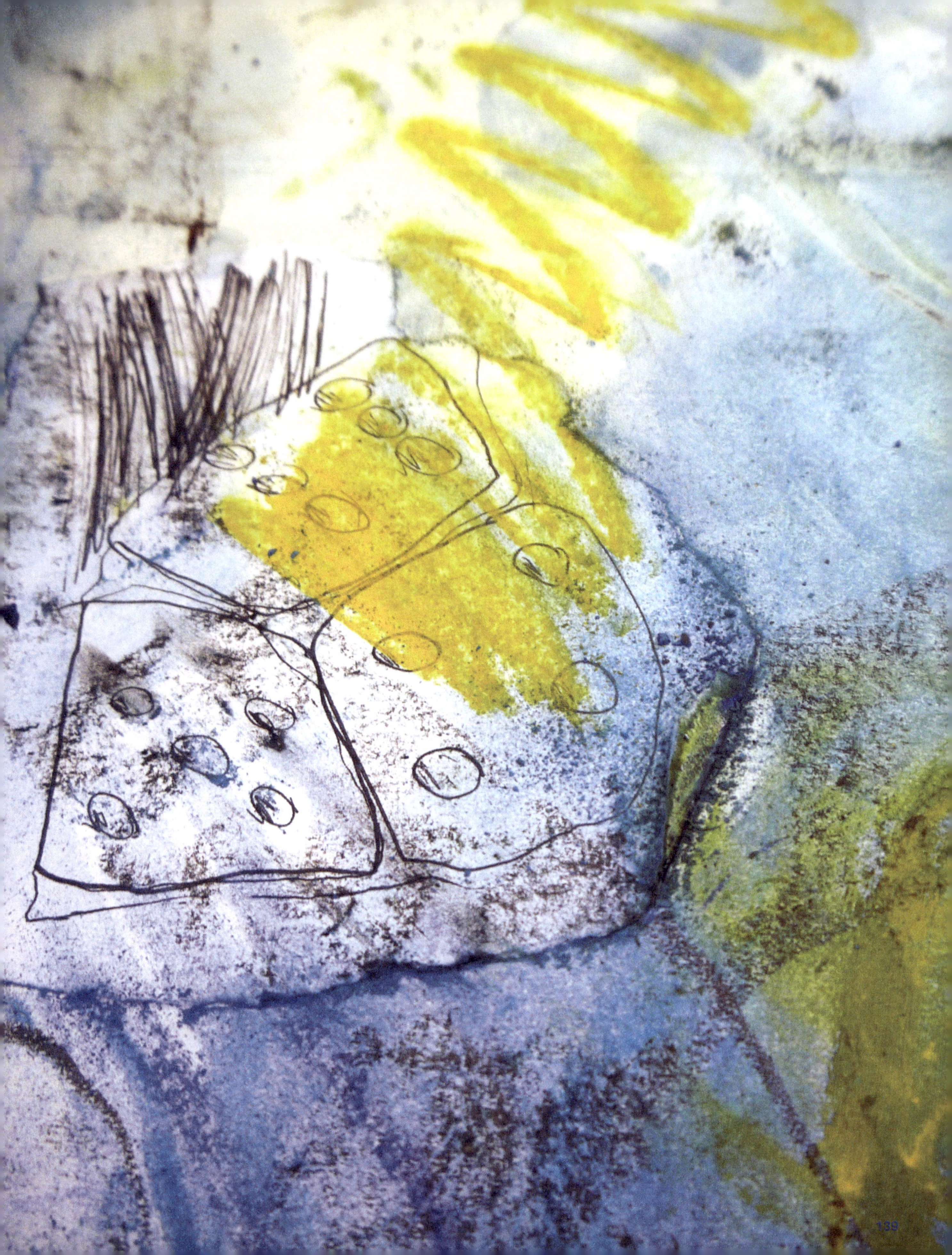

PICNIC DRAWING PARTY

In this project you will make drawings of picnic food directly onto a cotton sheet. When you eat the food, you will be left with a beautiful picnic drawing!

Materials

- Soft (B) pencils
- Graphite
- Handwriting pens
- Erasers
- Watercolours
- Brushes
- A large cotton sheet (an old white sheet from a charity or thrift shop works well, or otherwise a cheap 100 per cent cotton sheet from a supermarket).

Subject Matter

Collect a variety of picnic treats (crisps, cakes, buns, drinks, sandwiches, sausage rolls, etc) together with picnic utensils (cups, saucers, knives and forks). Aim for lots of colour, texture and pattern. Place these onto the cotton sheet, like you would put your picnic on a tablecloth or blanket. Make sure there is plenty of room between the items for you to sit and draw.

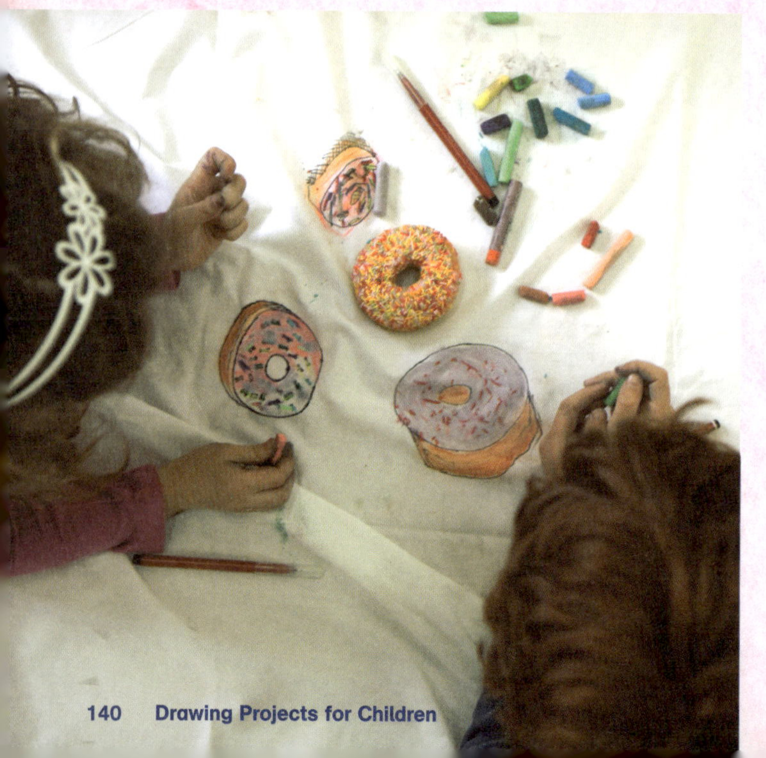

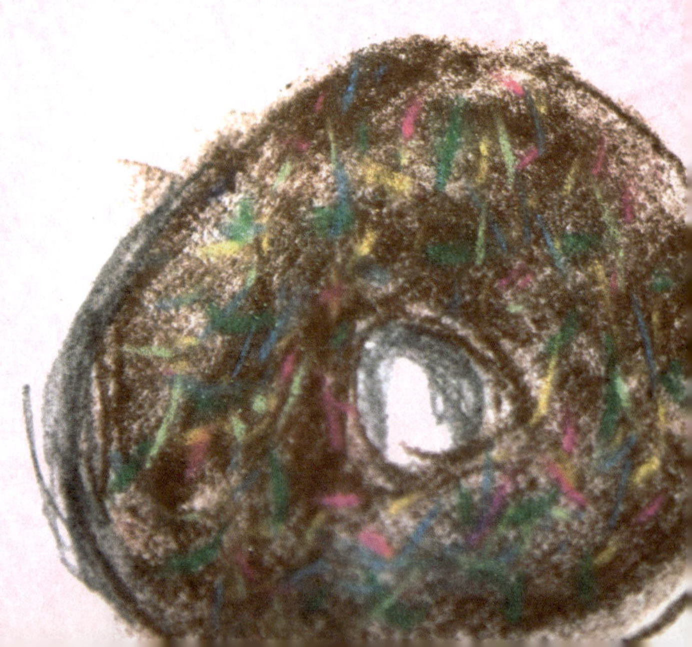

Choose a picnic food or object and make a drawing of it in anyway you wish directly next to the object, on the sheet.

The drawing materials may act differently to normal when you work directly onto the sheet. For example, the handwriting pens and watercolours may run into the cotton. Enjoy these new effects and experiment with what they can do.

Once you have drawn an object, remove it to make room for more drawings.

Once all the picnic elements have been drawn and removed, stand back (eat!) and enjoy the finished picnic rug drawing.

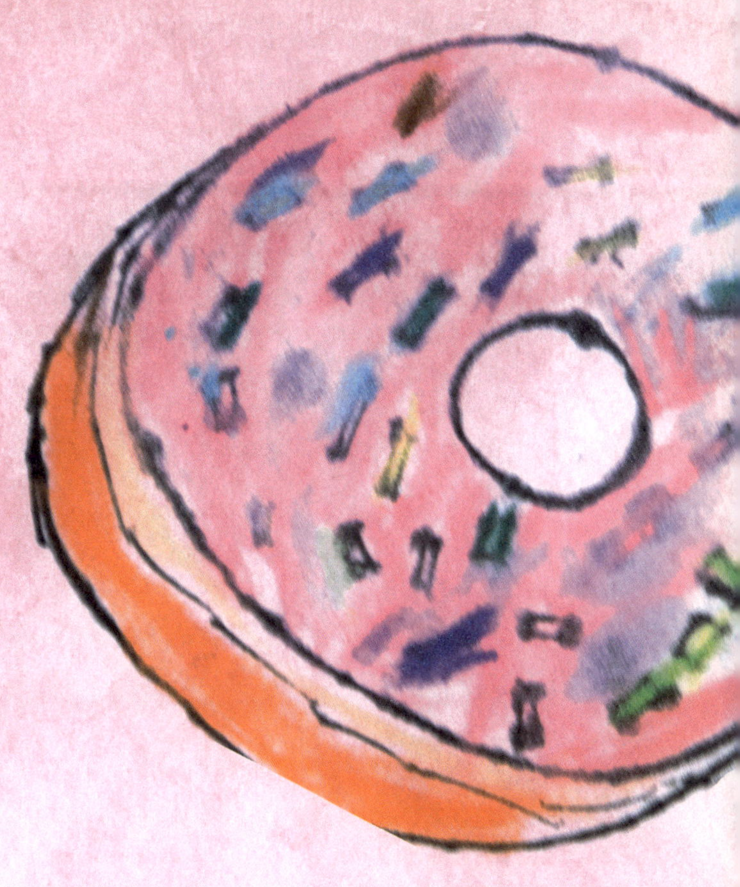

Facilitator's Note

If you are working with a group of children, this is an appealing and useful session to run at the end of a busy term, when the children have worked hard to experiment with lots of new materials and methods. A picnic drawing party is a great way to consolidate and celebrate their drawing progress.

Ideally have the space set up before the children arrive so there is an element of surprise.

As the drawing grows, you might need to keep reminding children to watch where they are sitting, though a certain chaotic element adds to the party feel!

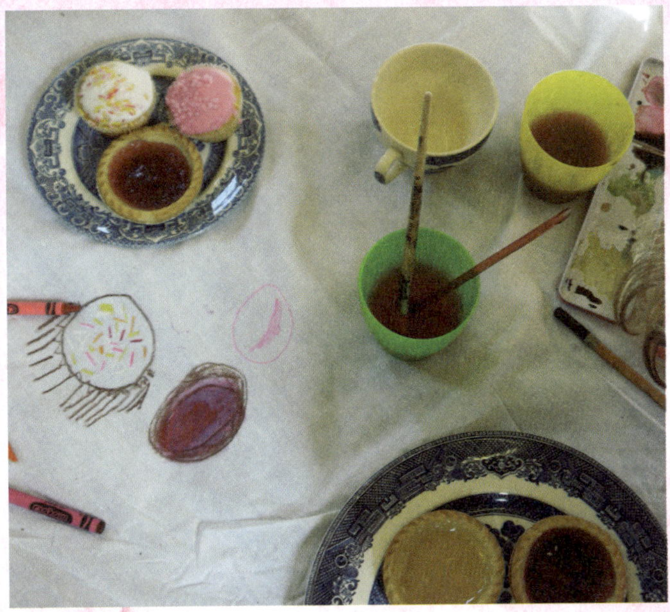

AFTERWORD

Every Tuesday after school, a group of children aged between six and eight have been coming to the AccessArt Drawing Workshop, which takes place in a village hall in the beautiful village of Grantchester, Cambridge. Like lots of village halls up and down the country, it is an unassuming place, with the entrance at the back, and no clue as to what takes place inside from the front.

Those sessions have been a joy—for me and, I think, for the children too. Winter nights and summer evenings, it has been wonderful to close the door on the world, forget school and settle into our routines. Some children have stayed for years, others have come and gone, but it has been fantastic to watch them grow in confidence handling materials and understanding processes which many adults may have thought were beyond their years. I love the concentrated quiet that falls in the room as the children begin to draw, and then the energy and momentum that gathers as they make their own drawing discoveries. Most of all I love the enthusiasm and openness with which children greet each new project.

We have been learning together, the children and I, about how you can help children discover drawing. How far to push, how much space to give, when to plant seeds, when to be studious, and how to have fun!

The warm up exercises and projects in this book all originate from those Tuesday afternoon sessions. The projects are completely transferable and adaptable, and can be used with a wide age range. I hope they give a flavour of my approach, and I hope that they will inspire.

One thing I am certain of is that we need to raise our expectations of the level of artwork children are capable of making. We need to give children access to more materials, more time and space, provide focused support, and we need to feed them with projects to give them a reason to explore further.

In return, they will demonstrate how fundamentally important drawing is to us as human beings, and they will reward us with the most beautiful, eloquent and remarkable drawings.

BIOGRAPHY

Paula Briggs received a First Class BA (HONS) in Fine Art (Sculpture) at Norwich School of Art, before going to the Royal College of Art, London to receive an MA Sculpture degree.

Paula has worked for 20 years with her colleague and friend Sheila Ceccarelli. Together they set up Cambridge Sculpture Workshops in 1995, and in 1999 established the UK charity AccessArt, which aims to inspire and enable high quality visual arts, teaching, learning and practice. AccessArt has become the leading provider of artist-led and artist-inspired digital resources for use by teachers, facilitators and creative practitioners. Find out more about AccessArt and sample resources at www.accessart.org.uk.

Paula continues to co-manage AccessArt and in addition to directing website content, continues to teach a wide audience of children, young people, adults and teachers in the Cambridgeshire area.

ACKNOWLEDGEMENTS

I feel very fortunate. Support and encouragement have been my enablers, and I could not have asked for more throughout my life. From my mum, dad and sister who have never doubted my direction and always kept faith, to my partner David who has been my rock throughout my adult life, to our wonderful daughter Rowan, who has attended every drawing class and who I think could actually facilitate them far better than me now! Thank you!

Thank you to all of the wonderful children I have been privileged enough to work with. I wish you well in your drawing.

Thank you to Leanne, Freddy, Vanessa and Duncan at Black Dog Publishing for all their work in bringing this book to print.

Most of all I need to thank Sheila Ceccarelli, who is the most generous, encouraging person I know. Sheila and I have been working together for 20 years, sharing our vision and creating our dream through the AccessArt website. Without Sheila there would be no AccessArt, and without our daily phone and email conversations my life would be so much less rich. Thanks Sheila for making it all possible.

Black Dog Publishing Limited
10a Acton Street
London
WC1X 9NG

Tel: +44 (0)20 7713 5097
Fax: +44 (0)20 7713 8682
info@blackdogonline.com
www.blackdogonline.com

Designed by Freddy Williams and Vanessa Wong
at Black Dog Publishing.

British Library Cataloguing-in-Publication Data.
A CIP record for this book is available from the British Library.

ISBN 978-1-908966-74-2

Black Dog Publishing Limited, London, UK, is an environmentally
responsible company. *Drawing Projects For Children* is printed
on an FSC certified paper.

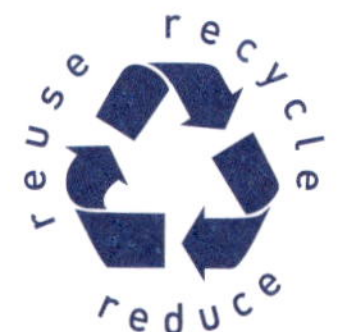

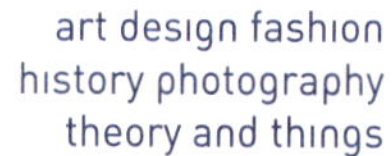

www.blackdogonline.com